Halsey Genealogy Since 1395 A.D.

Book Two

by

David Halsey

HERITAGE BOOKS
2008

HERITAGE BOOKS
AN IMPRINT OF HERITAGE BOOKS, INC.

Books, CDs, and more—Worldwide

For our listing of thousands of titles see our website
at
www.HeritageBooks.com

Published 2008 by
HERITAGE BOOKS, INC.
Publishing Division
100 Railroad Ave. #104
Westminster, Maryland 21157

Copyright © 2000 David Halsey

Other books by the author:
CD: Halsey Genealogy Since 1395 A.D.
Halsey Genealogy Since 1395 A.D.

International Standard Book Numbers
Paperbound: 978-0-7884-1432-9
Clothbound: 978-0-7884-8058-4

**HALSEY GENEALOGY
SINCE 1395 AD
BOOK II**

BY DAVID H. HALSEY

I dedicate this book to my mother. While in her teens she was seriously injured in a motorcycle accident. Following her healing, she came back to attend Milan High School, Wyoming County, West Virginia, and graduated in 1933 at the age of 22, one of ten graduates. It's her tenacity, some call stubbornness, that I admired the most. Since she was the youngest of a large closeknit family and lost her father when she was four, and because of her injuries, she was overprotected by her three older brothers and by my father. In my later years, it has become more obvious to me that her injuries left some subtle, lasting effects that slowly worsened as she aged. She was hampered all of her life as a result of these injuries, yet she birthed six babies, five at home.

Omeda Ellen Cook Halsey 1911-1973

TABLE OF CONTENTS

HALSEY GENEALOGY SINCE 1395
BOOK II

This book presents evidence as to the English ancestry of Thomas Halsey, Sr., our immigrant ancestor. Data are presented which represent results from genealogical research that was initiated more than one hundred years ago. Genealogists began questioning the ancestry of Thomas Halsey as late as the 1930's. He was NOT the Thomas Halsey whose ancestors lived at "The Parsonage", Great Gaddesden, Hertfordshire, England.

Ancestors for Thomas Halsey, Sr., the progenitor of this book, are presented from John Halsey alias Chambers, born circa 1498. Thus, this lineage covers more than eighteen generations.

Following the Introduction, descendants from Thomas Halsey, Sr., our immigrant ancestor, are presented using the "Henry Numbering System". The Henry System is used where the progenitor or in this case our immigrant ancestor, is given the number **1**. His oldest child is given the number **11**, the next child the number **12**, etc. The oldest child of number **11** is number **111**. If there are more than nine children the numbers are placed in parenthesis, thus the tenth child of number **111** is **111(10)** and his children become, etc. This format is compatible with the format used by Jacob **111(10)1**Lafayette and Edmund Drake Halsey in their book titled; "Thomas Halsey of Hertfordshire, England, and Southampton, Long Island, 1591 to 1679, with his American Descendants to the Eighth and Ninth Generations", printed at "The Jerseyman" Office, Morristown, NJ. in 1895.

The Index contains the names of all individuals, alphabetically by surnames and the pages on which they appear.

HALSEY GENEALOGY
SINCE 1395 AD
BOOK II

BY
DAVID HAROLD HALSEY

THE HALSEY NAME

There is some indication that the name Hals has a Norman origin; however, evidence seems to indicate a Saxon origin dating from the invasions of England in the Fifth Century. Folklore also seems to indicate that Hals is Danish and thus was brought over by the Vikings four centuries later. Hals as a surname is probably no older than the Conquest by William the Conqueror in 1085 or 86 when surnames first came into use in England.

English bearers of the name Halsey have been found as early as 1189. The earliest recorded Halsey name was "Halsey of Cornwall." Englishman who bore the name of Halsey, as far as known records show, lived in the extreme western edge of Cornwall, a portion of England so old that the ancient Phoenician navigators are believed to have visited it for the purpose of acquiring tin.

The estate of the Cornwall Halseys was Lanesley which is in the Gulval District near Mount's Bay next to the famous and picturesque ridge of rock which projects into the sea called St. Michael's Mount. At the time of Richard I, who was crowned in 1189, and of King John his successor, the Lanesley estate comprised the lands of a family called de Als who in 1895 were called Hals.

History insinuates that an estate of Als, called Alse and Alesa, in Buryan, was dismantled. Men by the name of Bar Alseton and Alston, in Devon, were called Lords, and one in particular was named William de Als who lived during the beginning of the reign of King Henry III. William de Als married Mary, the Daughter of Francis DeBray. He had a son called Simon de Als who lived in Halsham in Yorkshire.

As a common noun and verb the word "hals " was used in early times by the English and signifies in one case the neck and in the other to embrace or fall upon the neck of another. Hals occurs also in Icelandic, Gothic, Dutch, Old Frisian, and Danish, while the form "hawse" is Scotch. The word "halse" is found to be an obsolete (1895) form of "hawse", meaning that part of a ship's bow through which cables pass out. Today the word is spelled "h-a-w-s-e-r".

The origin of the "Halsey alias Chambers" designation has not been found. Though it was traced back for four generations from Thomas Halsey, the immigrant ancestor of the Halseys in America, it was apparently dropped in both America and England in subsequent generations.

THOMAS HALSEY, THE IMMIGRANT ANCESTOR

The Halsey family has been settled in America since 1638. Today members such as this writer's grandsons represent the eighteenth, and possibly the twentieth generation. Thomas Halsey, the Englishman, was the immigrant ancestor. Specific facts about his life in America are authentically recorded. Thomas Halsey was not the son of a family residing at "The Golden Parsonage", Great Gaddesden, Hertfordshire, England, as most believed.

Results from several comprehensive genealogical research endeavors have independently provided substantial documentation to ascertain the English ancestry of "our" Thomas Halsey.[1] Since the publication of the Halsey genealogy[2] and Howell's history of Southampton,[3] the authentication of Thomas Halsey's English ancestry has been a serious project for several researchers.[4][5]

Both references, "Halsey Family" and "Howell, Southampton", assumed that Thomas Halsey's ancestors lived at The Parsonage, Great Gaddesden, Hertfordshire. Also, they came to the conclusion, utilizing less sophisticated research techniques than is now available to genealogists, that Thomas Halsey, the settler of Southampton, Long Island, NY, was a mercer, sent a letter from Naples in 1621, and was a son from a family residing at "The Parsonage".

Seversmith first questioned these assumptions in 1939.[6] He was able to document that Thomas Halsey was "from Kempston, Bedfordshire" at the time of his immigration. Also, he found evidence that this Thomas was married to Elizabeth Wheeler, daughter of John Wheeler, Jr., of Cransfield, Bedfordshire.

Seversmith also questioned the dissimilarities in the signatures presented in the Halsey Genealogy.[7] He further identified the differences in personalities of the outspoken and argumentative Thomas of Southampton, contrasted to the modest Thomas of Naples, as recorded in his letter of 1621 to the family at The Parsonage. Seversmith came to the conclusion that "our" Thomas Halsey's English ancestry had been connected to the wrong family by the "Halsey Family" and "Howell, Southampton" references.

Seversmith found that "our" Thomas Halsey was a resident of Kempston, Bedfordshire, and that, in the Ship-Money Papers of Henry Chester and Sir William Boteler, 1637-1639, Thomas Halsey was assessed for one pound, five shillings and nine pence. There was a note, written at the time attached to these papers, that said, "Gone

---

[1] Raymond David Wheeler, "The English Ancestry of Thomas Halsey of Southampton, Long Island", (unpublished) October 1994, 28 pages; Copy from Dr. Hugh Halsey, II, President of "The Thomas Halsey Family Association" Southampton, NY; hereinafter "Wheeler Report".

[2] Jacob LaFayette Halsey and Edmund Drake Halsey, "Thomas Halsey of Hertfordshire, England, and Southampton, Long Island, 1591-1679, with his American Descendants to the Eight and Ninth Generations" 1895, Morristown, NJ; hereinafter "Halsey Family".

[3] George R. Howell, "The Early History of Southampton, Long Island, New York, with Genealogies, 2nd ed." 1887, 473 pages; hereinafter "Howell, Southampton".

[4] Herbert F. Seversmith, "Colonial Families of Long Island, New York and Connecticut", volume 2, 1939, typescript Library of Congress; published in four volumes 1944-1955; hereinafter "Seversmith".

[5] Hugh Halsey, II, M.D., President, "The Thomas Halsey Family Association, Southampton Colonial Society", Annual Reports, 1986, 1992, 1994; hereinafter "Hugh Halsey"

[6] "Seversmith".

[7] "Halsey Family".

๖ New England". Also, on the same page with Thomas Halsey was Thomas Wheeler's ่ame, a kinsman by marriage, with a note which said, "Gon out of the Contry". The part f the list which contained both Thomas' names was called the "List of Arrears, Arrerages ธig) of Shipping Money".   It is thought that one of the reasons that Thomas left ะngland was to avoid paying the tax levied for building the King's navy.

'HOMAS HALSEY'S ENGLISH ANCESTORS
          In the fall of 1985, "The Thomas Halsey Family Association" was founded by ่ugh Halsey, II, M.D., for the express purpose of funding research to ascertain the ่ncestry of Thomas Halsey. Dr. Halsey, the Association president, made arrangements ่hrough Mr. Nicholas G. Halsey of "The Golden Parsonage" to have various records ่earched.[8] [9]
          As part of his research into the Wheeler family, Colonel Raymond David ่Vheeler using wills, parish records, bishops transcripts and deeds, was able to distinguish ่etween the many "Thomases" (Halsey) that were born in the late 16th and early 17th ้entury, who could have been the one that came to America in 1638.[10] Colonel ่Vheeler's interest in "our" Thomas Halsey came about because Thomas married into the ่Vheeler family.
          Colonel Wheeler developed a lineage going back four generations in England ่howing Thomas as a descendant from John Halsey alias Chambers of Great ฿addesden, Hertfordshire, who was also the common ancestor of the Halsey family of ่he Golden Parsonage. Further, the lineage from John Halsey alias Chambers was ่aced to John Halsey alias Chambers, born circa 1548 who resided in Dunstable, ่ertfordshire at the time of his death. This John Halsey, in turn had a son Thomas ่alsey alias Chambers who died in Hemel Hempstead in 1600. One of this Thomas' ้ons is suggested to be the Robert Halsey alias Chambers of Holtsmerend who died in ่610 and is thought to be the father of Thomas Halsey alias Chambers, the immigrant. ่Vills have been found for all these individuals, but there are some minor gaps in the ่ocumentation.[11]
          It appears the reference, "Halsey Family" was correct in that Thomas Halsey ่riginally came from Hertfordshire and that his father was Robert, although not the Robert ่ving at the Parsonage.
          Since the greatest concentration of Halsey families lived in the adjoining parishes ่f Great Gaddesden, Flamstead, Kensworth, Hemel Hempstead, Redbourn, Harpenden, ฿erkhamstead, and St. Peters, all in Hertfordshire, and Caddington, Luton, Dunstable and ฿tudham, all in Bedfordshire, it is not too difficult to understand the confusion that early

---

[8]"Wheeler Report".

[9]Mrs. Pauline Sidell, B.A.,D.A.A., genealogist, of Hemel Hempstead searched records at: Hertfordshire and ฿uckinghamshire County Record Offices and the Public Record Office, London.
Mrs. Shelia Holgate, genealogist, of Kempston searched records at the Bedfordshire Record Office.

[10]"Wheeler Report".

[11]"Wheeler Report".

genealogists encountered in developing pedigrees. There were many Richard, Robert, William, Thomas, and John Halsey families living in these areas during the late 1500's and early 1600's[12].

"OUR" THOMAS HALSEY'S EARLY LIFE

Thomas Halsey grew up in an environment stirred by events that would shape the world into the twenty first century. Elizabeth, who was twelve years old when her father made the grant of "The Halsey Arms"[13] to William Halsey, had been seated on the throne, as Queen, for over thirty years. She had successfully resurrected the Protestant faith as the Church of England. About the time Thomas was born, Mary, Queen of Scots had been executed and Elizabeth had won England's mightiest naval victory with the overthrow of the Spanish Armada and thus established England as a great sea power. This victory severed England's dominance from Rome and Rome's Spanish ally and was the starting point for England's real activity in the affairs of the new world in America.

This English world in which Thomas was born has other memorable distinctions. It was the age of Bacon, Spencer, and Shakespeare. Thomas was born about the time that Spencer made public his "Faerie Queene", the most significant piece of English poetry ever. This poetry proved that English was to become a great literary language.

Shakespeare, in 1591, was 28 years old and had been working in London for about five years, winning fame and income as he could as an actor and mender of old plays. It was during Thomas' boyhood that Shakespeare's plays won fame. By this time Shakespeare had retired to Stratford and died. Francis Bacon was a young lawyer with fame yet to come. In 1597 his "Essays" laid the foundations for his future greatness. Bacon's home and birthplace was St. Albans, only six miles from Great Gaddesden Parsonage. Bacon was buried at St. Albans in 1626.

THOMAS HALSEY'S FIRST WIFE

One of the "debates" about Thomas Halsey was the name of his first wife, who was killed by the Pequot Indians. Was it "Phebe" or "Elizabeth Wheeler"? The only reference found to date which suggests her name as "Phebe" is the Halsey genealogy.[14] It is now accepted that her name was indeed "Elizabeth Wheeler".[15]

Seversmith also documents that Thomas Halsey first married Elizabeth Wheeler.

John Isley Coddington lists the wife of Thomas Halsey as a Cranfield Wheeler and states that the Wheeler families of New England were of the same connection.[16] A full copy of

---

[12]"Wheeler Report".

[13]1633

[14] "Halsey Family".

[15]"Wheeler Report"; "Seversmith".

[16]John Isley Coddington, "The Wheelers of Bedfordshire and New England", 1951; "hereinafter Coddington"

John Wheeler's will, dated 18 January 1642/3, lists the following: "I give and beequeath unto Elizabeth Halsie my daughter twelve pense of lawful English money".

EARLY RECORDS AT "THE PARSONAGE"
The earliest mention of "Halsey" found at "The Parsonage", Great Gaddesden, Hertfordshire, is dated 1424 when William Halsey, born circa 1395, received eighteen acres at Tags End[17]. Further, Richard Halsey, born circa 1420, was mentioned in a 16 July 1453 deed of the Priory of Kings Langley for providing for the poor of Great Gaddesden. The continuous lineage, found todate, of individuals residing at "The Parsonage" begins with John Halsey alias Chambers, born circa 1455. John's descendants are taken to and include the family of Thomas Halsey, the one that has been mistaken for "our" immigrant ancestor.
    Since early records were only kept by the churches, family records only existed as part of church records. Therefore, a discussion as to how the church records that apply to the Halsey family evolved is appropriate.
    The historian of Cornwall records that Simon de Als in 1266 gave the estate of Lanesley to the head of the religious house of St. Germain's, but later in the time of Henry VIII,[18] the estate again became a private estate. In 1620 its owner mortgaged the Lanesley estate to Sir Nicholas Halse of Fentongollan, a lineal descendant of Simon de Als.
    In the time of Edward II[19] the Lanesley estate embraced 16,000 to 17,000 acres. Fentongollan was also in Cornwall, but farther east than Lanesley and was originally the estate of another family called Hals. The mansion was older than the Conquest and because of the mortgage came into the possession of Sir Nicholas Halse. Sir Nicholas was originally from Efford near Plymouth in Devon County. In the time of Elizabeth I,[20] he had acquired property in Cornwall, and after he had been Captain of Pendennis Castle, James I[21] honored him with knighthood.
    Sir Nicholas' son, James Halse, fought at La Rochelle in 1628 and shortly thereafter went to the West Indies where he was Governor of Montserrat. The second son of James was William, the historian. Another William, the son of Sir Nicholas, became a Captain in the British Navy, and like his brother James, took part in the siege of La Rochelle.[22] [23]

---

[17]"Wheeler Report".

[18]He was king from 1509 to 1547.

[19]He was king from 1307 to 1327.

[20]She was queen from 1558 to 1603.

[21]He was the first Stuart king of England from 1603 to 1625. He also was James VI as king of Scotland from 1657 to 1625.

[22]Seaport in west France, 1627-1628.

[23]"Halsey Family".

William, the historian, was familiar with Fentongollan because his mother spent her later years there. He describes it as "including a church with an endowment for the saying of masses and prayers with many large and roomy houses". It was later sold to a member of the Boscawen family who dismantled the mansion completely.

From Cornwall members of the Hals family emigrated back to Devon. In the time of Edward II, Richard Hals was living at Kenedon, near Kingsbridge, close to the channel coast. In 1395 the estate of Kenedon by deed from John Govis "came to the genteel family of Halse[24] as recorded in a deed. The purchaser was John Hals, a descendant of Simon de Als, one of the Judges of the Court of Common Pleas. John Hals lived there until the latter part of the reign of Charles II[25]. Judge John Hals in 1423, the year Henry V died, built a mansion on the Kenedon estate. Judge Hals was the father of Bishop Halse of Lichfield and Coventry, who added the "e" to the name. The Bishop died at age 90 in 1490. He had taken part in the War of the Roses as a friend of Margaret of Anjou whom he escorted from the field of Bloreheath after the defeat of her army.[26]

During the reign of Charles Kenedon the estate passed out of the direct male line of descent through the will of Matthew Halse who gave it to his sisters, one of whom married into the Trelawney family of Cornwall. Sir Nicholas of Fentongollan was from these Kenedon Halses.

The relationships of the Halsey's of Cornwall and Devon to the Halsey's of the Great Gaddesden Parsonage in Hertfordshire in 1458 is not known.

This was a time of great unrest and ambition throughout England. It was the period of the War of the Roses, with the men of Cornwall and Devon taking part in this long conflict as followers of Margaret of Anjou. It can only be conjectured that some of the people named Halsey from these distant counties, when the War disrupted the Kingdom, took up a new home at Hertfordshire. What is known for certain is what Cussans recorded "that the Halsey family has been settled at Great Gaddesden for many generations".[27] He says "the earliest recorded mention of the Halsey name, at Great Gaddesden, was contained in a deed dated 10 July 1458, which states that Richard Halsey was a party, on behalf of the parishioners, to an agreement whereby the Prior of King's Langley covenanted to pay to the poor of Great Gaddesden the sum of 10 shillings annually".

In 1559, when the parochial registers commenced in England, there were four families with the Halsey name living at Great Gaddesden, located in Hertfordshire County near London, England. They were the Halsey of the Parsonage, Halsey of the Wood, Halsey of Northend, and Halsey of the Lane[28].

---

[24] Written "de Alse".

[25] He was king from 1660 to 1685.

[26] "War of the Roses" was a civil struggle between the houses of Lancaster and York, begun in 1455 and ended when King Henry VII became king and united both houses in 1485.

[27] John Edwin Cussans, "History of Hertfordshire", Volume 3, London, England, 1878; hereinafter "Cussans".

[28] "Halsey Family".

THE "GOLDEN PARSONAGE"

The origin of the "Golden" prefix to "Parsonage" is not known; however, the monks of Ashridge were formerly rectors or parsons of the church of Gaddesden. It is probable that there was a chapel or subsidiary house belonging to the Bens Hommes upon the site of the Parsonage. The church, which was dedicated to St. John the Baptist, was located in the valley of the Gade.

The style of architecture was in keeping with the period of its construction which appears to have been about the years 1280 to 1290. It is probable that there were originally transepts and that they were done away with about two centuries later when the roof of the nave was heightened and aisles with clerestories above were added.[29]

This church probably existed here at the time of the Conquest, for there is no mention of it in the Domesday Book, yet the record states that there was a priest at Gaddesden.[30]

Domesday was simply an inventory of the lands, etc., from which the King could derive revenue; hence many churches and castles, which are known to have been in existence at the time it was compiled, are omitted simply because they were not chargeable.

Another proof that the 1895 church[31] is not the earliest church exists in the fact that there was a Vicarage here before the year 1255 when the records of the See of Lincoln commence[32].

The Vicarage was within the Rural Deanery of Berkhamstead, and Archdeaconry and Diocese of St. Albans. In the Ecclesiastical Taxation, made in the year 1292, by order of Pope Nicholas IV, this Vicarage was rated at 13 pounds, 6 shillings, 8 pences, per annum. In the Survey taken in 1535, on the Dissolution of Religious Houses in England, its value was set down in the King's Books at 10 pounds, 1 shilling, 10 pence, per annum.

The manor or estate, with the Advowson of the church, remained vested in the family of de Holland until 1461, when, on the attainder of Henry de Holland, they were forfeited to the Crown[33]. A few months later King Edward IV restored the manor to his sister, Anne, wife of the attained Henry de Holland.

The Advowson of the rectory was probably granted at about the same time to the Dominican Nunnery of Dartford, in Kent, for the use of the Priory of Friars Preachers, or

[29] A transept is either of the two lateral arms of a church built in the shape of a cross.

[30] The Domesday Book was a Latin census of English property compiled by order of William the Conqueror. A census compiled usually from a comprehensive survey of geographical sector in which the merits and demerits of each individual were recorded.

[31] "Halsey Family".

[32] "See" is a church containing a cathedral; a seat or center of the power or authority of a bishop; a diocesan center; and, the jurisdiction of a bishop.

[33] English law provided the right of presenting a nominee to a vacant ecclesiastical benefice.

Black Friars, of King's Langley. The nunnery of Dartford was founded by King Edward III, who was also the great benefactor to King's Langley. King Richard II, in a grant which he made to Dartford Priory for the use of the Friars of Langley, states that such grant was made in accordance with the will of Edward, his grandfather. Whatever the connection between the two houses, it is certain that they were both interested in the Rectory before the Dissolution.

On the 20th of March, 1520, Thomas Cooper, Prior of King's Langley, leased to John Halsey, and William Halsey, his son, the Rectory of Great Gaddenson, for a term of 20 years; and by another deed dated the 24th of December 1529, Elizabeth, Prioress of the Monastery of our Lady and St. Margaret of Dartford, and Richard, Prior of the Friars Preachers of King's Langley, jointly leased the same Rectory to William Halsey for 31 years, which included the additional benefit of the unexpired time of 10 years from the former lease by John, his father.

On the Dissolution of Religious Houses, the Rectory at Great Gaddenson came to the Crown and was granted by Henry VIII, on the 12th of March, 1545, to the same William Halsey (Hawse), for the sum of 174 pounds, 13 shillings, 4 pence, and included the cost of the service of a fortieth part of a knight's fee and an annual payment of nineteen shillings and fourpence. The grant was one of several hundred made by Henry VIII after his suppression of the Monasteries. In this grant no mention is made of Dartford Nunnery.

The estate, known as the Golden Parsonage, together with the Advowson of the church and right of presentation to the vicarage, have since continued in the family of Halsey. Additions from time to time made the residence a large country place, sheltered in a small park of fine timber, including beech and holly, many of the latter having trunks three feet in diameter and being twenty feet tall. On the place exist a well of great depth from which water was drawn using donkeys walking on a large wheel, similar in design to a squirrel cage.

Great Gaddesden is a short distance west of the Parsonage and derives it's name from the River Gade which rises near the village. It is also about twenty eight miles north of London.

Around this new residence at Gaddesden Place were 3,000 acres, from which noble views may be had, such as one reaching to "Harrow-on-the-Hill," the famous school where Peel and Byron swam together in the pool and played on the grass.

In 1545, when the Rectory was granted to William Halsey, he is described as of the Parsonage, and by that name the residence has ever since been known.

THE HALSEY ARMS AND CREST

Based on Manuscripts in the British Museum, College of Heralds, and Record Office; Wills; Parochial Registers; Deeds in the possession of Thomas Frederick Halsey, of Gaddesden Place, Esquire, M.P., and other evidences (circa 1879) the "HALSEY ARMS" (Shield) was granted to William and James Halsey, on the 22nd of January 1633/4.[34] The Arms are described-"Argent; on a Pile sable three Griffins' heads erased of the first."[35] The "HALSEY CREST" is described as-"A cubit Arm gules, cuff argent, hand

---

[34]"Halsey Family".

proper, holding a Griffin's leg erased or"[36].

The "MOTTO" "Nescit vox missa reverti", translated means-"A word once uttered cannot be recalled."

These arms were granted to William Halsey and James Halsey, of Great Gaddesden, on 23 January 1633/4. Since only two names appeared on the grant, it suggest that the remaining brothers had died by this date. The "brother" Thomas, a London mercer who wrote a letter from Italy in 1621, was the same Thomas that was originally mistook for the immigrant ancestor[37], was excluded from the grant, since he probably died before 1633.[38]

TO AMERICA

Thomas Halsey coming to America was probably connected with the colonization enterprises of which John Winthrop became the leader. The men who founded the Massachusetts Bay Colony were Puritans of a milder and more worldly type than the older settlements. Winthrop's men were looking for a land where they could worship God after their own consciences, but one where towns, farms and property could grow. While still in England, Thomas had received a full and authentic report of the freedom which was enjoyed at Plymouth in America. In England Charles I wielded power oppressively, and Parliament ceased operation in 1629 so the desire to leave England grew in force.

Puritans, as they were in spiritual belief, their leader, Winthrop, had originally been a member of the Church of England. Winthrop sailed in 1630 and many shiploads followed him into Boston Bay in the years to follow. Settlements spread rapidly from the town of Beacon Hill, forming the towns of Salem and Lynn.

IN AMERICA

Documents in the Clerk of Courts at Salem, MA, present the divisions of land among the inhabitants of Lynn, MA in April 1638.[39] Thomas Halsey received 100 acres which, therefore, means that he was in America in April 1638. He was resident of Lynn in 1639 and most of 1640.

Thomas Halsey and his brother-in-law, Thomas Wheeler, made a survey trip to New England in the fall of 1637.[40] Thomas Halsey returned to England in early 1638 before selling his land at Kempston. Thomas and his family had returned to America by April 1638.

---

[35]Translation: "Silver, on a black wedge three jagged silver griffin's heads".

[36]Translation: "A right hand natural, sleeved red, cuffed silver, holding a griffin's claw jagged in gold".

[37]"Halsey Family".

[38]"Wheeler Report"; "Hugh Halsey".

[39]"Seversmith".

[40]"Wheeler Report".

Seversmith also agrees that a number of colonists of Lynn decided to leave and settle in another place. On 10 March 1639, Edward Howell and others contracted for transport to the future Southampton, Long Island, NY. We know that Thomas Halsey was not on the first ship that sailed, but, after he contributed his 80 pounds, he was included. The final agreement to settle Southampton was dated at Lynn on 17 April 1640. The last of the three shiploads arrived in Southampton on 13 December 1640.

OTHER HALSEY FAMILIES IN AMERICA

A family named Halsey has been found in Boston, MA, records of 1635, but it appears to have died out with the second generation.

Also, from Boston came a Captain John Halsey of whose deeds on the high seas have been recorded.[41] Henry Benton remarked that Captain Halsey, though he resolved upon turning pirate, intended to rob only Moor ships. After an adventurous career he died of a fever in Madagascar, and was buried with "great solemnity and ceremony. The prayers of the Church of England were read over him, colors were flying, and his sword and pistol laid on his coffin which was covered with a ship's jack; as many minute guns fired as he was years old, (46), and three English volleys and one French volley of small arms. He was brave in his person, courteous to all his prisoners, lived beloved, and died regretted by his own people. His grave was made in a garden of watermelons and fenced in with palisades to prevent his being rooted up by wild hogs of which there are plenty in these parts".

Another family of Halseys existed in Providence, RI; one was Thomas Lloyd Halsey, a quartermaster in the Revolutionary army, but they disappeared some years since in South America.

TO LONG ISLAND, NY

Thomas was able to make the break with Winthrop peaceably having obtained his consent. On March 10, 1639, articles of agreement had been signed at Lynn. Thomas Halsey being one of the signers, described the conditions and terms under which the new settlement was to be founded. Captain Daniel Howe was engaged to transport the company. It was provided that his ship should be at Lynn three times during the year, March, June, and October, ready to convey goods and people to the new Long Island lands.

The lands on Long Island were to be purchased and laid out but not divided. "Whatsoever we lay out as farms shall remain so," they said, and in case any person who sold his property was not to divide it but was to sell "house, lot and plantings, or lots and meadows, entirely, and if he sell his farm he shall not divide it but sell it together." There was a limit of four acres to house lots and twelve acres to the planting lot, while the meadows and uplands might make thirty-four or fifty acres for each holder. Other lands were held in common.

One of the clauses on religion had been interpreted as meaning that they were forming a kind of union between church and state the same as existed in the Bay Colony.

---

[41] Henry Benton, "The History of the Pirates, containing the Lives of those noted Pirate Captains Misson, Bowen, Kidd, Tew, Halsey", Hartford, CT, 1829.

It was agreed in April, 1640, that they should settle on eight square miles in any part of Long Island, the amount to be paid fixed by Governor Winthrop, who said that since this was wilderness, four bushels of corn would be fair. The purchase was made from Lord Stirling through his agent, James Farrett.

The first ship arrived at Long Island early in May at a place called Cow Bay and now called Manhasset, a bay which indents the shore from Long Island Sound in the town of North Hempstead, about twenty miles east of Hell Gate. Here they landed and finding the Dutch arms set up, Captain Howe took them down, and an Indian drew in their place "an unhandsome face". Only a few of the Lynn company went with the first voyage, and Thomas probably was one of those who did not go.

When the Dutch on Manhattan Island heard that their arms had been taken down, they sent Cornelius Van Tienhoven to Cow Bay with twenty-five soldiers under orders to bring the offenders to New Amsterdam, "taking care above all things to avoid all bloodshed." Six men were taken to New Amsterdam and after it was shown that Captain Howe and not the settlers had taken down the arms they were turned loose on the conditions that they depart from the territory and never return without the Director's consent. Before being discharged they were obliged to sign an agreement to leave Cow Bay on "pain of being punish as perverse usurpers subjecting ourselves not only to this but to all other courts in the world." During their imprisonment in New Amsterdam these men sent a letter to Governor Winthrop which gave evidence that they were men of some learning for the letter was written in Latin.

On leaving Cow Bay the settlers sought another place to settle. They found it at the eastern end of Long Island and called it Southampton. They reached these lands in early June, 1640, and it is contended that here was founded the first settlement ever made by Englishmen within the present limits of New York State. To the Indians for their interest in the lands at Southampton, they gave sixteen coats and sixty bushels of corn, with a promise to defend them against other Indians. This agreement was dated December 13, 1640.

Before winter set in, a crude church was erected in the new settlement. It remained Congregational for a time but was soon changed to the Presbyterian faith. Church and town were practically one body for in the town meetings resided all power. Southampton offered an example of a pure democracy, with the town meeting voting taxes, sitting as a court and imposing fines. For these reasons they met once per month and every freeholder was required to be present and was fined if absent. During the first five years, the dangers of attack by the Indians were great so individuals carried weapons to church.

In 1645 the rules were changed so that carrying arms was permitted only in the winter months, from November 1st to March 1st.

The town of Southampton grew slowly in population. In 1650 only ten or twelve houses were standing. It was an exposed kind of life that the settlers were forced to live being surrounded by Indians. Thomas' house was erected south of the first mill on Horse Mill Lane, where in 1649 Elizabeth, his first wife, was murdered by Pequot Indians. Wyandoch, a friendly chief, was suspected of the murder and at once gave himself up, declaring his innocence. He had already caught the true murderers, the two Pequot Indians from the mainland. They were sent to Hartford, tried, convicted, and executed.

In July 1660, Thomas Halsey, described as "of Southampton in the jurisdiction of

Connecticut, husbandman," declared that he took "Ann Jones, the wife of Edward Jones, lately deceased, in marriage contract to be my espoused wife." He renounced all claim to any of Jones' property.

It is recorded that Thomas Halsey remained in Southampton for many years and was the richest man in the place.

HALSEYS IN AMERICA

From Southampton future generations of Halsey kith and kin would fan out into these United States. This genealogy of the Halsey family bears witness to that fact!

1   HALSEY, Thomas, Sr.

He married **WHEELER**, Elizabeth in Cranfield, Bedfordshire,
England, circa 1625. He married **JOHNS**, Ann Mrs. in Southampton, L.I.,
NY, 25 July 1660. Thomas, died 27 August 1678 in Southampton, L.I. NY

It is conceivable the Thomas Halsey of Kempston and Southampton,
might be one of the other Thomas Halseys born near Flamstead,
Hertfordshire, because the researchers were unable to document the age of
Thomas Halsey from his will or other documents located in the Southampton
archives. Since Thomas' first child was baptised in 1626, it can be estimated
that Thomas was born by 1600. Since he died in 1678, it can be reasoned
that he was born after 1578. During this period there were ten other Thomas
Halseys found to have lived in this area. Seven were identified with other
families, however the fate of the other three are unknown. There is no
documented evidence to suspect that any of the unknown three may have
settled at Southampton, L.I., NY.

From 1632 until he left Kempston, for America, in 1638, Thomas
Halsey was mentioned on the court records of the manors of Kempston
Greys alias Hastingbury and Kempston Hardwick.

By 22 April 1638, Elizabeth and her husband evidently relocated to
Cranfield, where their son, Daniel, was baptized on this date. On 28 April
1638, "Thomas Halsey als. Chambers, Kempston, Bedfordshire, yeo."
and Elizabeth Halsey, his wife" sold their eleven acres to Kempston Charties
for 77 pounds. Among the witness were William Wheeler, Richard Mouse
and Richard Halsey. The signature of Thomas Halsey is identical to that of
Thomas Halsey of Southampton, NY. Also the signature of William Wheeler,
Elizabeth's brother, matches the signature on his will. On this same day there
was a second conveyance by lease to "Richard Halsey, als. Chambers,
Flamstead, Hertfordshire, yeo." witnesses among others by Thomas Halsey.
The lands were in Ridgeway Field.

The Ship "Money Arrears" List of 1637 for Kempston was noted,
"Thomas Halsey gone to New England". Thomas Wheeler of Cranfield was
also noted as having "gone into New England" in the 1637 list. Evidently
Thomas Halsey and his brother-in-law Thomas Wheeler made a survey trip
to New England in the fall of 1637, with at least Thomas Halsey returning
early in 1638 before selling his land. Soon thereafter Thomas Halsey
embarked for Lynn, MA, where he in that same year 1638, land was
distributed: "...Thomas Halsye, 100 acres;..."

On 10 March 1639/40, arrangements were made at Lynn, MA, for
the settlement of Southampton, and Thomas Halsey was added to the list:
"...Furthermore for as much as Allen Bread, Thomas Halsey & William
Harker, Are by the Consent of the Company come into and pty vndertakers
with us, we Edward Howell, Daniel How & Henry Walton have consigned
three of our pts. that each man a howse lott, plantinge lott and farme
answerable to the rest of the vndertakers for their disbursement of five
pounds A man to vs the aboue said vndertakers."

From the town of Southampton, Long Island, NY., records it is plain
that Thomas Halsey was not only an active citizen, but one possessed of

independent spirit and strong will, and not always respectful to his fellow townsmen. He was well educated and considered a "gentleman" by all records. The first recorded instant of his independent will, in America, was dated March 15, 1643, when he was censured in a town meeting "for some irreverent speech to Daniel Howe in Court, being then a Magistrate, who acknowledged his offense and promised to make the like acknowledgement the next quarter court." In 1646 Thomas was Marshall and in March he was censured "for hindering the quite proceedings of the Court and causing them to loose their time by his willful obstinacy and for the unjust charging of the Court for justifying the actions of Mr. Howe, for which offense he is required forthwith to make public acknowledgement and to pay five shillings for his fine." Under the same date in the record "Thomas Halsey upon his refusal to make acknowledgement of those things for which he was censured is fined to pay the sum of 40s;" but in a note it is explained that "Thomas Halsey had his fine remitted by the General Court on March 3, 1647."

In June 1654, there was "great disturbance" at court by reason of the departure of some of the members there of." Fines were imposed and it was ordered that Thomas Halsey "shall pay moreover 5s. for his contemptuous carriage unto the court at his departure." He was a looser in a suit for trespass in 1654 and appealed to Hartford, being "bound in the sum of 40 pounds to prosecute there."

Other suits he won, according to the town records. In October 1655, he had some differences with the town in regard to fences which he acknowledged himself "sorry for his fault therein and desireth of the town their courtsey therein, whereupon the town does consent unto the said Thomas Halsey that he shall have his said closes in particular to himself," he agreeing to keep up his fences.

On November 23, 1663, Thomas Halsey was appointed to a Committee to act for the town in dividing up money due Captain Scott, who appeared to have purchased property for the town of Southampton, NY. There was some dispute as to jurisdiction; NY or Conn.? Thomas was of the opinion that Conn. had jurisdiction but evidently lost. On February 10, 1663-4, Thomas Halsey, Senior, "absolutely refusing to do town service in that occasion as specified", John Jessup was appointed in his place.

It was not until six years of Thomas' death that the threat of Dutch agression on Long Island would cease forever. It was obvious that the Dutch looked upon the settlement of Southampton as an intrusion to their territory. We know that as late as 1650 the Dutch desired to purchase Long Island and thus shut Southampton out so Long Island would be secured to New Netherland (NY). In 1651 the Dutch state paper said that Peter Stuyvesant declared that Long Island rightfully belong to the Dutch, both by first purchase, possession and ancient resort. Thirteen years later the island of Manhattan passed from Dutch to English hands. There had been an act of war but no blood shed. This was one of the greatest events in the history of the English people, for out of it determine which peoples should dominate the North American Continent. After this event the eastern part of Long Island transferred from Conn. jurisdiction to NY.

Thomas, Senior's will of June 1677 was probated at New York on 8 July 1679.
11   HALSEY, Thomas, Jr.
Thomas was born in England. His body was interred in Hay Ground g.y. Bridgehampton, LI. He married **BARRETT**, Mary in Southampton, NY, circa 1651. Thomas, died 1688 in Southampton, L.I., NY. He was first mentioned in the records of Southampton, L.I, NY, on March 7, 1644, when he was enrolled among those sixteen year old and over in a whaling ward. In 1657 he was living among "Eastern men" probably at Mecox. His will was signed 3 August 1688.
111   HALSEY, Mary
Mary was born 29 August 1654. She married **HOWELL**, Matthew 8 November 1677. Mary died circa 1710.
1111   HOWELL, Jerusha
1112   HOWELL, Eunice
Eunice was born 18 August 1678.
1113   HOWELL, Nathan
Nathan was born 24 November 1681.
1114   HOWELL, Israel
He married **ROGERS**, Mary. He married **COOPER**, Abigail. Israel was born in Southampton, L.I 17 April 1686. Israel died 2 May 1739 in Moriches, NY, at 53 years of age.
11141   HOWELL, Matthew
Matthew died 24 December 1715 in Southampton, L.I., NY.
11142   HOWELL, Eunice
11143   HOWELL, Israel
Israel was born 14 March 1714/5.
11144   HOWELL, Jerusha
Jerusha was born 30 July 1720.
11145   HOWELL, Abigail
Abigail was born 9 January 1721/2. She married **HALSEY**, Silas (Jerusha) 19 June 1750.
11146   HOWELL, David
David was born 13 June 1724.
11147   HOWELL, Matthew
Matthew was born 14 February 1725/6.
11148   HOWELL, Nathan
Nathan was born 12 July 1728.
11149   HOWELL, Eunice
Eunice was born 10 January 1733/4.
1115   HOWELL, Ezekiel
Ezekiel was born 21 January 1687/8.
112   HALSEY, Elizabeth
Elizabeth was born 15 October 1655. Elizabeth died circa 1715.
113   HALSEY, Josiah
His body was interred in Wickapogue g.y., NY. Josiah was born 15 February 1655/6. He married **TOPPING**, Sarah 12 September 1678. Josiah

died circa 1732.

1131   HALSEY, Martha

1132   HALSEY, Elizabeth

1133   HALSEY, Mary

1134   HALSEY, Josiah

Josiah was born circa 1691. Josiah died circa 1744.

11341   HALSEY, Israel

He married **HALSEY**, Mary. Israel died 19 March 1774.

11342   HALSEY, Temperance

She married **FOSTER**, Daniel.

11343   HALSEY, Esther

She married **HALSEY**, Sylvanus

11344   HALSEY, Ruth

She married **BURNET**, James.

11345   HALSEY, Zebulon

His body was interred in Wickapogue g. y., LI, NY. He married **SAYRE**, Sarah. Zebulon was born in Southampton, LI, NY circa 1729. Zebulon died 6 May 1806 at 76 years of age.

113451 HALSEY, Zebulon, Jr.

He married **HOWELL**, Pamela. Zebulon, was born 26 February 1755. Zebulon, died 21 December 1817 at 62 years of age.

114   HALSEY, Sarah

She married **MOORE**, Joseph. Sarah was born 29 October 1658. Sarah died after 1725/6.

1141   MOORE, Sarah

Sarah was born in Suffolk Co., NY 29 October 1683. She married **COOK**, Abiel circa 1702.

11411   COOK, Ellis

Ellis was born in Southampton, L.I, NY circa 1703. He married Temperance circa 1723. He married **WILLIAMS**, Mary in Southampton, L.I, g.y. circa 1730. Ellis died 31 August 1756 in Fort Oswego, NY, at 53 years of age. On 22 Jun 1747, Ellis Cook, husbandman, bought from Cornelius Drake, of Hanover, a farm of 110 acres, on south side of road to old "iron works" and extending from the Passaic River 62 chains west. This lot had been sold by James Ball and Sarah Ball, and was bounded on south by John Canfield and a meadow belonging to Caleb Ball, and on west by Mrs. Wheeler's land. Indians killed Ellis in 1756 while going with his two youngest sons, John and Epaphras, with the Jersey Blues, to the relief of Oswego, then besieged by Montcalm. The Jersey regiment was under Col. Peter Schuyler. Both sons returned safely. In Book F. Wills, p. 404, in office of Secretary of State, Trenton, NJ, is recorded the will of Ellis. It is dated March 11, 1756, and it is said that the occasion for the will was the drafting or enlistment of his sons in the Jersey regiment. The will was proved 31 August 1756, and it names sons Williams, Ellis, Jonathon, Epaphras and John. The will gave the property in Hanover to Williams and Ellis (the oldest sons) and legacies to the other sons. Williams sold out his share to Ellis--"and much of the land is still held" by his descendants. Ellis probably moved to NJ after his first wife died in 1723.

114111 COOK, Williams

Williams died in Troy, NJ. Williams was born in Hanover, Morris Co, NJ circa 1732. He married **COCKER**, Sarah in Hanover, Morris Co, NJ, 5 June 1755. He married **COOPER**, Margaret in Hanover, Morris Co, NJ, 12 February 1778.

1141111   COOK, Williams

Williams was born circa 1748.

1141112   COOK, Ellis (Capt.)

Ellis was born in Hanover, Morris Co, NJ circa 1756. He married **DAVIS**, Isabella in Hanover, Morris Co, NJ, 1777. Ellis died 1832 in Hanover, Morris Co, NJ, at 76 years of age. His body was interred 1833 in Hanover, Morris Co, NJ. Per Mrs. E. Dodd Condit (Anna Cecelia Thompson, granddaughter of William Cook Ball and Margaret Ann Ten Broeck), in letter of 20 Jul 1931 to Mrs. Stephen L. Morgan, the date of birth was 1740 and date of death was 1830. However, she sent a photo of the tombstones of Ellis Cook and his wife, Isabella Davis, taken at Hanover, NJ cemetery. The inscription stating "Sacred in the Memory of Ellis Cook, A captain in the Revolutionary War, who died AD 1832 and of Isabel Cook, his wife who died AD 1825", and below "Erected by their descendants AD 1860". Whether dates were accurate is unknown. In her letter of 22 Aug 1933 to "Emmie" (Mrs. S.L. Morgan), she describes her search for the tombstones. It was a cemetery by a church, and the records of the church showed their monuments. Next to that monument was a tablet "In memory of Martha, widow of Phineahas Beach, who died March 2nd 1847 in the 63rd year of her age."--This is the wife of Daniel Ball (their child Cyrus married the daughter of Ellis Cook and Sarah Cook). Apparently many of the related families are buried at Hanover. In 1933 some Cook descendants still lived there--namely, daughter of James Cook. See Revolutionary War Pension file Series M805 Roll 214, pension file #S34224. Per declaration, enlisted 12 Feb 1776 as private and continued in service until Yorktown. He was a commisioned as a "Waggon Master", which apparently entitled him to be called a captain. There is discrepancy as to birth date of Ellis--The pension file implies that he was born in 1754; Condit shows lineal chart with Ellis born in 1740. Fisk alleges the father and mother married 5 June 1755, thus circa 1756 is chosen.

11411121   COOK, Williams

Williams was born in Hanover, Morris Co, NJ 8 December 1779.

11411122   COOK, Sarah

Sarah was born in Hanover, Morris Co, NJ 21 January 1783. She married **BALL**, Cyrus in Hanover, Morris Co, NJ, 3 November 1802. Sarah died circa 1811 in Hanover, Morris Co, NJ.

114111221   BALL, William Cook

He married **TEN BROECK**, Margaret. William was born in Hanover, Morris Co, NJ 24 August 1805.

1141112211   BALL, Caroline Elizabeth 'Carrie'

Caroline was born 22 April 1827. Caroline died 30 December 1878.

1141112212   BALL, Frances 'Fanny' Amelia

She married **FISK**, Anthony (Fick). Frances was born 30 November 1828.

11411122121 FISK, Ella Frances
Ella was born circa 1855.

11411122122 FISK, Charles William
He married Emma. Charles was born circa 1860.

114111221221 FISK, Aylmer

114111221222 FISK, Arthur
Arthur was born circa 1890.

1141112213 BALL, Ann Louise 'Wesey'
She married **PHAIR**, Harry 'Henry'. Ann was born 16 October 1830.

11411122131 PHAIR, Henry
Henry was born circa 1855.

11411122132 PHAIR, William
William was born circa 1856.

11411122133 PHAIR, Mary
Mary was born circa 1857.

1141112214 BALL, Mary Josephine 'Josey'
She married **ROGERS**, Joseph. Mary was born 17 November 1832.

11411122141 ROGERS, Frances

11411122142 ROGERS, Warren
Warren was born circa 1855.

11411122143 ROGERS, Carrie
Carrie was born circa 1856.

1141112215 BALL, Eleanora 'Nora'
She married **PETTY**, George. Eleanora was born 2 April 1834.

11411122151 PETTY, Annie
She married **BUGELLEN**, Henry. Annie was born circa 1853.

11411122152 PETTY, John
John was born circa 1855.

11411122153 PETTY, Harry
Harry was born circa 1859.

11411122154 PETTY, George
George was born circa 1859.

11411122155 PETTY, Robert
Robert was born circa 1861.

1141112216 BALL, Maria Theresa 'Ressie'
She married **WALDRON**, James. Maria was born 1 January 1836.

11411122161 WALDRON, Arthur
Arthur was born circa 1860.

1141112217 BALL, Cecelia Emilie 'Celie'
She married **THOMPSON**, Samuel. Cecelia was born 30 September 1837.

11411122171 THOMPSON, William Ward
He married **MCBRIAN**, Martha Ann. William was born 11 June 1856.

114111221711 THOMPSON, Anna Cecelia

She married **CONDIT**, Ernest Dodd. Anna was born circa 1880. There are two letters to Mrs. Stephen L. Morgan (Emilie Stevens) from Mrs. E. Dodd Condit--nee Anna Cecelia Thompson. One letter postmarked 20 Jul 1931 from Oakdale Avenue, Norristown, PA, refers to fact that Grandma told her the Daughters of the American Revolution (DAR) membership of MRS. Ella L. Fisk Josselyn, (#56578) daughter of Frances Amelia Ball and ? Anthony Fisk. The DAR records were found in the Norristown Historical Society records. Mrs. Mary Phair Ellis, (#58528), was the daughter of Ann Louise Ball and Henry Wood Phair, and Mrs. Alice Weed Coulter, (#69960) who was granddaughter of Caroline Ball (1803-91) and Robert Baxter Moores--who had become members because of Ellis Cook and Daniel Ball for Revolutionary War. She also attaches her ancestry to Daniel Ball and Ellis Cook. A letter of 22 Aug 1933 tells of trying to reach Arthur Fisk while at East Orange, NJ. She then drove to Hanover and saw monuments of Ellis Cook and his wife, Isabel; and adjacent stone of MARTHA, wife of Phineahas Beach (also widow of Daniel Ball). She located some Cook descendants in Hanover; and many of related families are buried there.

11411122172   THOMPSON, Cecelia
Cecelia was born 26 October 1859.

11411122173   THOMPSON, Jenny
Jenny was born circa 1861.

1141112218   BALL, Charles Henry
Charles was born 10 December 1839. Charles died 23 February 1840 at less than one year of age.

1141112219   BALL, Martha Cook
Martha was born 28 August 1841. Martha died 22 December 1843.

114111221(10) BALL, Fredricka Freddie Bremer
Fredricka was born in New York, NY 13 September 1844. She married **STEVENS**, William Henry, Jr. in NY, NY, 11 October 1866. Fredricka died 17 August 1926 in Skaneateles, Onondaga Co, NY, at 81 years of age. Her body was interred 19 August 1926 in Paterson, Passaic Co, NJ.

114111221(10)1   STEVENS, Emilie Louise
Emilie was born in New York, NY 13 September 1867. She married **MORGAN**, Stephen Lincoln in Rutherford, Bergen Co, NJ, 26 June 1889. Emilie died 30 May 1961 in Lake Geneva, Walworth Co, WI, at 93 years of age. Her body was interred June 1961 in Skaneateles, Onondaga Co, NY.

114111221(10)11   MORGAN, Almira Smith
Almira was born in Rutherford, Bergen Co, NJ 19 December 1890. She married **MCNALLY**, Robert Everett in Skaneateles, Onondaga Co, NY, 8 August 1915.

114111221(10)111   MCNALLY, Emilie Elizabeth
Emilie was born in Glens Falls, Warren Co, NY 17 June 1916. She married **HARTNETT**, William Edward in Lake Geneva, Walworth Co, WI, 23 November 1944.

114111221(10)1111   HARTNETT, Emilie Louise
Emilie was born in Charlottesville, Albermarle Co, VA 22 March

1946. She married **DOWNS**, Clark Evans in Lake Geneva, Walworth Co, WI, 17 August 1968.

114111221(10)11111   DOWNS, Morgan Elizabeth
Morgan was born in Lake Forest, Lake Co, IL 24 November 1975.

114111221(10)11112   DOWNS, Julia Evans
Julia was born in Lake Forest, Lake Co, IL 25 May 1978.

114111221(10)1112   HARTNETT, Jeffrey Edward
Jeffrey was born in Elkhorn, Walworth Co, WI 15 July 1948. He married **BERG**, Diana in Bradley, Kankakee Co, IL, December 1972.

114111221(10)11121   HARTNETT, Andrew McNally
Andrew was born in St. Louis, St. Louis Co, MO 19 January 1981.

114111221(10)11122   HARTNETT, Elizabeth Hutchings
Elizabeth was born in St. Louis, St. Louis Co, MO 10 June 1986.

114111221(10)1113   HARTNETT, Merry Alice
Merry was born in Woodstock, McHenry Co, IL 25 December 1950. Merry died 25 October 1953 in Lincoln, Logan Co, IL, at 2 years of age.

114111221(10)1114   HARTNETT, William Robert
William was born in Woodstock, McHenry Co, IL 24 February 1953. He married **HUDOCK**, Patricia in Lake Forest, Lake Co, IL, 6 July 1977.

114111221(10)11141   HARTNETT, Abigail Frances
Abigail was born in Waukegan, Lake Co, IL 9 August 1978.

114111221(10)11142   HARTNETT, Christop Aidan
Christop was born in Waukegan, Lake Co, IL 3 January 1980.

114111221(10)11143   HARTNETT, Emilie Elizabeth
Emilie was born in Lake Forest, Lake Co, IL 17 May 1981.

114111221(10)11144   HARTNETT, Kara Adelaide
Kara was born in Lake Forest, Lake Co, IL 4 April 1983.

114111221(10)11145   HARNETT, O'Connor William Jeffrey
O'Connor was born in Lake Forest, Lake Co, IL 9 January 1989.

114111221(10)1115   HARTNETT, Elizabeth Ann
Elizabeth was born in Waukegan, Lake Co, IL 2 April 1957. She married **WHITE**, Matthew Hagy in Antioch, Lake Co, IL, 22 August 1981.

114111221(10)11151   WHITE, Thaddeus Edward
Thaddeus was born in Evanston, Cook Co, IL 12 December 1989.

114111221(10)112   MCNALLY, Robert Morgan
Robert was born in Lake Geneva, Walworth Co, WI 17 May 1920. He married **HATTEN**, Rose Emma in Santa Monica, Los Angeles Co., CA, 19 April 1946.

114111221(10)1121   MCNALLY, Stephen Campbell
Stephen was born in Los Angeles, Los Angeles Co, CA 19 June 1948. Stephen died 31 July 1968 in Sherman Oaks, Los Angeles Co, CA.

114111221(10)1122   MCNALLY, Mark Everett
Mark was born in Los Angeles, Los Angeles Co, CA 8 August 1951. He married **SIMPKINS**, Cindy Sue in Palos Verdes, Los Angeles Co, CA, 5 February 1977.

114111221(10)113   MCNALLY, Stephen Bolles
Stephen was born in Skaneateles, Onondaga Co, NY 21 May 1922.

He married **WALTERS**, Mavis Adell in Sherman Oaks, Los Angeles Co, CA, 20 August 1950.

114111221(10)1131   MCNALLY, Stuart Morgan
Stuart was born in Los Angeles, Los Angeles Co, CA 22 August 1954.

114111221(10)1132   MCNALLY, Kim Elizabeth
Kim was born in Los Angeles, Los Angeles Co, CA 21 April 1956.

114111221(10)2   STEVENS, William Frederick, Sr.
William was born in Rutherford, Bergen Co, NJ 16 December 1870. He married **PECK**, Maude in Haverstraw, Rockland Co, NY, 24 April 1901. William died 15 February 1962 in Hasbrouck Hts, Bergen Co, NJ, at 91 years of age. His body was interred 1962 in East Paterson, Passaic Co, NJ.

114111221(10)21   STEVENS, Maude Evelyn
Maude was born in Rutherford, Bergen Co, NJ 15 September 1902. She married **ROYLANCE**, Raymond in Arlington, Arlington Co, VA, 28 June 1939.

114111221(10)22   STEVENS, Ruth Gordon
Ruth was born in Rutherford, Bergen Co, NJ 23 August 1905. She married **CARR**, George Nelson in Hasbrouck Hts, Bergen Co, NJ, 20 December 1935.

114111221(10)221   CARR, Cynthia
She married **SUSTAD**.

114111221(10)2211   SUSTAD, Debbie
114111221(10)2212   SUSTAD, Diane
114111221(10)2213   SUSTAD, David

114111221(10)23   STEVENS, William Howard
William was born in Rutherford, Bergen Co, NJ 16 July 1907. He married **DELAMATER**, M. Elizabeth (Betty) in Hasbrouck Hts, Bergen Co, NJ, circa 1930. William died 1974 in Hartford, Hartford Co, CT.

114111221(10)231   STEVENS, William Anthony (Tony)
He married **NOLES**, Jo Ann. William was born in Hasbrouck Hts, Bergen Co, NJ 8 January 1939.

114111221(10)2311   STEVENS, William Anthony (Tony), Jr.
William was born in Hasbrouck Hts, Bergen Co, NJ 1965.

114111221(10)2312   STEVENS, Jennifer
Jennifer was born in West Hartford, Hartford Co, CT 1971.

114111221(10)232   STEVENS, Diane Mary
She married **HALEY**, Thomas. Diane was born in Hasbrouck Hts, Bergen Co, NJ 13 February 1941.

114111221(10)2321   HALEY, Deborah (Debbie)
Deborah was born in Larchmont, CT 18 March 1964.

114111221(10)2322   HALEY, Elizabeth (Beth)
Elizabeth was born in Larchmont, CT 1965.

114111221(10)2323   HALEY, Theodore (Ted)
Theodore was born in Larchmont, CT 1970.

114111221(10)233   STEVENS, Jeffrey Howard
Jeffrey was born in Ridgewood, Bergen Co, NJ 1948. He married

LA BLANC, Patricia in West Hartford, Hartford Co, CT, 14 February 1975.
114111221(10)2331   STEVENS, Erich
     Erich was born 1970.
114111221(10)2332   STEVENS, Ashleigh
     Ashleigh was born in Hollywood, Broward Co, FL 7 January 1977.
114111221(10)2333   STEVENS, Jeffrey William
     Jeffrey was born in Plantation, Broward Co, FL 4 August 1980.
114111221(10)3   STEVENS, Caroline Ball
     Caroline was born in New York, NY 23 April 1873. Caroline died 30
December 1878 in New York, NY, at 5 years of age.
114111221(10)4   STEVENS, Arthur Waldron
     Arthur was born in Rutherford, Bergen Co, NJ 2 August 1876. He
married **FOWLER**, Edna Belle circa 1900. His body was interred 1910 in
East Paterson, Passaic Co, NJ. Arthur died 29 August 1910 in Rutherford,
Bergen Co, NJ, at 34 years of age. Arthur received his education in
Rutherford. He served in the Army during the Spanish American War. The
Company Muster Roll of Company L, 2 Reg't NJ Infantry (National Archives)
show he enlisted May 2, 1898 in Rutherford; mustered in at Sea Girt, NJ on
May 14, at age 21. He was listed as 5'8 1/5", with a dark complexion, eyes
brown, hair black, born Rutherford, occupation laundryman. He mustered
out as a private 17 Nov 1898 at Rutherford. According to Arthur's obituary, at
the time of the war he went to Jacksonville with Company L, Second
Regiment. After the war he was active with the Sp War Veterans, being a
commander of Hilton Camp, and being Dept Quartermaster during the term
of John T.7 Collins as State Dept Commander.
114111221(10)41   STEVENS, William Henry
     William was born in Rutherford, Bergen Co, NJ 17 March 1903.
William died 20 March 1903 in Rutherford, Bergen Co, NJ.
114111221(10)42   STEVENS, Helen Miriam
     She married **PARRISH**, Maxwell. Helen was born in Rutherford,
Bergen Co, NJ 11 December 1906. She married **LIGHTHALL**, Edwin
Howard 20 June 1923. Her body was interred 1983 in Pulaski, Oswego Co,
NY. Helen died 16 October 1983 at 76 years of age.
114111221(10)421   LIGHTHALL, Edna Ann
114111221(10)422   LIGHTHALL, Edwin Howard, Jr.
     Edwin was born in Sommerville, Middlesex Co, MA 6 February 1930.
He married **KELLY**, Barbara Jean 24 August 1952.
114111221(10)4221   LIGHTHALL, Donald Edwin
     His body was interred in Mexico, Oswego Co, NY. Donald was born
in Fulton, Oswego Co, NY 24 July 1953. Donald died 25 July 1973 in
Fairbanks, FNS Borough, AL, at 20 years of age.
114111221(10)4222   LIGHTHALL, Diane Emilie
     Diane was born in Fulton, Oswego Co, NY 24 July 1953. She
married **WATSON**, William Robert 3 October 1975. She married **GILLINGS**,
Thomas Anthony 21 April 1989.
114111221(10)42221   WATSON, Robecca Lolita
     Robecca was born in Ewa Beach, Honolulu Co, HI 3 April 1977.

114111221(10)42222   WATSON, David James
David was born in Ewa Beach, Honolulu Co, HI 23 January 1979.
114111221(10)4223   LIGHTHALL, Edwin Howard III
Edwin was born in Fulton, Oswego Co, NY 12 November 1954. He
married **FISCHER**, Lorraine Kay 29 May 1975.
114111221(10)42231   LIGHTHALL, Regina Louise   Regina was born in
Potsdam, St. Lawrence Co, NY 19 May 1977.
114111221(10)42232   LIGHTHALL, Kelly Jean
Kelly was born in Syracuse, Onondaga Co, NY 13 December 1979.
114111221(10)42233   LIGHTHALL, Louise Ann
Louise was born in Syracuse, Onondaga Co, NY 19 November 1982.
114111221(10)42234   LIGHTHALL, Jason Stewart
Jason was born in Syracuse, Onondaga Co, NY 19 July 1986.
114111221(10)4224   LIGHTHALL, William Arthur
William was born in Fulton, Oswego Co, NY 5 December 1955. He
married **DAVIS**, Christine Janet in Fulton, Oswego Co, NY, 19 September
1981.
114111221(10)42241   LIGHTHALL, Bethany Joy
Bethany was born in Oswego, Oswego Co, NY 18 December 1986.
114111221(10)4225   LIGHTHALL, Robert James
Robert was born in Fulton, Oswego Co, NY 14 September 1957. He
married **ROWELEE**, Lynn Louise 14 August 1976. He married **WOODARD**,
Christine Edith 1 January 1982.
114111221(10)42251   LIGHTHALL, Michael Alan
Michael was born in Oswego, Oswego Co, NY 25 January 1978.
114111221(10)42252   LIGHTHALL, Jessica Lea
Jessica was born in Oswego, Oswego Co, NY 20 January 1980.
114111221(10)42253   LIGHTHALL, Sara Jean
Sara was born in Oswego, Oswego Co, NY 15 October 1983.
114111221(10)42254   LIGHTHALL, Stacey Ann
Stacey was born in Oswego, Oswego Co, NY 15 October 1983.
114111221(10)4226   LIGHTHALL, Susan Ellen
Susan was born in Fulton, Oswego Co, NY 12 March 1959. She
married **ALEXANDER**, Paul Herbert in Mexico, Oswego Co, NY, 16 June
1979. She married **BUSKE**, David Michael 20 July 1985.
114111221(10)42261   BUSKE, David Michael II
David was born in Syracuse, Onondaga Co, NY 9 February 1987.
114111221(10)42262   BUSKE, Adam Paul
Adam was born in Syracuse, Onondaga Co, NY 5 May 1989.
114111221(10)4227   LIGHTHALL, Marcia Jean
Marcia was born in Fulton, Oswego Co, NY 20 March 1961. She
married **ALBRECHT**, Jeffrey Scott 11 August 1979.
114111221(10)42271   ALBRECHT, Aaron Robert
Aaron was born in Syracuse, Onondaga Co, NY 10 May 1986.
114111221(10)42272   ALBRECHT, Eric James
Eric was born in Syracuse, Onondaga Co, NY 10 May 1986.
114111221(10)42273   ALBRECHT, Donald Scott

Donald was born in Syracuse, Onondaga Co, NY 12 October 1989.
114111221(10)5   STEVENS, Frank
Frank was born 17 September 1881. Frank died 16 January 1902.
114111221(10)6   STEVENS, Harry Phair
Harry was born 11 November 1888. Harry died 30 March 1891.
114111222   BALL, Daniel
Daniel was born in Hanover, Morris Co, NJ circa 1806.
114111223   BALL, Jacob
Jacob was born in Hanover, Morris Co, NJ circa 1807.
114111224   BALL, Caroline
She married **MOORES**, R. B.. Caroline was born in Hanover, Morris Co, NJ circa 1808.
11411123   COOK, Martha 'Grandma Beach'
Martha was born in Hanover, Morris Co, NJ 19 August 1784. She married **BALL**, Cyrus circa 1812. She married **BEACH**, Phineas circa 1820. Martha died 2 March 1847 in Hanover, Morris Co, NJ, at 62 years of age. Her body was interred 1847 in Hanover, Morris Co, NJ. Martha Cook was the second wife of Cyrus Ball (whose first wife was her sister Sarah). She had three sons of Cyrus; and after the death of Cyrus married Phineas Beach and had one daughter. She was called "Grandma Beach". Per Condit letter, next to monument of Capt. Ellis Cook is tablet, which says, "In memory of Martha, widow of Phineahas Beach, who died March 2nd. 1847 in the 63rd year of her age." It is in a cemetery next to a church in Hanover.
11411124   COOK, Margaret

Margaret was born in Hanover, Morris Co, NJ 15 December 1785.
11411125   COOK, Samuel
Samuel was born in Hanover, Morris Co, NJ 5 December 1787.
114111251   COOK, Martindale
Martindale was born in Hanover, Morris Co, NJ circa 1800.
1141112511   COOK, Raymond
114111252   COOK, James
James was born in Hanover, Morris Co, NJ circa 1801.
11411126   COOK, Maria
Maria was born in Hanover, Morris Co, NJ 11 October 1789.
11411127   COOK, Louis B.
Louis was born in Hanover, Morris Co, NJ 21 June 1795.
1141113   COOK, Calvin
Calvin was born circa 1780.
114112 COOK, Ellis (Col.)
He married **PERKINS**, Lucy (Ely). Ellis was born in Hanover, Morris Co, NJ circa 1732. He married **COCKER**, Margaret Griswold 12 July 1753. Ellis died 17 April 1797 in Troy, Rensselaer Co, NY, at 64 years of age. Colonel Ellis was a member of the Morris County, NJ Militia, and was an aide for Washington's staff during the encampments at Morristown, NJ. He was a member of the Provincial Assembly.
1141121   COOK, Jabez

Jabez was born in Hanover, Morris Co., NJ before 1755.

1141122   COOK, Zebulon

Zebulon was born 22 March 1755. Zebulon died 12 December 1810.

1141123   COOK, James

James was born in Hanover, Morris Co., NJ 25 March 1760. He married **CONDIT**, Elizabeth P. 25 November 1781. He married **PIERSON**, Ruth 3 August 1786. James died 26 March 1836 at 76 years of age.

1141124   COOK, Ambrose

Ambrose died in Monmouth Co., NJ. Ambrose was born in Hanover, Morris Co., NJ after 1760. He married **WHEELER**, Sally P. 27 June 1794.

1141125   COOK, Matilda

Matilda was born in Hanover, Morris Co., NJ after 1761. She married **PLUMB**, David 27 February 1794.

1141126   COOK, Margaret

She married **KITCHELL**, William in Hanover, NJ. Margaret was born in Hanover, Morris Co., NJ after 1761.

1141127   COOK, Rulatte

Rulatte was born in Hanover, Morris Co., NJ after 1762. She married **GREGORY**, William O. September 1792.

1141128   COOK, Elizabeth

Elizabeth was born 28 May 1779. Elizabeth died 30 September 1780 at 1 year of age.

1141129   COOK, George Whitefield

George was born 1790.

114113 COOK, Jonathon

Jonathon was born in Hanover, Morris Co, NJ circa 1734. He married **TAPPAN**, Margaret 30 November 1757.

114114 COOK, Epaphras

Epaphras was born in Hanover, Morris Co, NJ circa 1736. He married **SMITH**, Sarah 4 October 1762.

1141141   COOK, Peter

Peter was born 1767.

114115 COOK, John

He married **PARROTT**, Sarah. John was born in Hanover, Morris Co, NJ circa 1738.

1141151   COOK, Silas

Silas was born 1767.

11412 COOK, Phebe

Phebe was born circa 1704.

11413 COOK, Susanna

Susanna was born circa 1705.

11414 COOK, Mathew

Mathew was born circa 1708.

11415 COOK, Abiel

Abiel was born circa 1710. He married **LEONARD**, Parthenia 1722. Abiel died 1781 in Imlaystown, NJ, at 71 years of age.

114151 COOK, Abiel

Abiel was born in Monmouth Co., NJ 15 November 1723. He married **THOMPSON**, Mary in Monmouth Co., NJ, 17 June 1765. Abiel died 24 January 1797 in Monmouth Co., NJ, at 73 years of age.

1141511   **COOK, Susannah**
1141512   **COOK, Samuel**
1141513   **COOK, Elizabeth**
1141514   **COOK, Nathaniel**
1141515   **COOK, Sarah**

Sarah was born 1765.

1141516   **COOK, William**

William was born 1765.

1141517   **COOK, Hannah**

She married **STEPHENS**, Joseph. Hannah was born 1775. Hannah died 1817 at 42 years of age.

114152 COOK, Sarah

She married **MATTISON**, Aaron. Sarah was born 23 January 1726.

114153 COOK, Nathaniel

Nathaniel was born in Imlaystown, NJ 10 April 1728. He married **ROBBINS**, Margaret in NJ, before 1756. Nathaniel died 10 June 1812 in Charlton, Saratoga Co., NY, at 84 years of age.

1141531   **COOK, Asher**

Asher was born in Imlaystown, NJ 5 October 1756. He married **BARCALOW**, Helena in NJ, before 1778. Asher died 5 February 1822 in Charlton, Saratoga Co., NY, at 65 years of age.

11415311   **COOK, Nathaniel**

Nathaniel was born 21 October 1781.

11415312   **COOK, William**

He married **CRANE**, Sarah. William was born in Charlton, Saratoga Co., NY 24 December 1783. William died 1859 at 75 years of age.

11415313   **COOK, Anna**

Anna was born 26 July 1786.

11415314   **COOK, Margaret**

Margaret was born 10 December 1788.

11415315   **COOK, John C.**

John was born 19 April 1791.

11415316   **COOK, Arthur**

Arthur was born 14 August 1793.

11415317   **COOK, Zebulon**

Zebulon was born 3 March 1796.

11415318   **COOK, Asher**

Asher was born in Charlton, NY 19 August 1798. Asher died 6 August 1799 in Charlton, NY, at less than one year of age.

11415319   **COOK, Sarah**

She married **OLMSTEAD**, Ebenezer. Sarah was born in Charlton, NY 12 June 1800. Sarah died 11 June 1838 in Charlton, NY.

1141532   **COOK, Zebulon**

Zebulon was born in Imlaystown, NJ 7 August 1758. Zebulon died

1784 in Charlton, Saratoga Co., NY, at 25 years of age.
1141533   COOK, Aaron
Aaron was born in Imlaystown, NJ 22 October 1760. Aaron died 30
July 1841 in Charlton, Saratoga Co., NY, at 80 years of age.
1141534   COOK, Samuel
He married **LORD**, Abigail. Samuel was born in Imlaystown, NJ 6
August 1762. Samuel died 28 July 1834 at 71 years of age.
11415341   COOK, Aaron
Aaron was born 1799.
1141535   COOK, Joseph
Joseph was born in NJ 12 May 1764. He married **GORDON**,
Rebecca in Ballston Center, NY, 27 January 1790. Joseph died 7 January
1823 in Galway, NY, at 58 years of age.
1141536   COOK, Nathaniel
Nathaniel was born in Imlaystown, NJ 1 September 1766.
1141537   COOK, John
He married **JOHNSON**, Anna Nancy. John was born in
Imlaystown,NJ 25 November 1768. John died 4 August 1811.
11415371   COOK, Nathaniel
11415372   COOK, Aaron
11415373   COOK, William Johnson
11415374   COOK, Polly
11415375   COOK, Phoebe
11415376   COOK, Orpha
11415377   COOK, Sarah "Sally"
Sarah was born 28 March 1808.
1141538   COOK, Thomas C.
Thomas was born in Imlaystown, NJ 10 March 1772. Thomas died
1828 in Charlton, Saratoga Co., NY, at 56 years of age.
1141539   COOK, Sarah C.
She married **FINLEY**, James. Sarah was born in Charlton, Saratoga
Co., NY 25 May 1774. Sarah died 1859 in Charlton, NY, at 85 years of age.
114154 COOK, Frances
She married **MOUNT**, Samuel. Frances was born 16 September
1731.
114155 COOK, Susanna
She married **IMLAY**, Peter. Susanna was born 3 April 1735.
114156 COOK, Mary C.
She married **LIPPINCOTT**, Jonathon. Mary was born about 1736.
114157 COOK, Phebe
She married **DEWITT**, Peter. Phebe was born about 1737.
114158 COOK, Abigail
She married **STRICKLIN**, . Abigail was born about 1739.
11416   COOK, Zebulon
Zebulon was born circa 1712.
11417   COOK, Samuel
Samuel was born circa 1714.

11418   COOK, Elemuel
Elemuel was born circa 1715.
11419   COOK, Abigail
Abigail was born circa 1716.
1141(10)   COOK, Anna
Anna was born circa 1718.
115   HALSEY, Isaac Captain
His body was interred in Old South g.y., LI. Isaac was born 29
August 1660. He married **STRATTON**, Hannah 19 November 1699. He
married **HUDSON**, Mary 14 July 1736. Isaac died circa 1757. He was
engaged in the French and Indian war. His will was dated 10 January 1751,
as recorded in NY county, in 1757. References agree that he was married to
Hannah Stratton and Mary Hudson. However, which is the mother of his
three children remains an unknown to this researcher.
1151   HALSEY, Ephraim
Ephraim was born circa 1693. He married **CONKLING**, Martha 22
December 1713. Ephraim died 20 August 1764 at 71 years of age.
11511   HALSEY, Cornelius
Cornelius was born 15 June 1715. He married **ROGERS**, Obadiah
10 January 1750/1. Cornelius died 12 April 1782 at 66 years of age.
11512   HALSEY, Lemuel
Lemuel was born 14 December 1715. Lemuel died 30 May 1735.
11513   HALSEY, Matthew
Matthew was born 3 March 1717/8. Matthew died 31 December
1722 at 4 years of age.
11514   HALSEY, Sylvanus
He married **HALSEY**, Esther. He married **CHARD**, . Sylvanus was
born 18 November 1722. Sylvanus died 14 February 1815 in Blooming
Grove, Orange Co., NY, at 92 years of age.
11515   HALSEY, James (or Abraham)
James was born 16 November 1724. James died 22 December
1746 in Albany, NY, at 22 years of age.
11516   HALSEY, Timothy
Timothy was born 23 September 1727. Timothy died 9 August 1732.
11517   HALSEY, Waitglil
Waitglil was born 28 December 1729. Waitglil died 21 April 1731.
11518   HALSEY, Abigal
She married **ELY**, Simon. Abigal was born 8 February 1731/2.
11519   HALSEY, Zophar
Zophar was born 15 March 1734/5. Zophar died 20 December 1751.
1151(10)   HALSEY, Mary
She married **JESSUP**, John. Mary was born 19 June 1738.
1152   HALSEY, Isaac
Isaac was born circa 1693. Isaac died 3 January 1724/5.
1153   HALSEY, Timothy
His body was interred in Southampton g.y., LI. Timothy was born
circa 1703. Timothy died 12 July 1723 at 20 years of age.

116   HALSEY, David
His body was interred in Water Mills, LI. David was born 12 April 1663. He married Hannah circa 1696. David died 18 February 1731/2.
1161   HALSEY, Phebe
She married Hezekiah Howell.
1162   HALSEY, Hannah
1163   HALSEY, Mehitabel
1164   HALSEY, Abigail
Her body was interred in Southampton, LI. Abigail was born in Southampton, LI circa 1690. Abigail died 10 October 1696 at 6 years of age.
1165   HALSEY, Abraham
His body was interred in Water Mill, LI. He married **HALSEY**, Amy. Abraham was born circa 1695. Abraham died 28 November 1759.
11651   HALSEY, Lemuel
Lemuel was born in Southampton, LI, NY. He married **WHITE**, Abigail.
11652   HALSEY, David
His body was interred in Water Mill g.y.. He married **COOPER**, Mary. David was born 6 October 1722. David died circa 1805.
11653   HALSEY, Amy
She married **SAYRE**, John. Amy was born 24 August 1724.
11654   HALSEY, Jonathan
Jonathan was born 1 May 1727. He married **COOPER**, Jane 31 December 1761. Jonathan died 2 January 1797 at 69 years of age.
11655   HALSEY, Elias
Elias was born 3 February 1729/0. He married **HOWELL**, Hannah circa 1760. He was a Lieutenant in the French and Indian war station at Brewton and Oneida Lake. He was living in 1815.
116551   HALSEY, Elihu Howell
Elihu was born. He received land in will of uncle Theophilus Howell, dated 18 January 1775.
116552   HALSEY, Prudence
Prudence was born circa 1768. She married Hezekiah Sandford.
116553   HALSEY, Elias
Elias was born circa 1770. He married Jerusha Sandford.
116554   HALSEY, Hezekiah
Hezekiah was born 8 September 1771. He married Elizabeth Sandford.
11656   HALSEY, Hannah
She married **SANFORD**, Joel. Hannah was born 7 January 1731/2.
116561   SANFORD, Jared
11657   HALSEY, Stephen
Stephen was born in Bridge Hampton, LI, NY 13 April 1733.
117   HALSEY, Hannah
Hannah was born 5 February 1664/5. She married **HOWELL**, Nathaniel 3 August 1688. Hannah died circa 1732.
1171   HOWELL, Susannah

1172   HOWELL, Eunice
She was living in 1725.
1173   HOWELL, Mehetable
Mehetable was born circa 1690. She married John Cook.
1174   HOWELL, Martha
Martha was born circa 1692.
1175   HOWELL, Nehemiah
Nehemiah was born circa 1696. He married Martha.
1176   HOWELL, Henry
Henry was born circa 1698. He died young.
1177   HOWELL, Nathaniel, Jr.
Nathaniel, was born after 1703/4. He married Esther Johnes.
118   HALSEY, Jeremiah
His body was interred in Mecox g.y., LI, nr Mecox Bay. Jeremiah
was born 7 September 1667. He married Ruth circa 1689. He married
HALSEY, Deborah after 1705/6. Jeremiah died 29 December 1737.
1181   HALSEY, Jeremiah, Jr.
He married Hannah. Jeremiah, was born circa 1690. He married
CONKLING, Mary in East Hampton, LI, NY, 25 November 1721. Jeremiah,
died circa 1768. His will was dated 21 January 1767 (On file in the
Surrogate's Office, City of New York).
11811   HALSEY, Stephen
He married **ROGERS**, Mary.
11812   HALSEY, Isaac
11813   HALSEY, Jabez
11814   HALSEY, Amos
11815   HALSEY, Hannah
11816   HALSEY, Martha
11817   HALSEY, Matthew
He married **HAINES**, Sarah. Matthew was born 24 February 1724/5.
Matthew died circa 1802.
118171 HALSEY, Jacob
Jacob was born in Bridgehampton, L.I., NY 4 November 1769. He
married **WOODRUFF**, Sarah circa 1791. Jacob died 10 April 1847 in
Bridgehampton, L.I., NY, at 77 years of age.
1181711   HALSEY, Gurden
Gurden was born in Bridgehampton, L.I., NY 12 February 1797. He
married **OSBORN**, Elizabeth July 1822. Gurden died 25 September 1852 in
New York City, NY, at 55 years of age.
11817111   HALSEY, George
George was born in Wainscott, NY 15 April 1823. He married
MEAD, Josephine A. 5 September 1850.
11817112   HALSEY, Jacob L.
Jacob was born in New York City, NY 18 August 1828. He married
HARVEY, Mary C. 3 April 1850. He married **PIERSON**, Sarah F. 4 October
1864.
11817113   HALSEY, Jonathan O.

Jonathan was born in Wainscott, NY 6 August 1836. He married **NICHOLS**, Virginia B. 25 December 1859.

118172 HALSEY, Samuel

Samuel was born 6 January 1773. Samuel died 22 September 1839

11818   HALSEY, Jeremiah III

His body was interred in Scuttle Hole, LI, NY. He married **WOODRUFF**, Elizabeth. Jeremiah was born circa 1737. Jeremiah died September 1782 at 45 years of age. His will of 7 September 1782 was proved on 31 December 1782 (On file in the Surrogate's Office, City Of New York).

118181 HALSEY, Simeon

118182 HALSEY, Luther

118183 HALSEY, Amos

118184 HALSEY, Jerusha

118185 HALSEY, Unice

118186 HALSEY, Elizabeth

Elizabeth was born 1 January 1766. Elizabeth died 11 August 1834.

118187 HALSEY, Jeremiah

Jeremiah was born circa 1771. He married **SANDFORD**, Jerusha 29 May 1791. Jeremiah died 9 October 1806 at 35 years of age. He was killed by a stick of timber or "shears" which he was assisting in raising. The timber fell on him in Bridgehampton, NY.

11819   HALSEY, Paul

His body was interred in g.y., near Mecox Bay, LI. He married **HUDSON**, Anna. Paul was born December 1741. Paul died 1 April 1830 in Scuttle Hole, LI, NY, at 88 years of age.

1181(10)   HALSEY, Silas

Silas was born 12 June 1753. Silas died 26 October 1801 in Sag Harbor, MI, at 48 years of age. He married Jane Ludlow, born 10 December 1756 and died 9 October 1836.

1181(11)   HALSEY, William Rogers

William was born circa 1757. William died 4 March 1835 in Franklin, Del. Co., NY, at 77 years of age.

1182   HALSEY, Nathan

Nathan was born circa 1692. He married **HOWELL**, Charity in Hampton, NY, circa 1729. Nathan died circa 1760.

11821   HALSEY, Timothy

He married **TOPPING**, Phebe. Timothy was born in Bridge Hampton, NY 16 October 1730. Timothy died 1812 at 81 years of age.

11822   HALSEY, Nathaniel

Nathaniel was born in Hampton, NY circa 1731. He married Mary circa 1756. Nathaniel died 1768 in Bridgehampton, NY, at 37 years of age.

118221 HALSEY, Daniel

Daniel was born in Scuttle Hale, NY 29 May 1757. Daniel died 14 January 1827 at 69 years of age.

118222 HALSEY, Moses

Moses was born in Scuttle Hale, N.Y. circa 1759. He married

HALSEY, Margaret circa 1800. Moses died circa 1830 in Mouth of Wilson, Grayson County, VA. Migrated to Mouth of Wilson, Grayson County, VA, Circa 1780- 1800. Supplemental to the Grayson County 1810 tax list shows that Moses was a white tithable with no slaves over 12 years old and he had 4 horses. Grayson County, VA, records indicate that a deed, dated March 24, 1806, from James Lynch and wife Elizabeth, to Moses Halsey, was recorded. There was 100 acres of land, located on the New River at the mouth of Dotes Branch (B2P185 Grayson County Clerk, VA), sold for a price of $146.00. Another deed, dated September 2, 1812, from John Stogil and wife Jemima to Moses Halsey, for $200.00 for 156 acres of land near the New River at the Mouth of Wilson Creek, and a stake in Doty's Branch, is recorded (B3P337 Grayson County Clerk, VA, witnessed by James Halsey, Amos Halsey and William Halsey).

1182221   HALSEY, Elizabeth
Elizabeth was born circa 1792. Elizabeth died circa 1856.

1182222   HALSEY, Robert
Robert was born in Mou of Wilson, Virginia 1 July 1801. He married ALLEN, Mary Polly 26 March 1819. His body was interred November 1876 in Coy Halsey Cem.. Robert died 20 November 1876 in Mou of Wilson, VA.

11822221   HALSEY, Lewis Hamilton
Lewis was born in Mou of Wilson, Virginia 27 December 1819. He married STURGILL, Rebecca in Ashe Co., NC, 2 May 1841. Lewis died 17 September 1888 at 68 years of age.

118222211   HALSEY, Mary Jane
Mary was born 6 February 1842. She married MAXLEY, David Martin 22 February 1877. Mary died 12 December 1917 at 75 years of age.

1182222111   MAXLEY,
He was born 24 April 1878. He died 27 April 1878.

1182222112   MAXLEY, Mellissie
Mellissie was born 4 February 1881. Mellissie died 30 March 1932.

1182222113   MAXLEY, Frank J.
Frank was born 16 September 1882. Frank died 24 April 1959.

1182222114   MAXLEY, Laura E.
Laura was born 19 October 1885. Laura died 14 February 1959.

1182222115   MAXLEY, Cora Ennice
Cora was born 19 October 1885. Cora died 11 September 1953.

1182222116   MAXLEY, Rebecca 'Becky Ann'
Rebecca was born 28 August 1889.

118222212   HALSEY, Robert Franklin
Robert was born 3 October 1843. He married FRANCIS, Elizabeth in Ashe Co., NC, 23 January 1872. Robert died 25 April 1877.

1182222121   HALSEY, James Kenney
1182222122   HALSEY, Eli Hamilton
Eli was born 21 July 1876. He married SMITH, Lilian Blanche in Ashe Co., NC, 4 April 1894. Eli died 5 December 1951 at 75 years of age.

11822221221   HALSEY, Walter Franklin
Walter was born 20 January 1895. Walter died circa 1959.

11822221222   HALSEY, Leonard Kenney
Leonard was born 8 August 1897. He married **PARSONS**, Sarah 22 August 1932. Leonard died 6 September 1975 at 78 years of age.
118222212221   HALSEY, Lenna
Lenna was born 21 May 1944.
118222212222   HALSEY, Sarah Elizabeth
Sarah was born 19 January 1946.
11822221223   HALSEY, Lena Elizabeth
Lena was born 8 August 1897. She married **JENKINS**, Everette Jackson 24 September 1921.
118222212231   JENKINS, Georgia Maxine
Georgia was born 28 December 1922.
118222212232   JENKINS, Everette Jackson, Jr.
Everette was born 8 March 1924.
118222212233   JENKINS, Evon Halsey
Evon was born 7 November 1926.
118222212234   JENKINS, Ronald Hamilton
Ronald was born 22 July 1928.
118222212235   JENKINS, Billy Hazeltine
Billy was born 12 November 1930.
11822221224   HALSEY, Roy Lee
Roy was born 16 February 1900. Roy died 19 April 1916.
11822221225   HALSEY, Ray McCoy
Ray was born 15 August 1902. He married **TUGGLE**, Georgia 3 January 1925. Ray died 27 August 1976 in Mouth Of Wilson, VA.
118222212251   HALSEY, Bettie Ray
Bettie was born 10 February 1926.
118222212252   HALSEY, Mary Frances
Mary was born 21 October 1932.
118222212253   HALSEY, Raymond McCoy, Jr.
Raymond was born 10 January 1934.
118222212254   HALSEY, James Walter
James was born 16 June 1940.
11822221226   HALSEY, Robert Greek
Robert was born 4 June 1909. He married **LYONS**, Clara Norman in Sparta, NC, 25 December 1933. Robert died May 1983 in Sparta, NC.
118222212261   HALSEY, Ronald Lee
Ronald was born 11 August 1934.
118222212262   HALSEY, Robert Cleff
Robert was born 18 September 1936.
118222212263   HALSEY, Ralph Benton
Ralph was born 4 May 1938.
118222213   HALSEY, James W.
James was born circa 1846. He married **BELL**, Elizabeth in Sparta, NC, 5 March 1875.
1182222131   HALSEY, Drewey Cesero
Drewey was born. He married **GORE**, Capitola 27 July 1926.

Drewey died 7 July 1957.
11822221311   HALSEY, Elizabeth
She married **COX**, Jesse Long.
118222213111 COX, Mary Caroline
Mary was born 19 October 1950.
118222213112 COX, A.
A. was born circa 1951. A. died circa 1951.
118222213113 COX, A.
A. was born circa 1951. A. died circa 1951.
118222213114 COX, Bobby Ray
Bobby was born 23 May 1953.
118222213115 COX, Billy Dean
Billy was born 23 May 1953.
118222213116 COX, Johnnie Franklin
Johnnie was born 9 September 1955.
118222213117 COX, Judy Rose
Judy was born 15 August 1958.
11822221312   HALSEY, Minerva
11822221313   HALSEY, Mildred Virginia
Mildred was born 24 August 1930.
1182222132   HALSEY, Minerva
118222214   HALSEY, Rosamond E.
Rosamond was born 22 May 1849. Rosamond died 18 October
1862 at 13 years of age.
118222215   HALSEY, Martha Ann
Martha was born circa 1853.
118222216   HALSEY, Rebecca M.
Rebecca was born 4 May 1858. Rebecca died 2 July 1863.
11822222   HALSEY, William B.
William was born in Mou of Wilson, Virginia 9 July 1829. He married
BISHOP, Mahala 30 November 1850. William died 21 June 1890.
118222221   HALSEY, Granville F.
Granville was born 1 May 1852. Granville died 25 September 1853.
118222222   HALSEY, Samuel Freeland
His body was interred in Piney Creek Cem., NC. Samuel was born 5
December 1853. He married **HALSEY**, Mary Elizabeth 'Molly' 25 December
1882. Samuel died 27 April 1934 at 80 years of age.
1182222221   HALSEY, Cora Alice
Cora was born 27 September 1883. Cora died 25 January 1970.
1182222222   HALSEY, Dora Mahala
Dora was born 14 December 1885. Dora died 10 September 1942.
1182222223   HALSEY, William Caswell
William was born 14 December 1885. William died 28 December
1885 at less than one year of age.
1182222224   HALSEY, John Reed
John was born 10 September 1887. He married **ROBBINS**, Flossie
L. in Sparta, NC, 12 November 1919. John died 8 May 1969.

11822222241   HALSEY, Alice Marie
Alice was born 7 August 1920. She married **STURGILL**, David Andrew 18 May 1942.
118222222411 STURGILL, David Joseph
David was born 30 August 1943.
118222222412 STURGILL, John David
John was born 30 June 1945.
118222222413 STURGILL, Thomas Halsey
Thomas was born 9 October 1948.
118222222414 STURGILL, Rebecca Ruth
Rebecca was born 17 November 1953.
118222222415 STURGILL, Barbara Sue
Barbara was born 17 November 1953.
11822222242   HALSEY, Hazel Fern
Hazel was born 1 January 1922. Hazel died 4 January 1922.
11822222243   HALSEY, Rodney Lawurence
Rodney was born 23 June 1923. Rodney died 1 July 1923.
11822222244   HALSEY, Samuel Lyda
Samuel was born 13 September 1934. He married **ASHLEY**, Peggy Ann 20 June 1959.
118222222441 HALSEY, Sharon Elizabeth
Sharon was born 24 February 1961.
118222222442 HALSEY, Brenda Lynn
Brenda was born 5 April 1962.
118222222443 HALSEY, Charles Allen
Charles was born 11 October 1964.
118222222444 HALSEY, Patricia Ann
Patricia was born 21 September 1966.
1182222225   HALSEY, Fitchugh L.
Fitchugh was born 20 October 1889. Fitchugh died 10 July 1976.
1182222226   HALSEY, Samuel Carl
Samuel was born 22 March 1891. Samuel died 19 February 1955.
1182222227   HALSEY, Ora
Ora was born 1 September 1894. Ora died 25 September 1895.
1182222228   HALSEY, Rachel French
Rachel was born 10 October 1897. Rachel died 11 April 1973.
1182222229   HALSEY, Paul Jones
Paul was born 20 April 1900. Paul died 19 January 1969.
118222222(10) HALSEY, George Bland
George was born 3 July 1903. He married **KENYON**, Mercedes 20 December 1927. George died 23 February 1978 in Piney Cr., NC.
118222222(10)1   HALSEY, William Beverly
William was born 13 September 1930. William died 3 July 1950.
118222222(10)2   HALSEY, Walter Freeland
Walter was born 25 January 1943.
118222223   HALSEY, Robert M.
Robert was born 8 September 1855. Robert died 16 July 1862.

118222224   HALSEY, Levi F.
Levi was born 12 March 1857. Levi died 2 July 1862.
118222225   HALSEY, Drury Miles
Drury was born 4 April 1859. Drury died 22 February 1861.
118222226   HALSEY, Baley
Baley was born 31 May 1861. Baley died 5 September 1861.
118222227   HALSEY, Mary Elizabeth
Mary was born 8 July 1862. She married **ROUP**, Freeland Norman in Sparta, NC, 7 April 1878. Mary died 19 March 1941 at 78 years of age.
1182222271   ROUP, George Washington
George was born 3 April 1879. George died 16 December 1970 in Clarkston, WA, at 91 years of age.
1182222272   ROUP, William Howard
William was born 10 March 1881. William died 4 August 1967.
1182222273   ROUP, Jacob Leonard
Jacob was born 19 June 1883. Jacob died 4 February 1965 in Avondale, PA, at 81 years of age.
1182222274   ROUP, Nannie Alice
Nannie was born 18 July 1885.
1182222275   ROUP, John Lester
John was born 19 August 1888. John died 8 December 1956 in San Antonio, TX, at 68 years of age.
1182222276   ROUP, Mayme Virginia
Mayme was born 15 July 1893. She married **HALSEY**, Luther Fields in Sparta, NC, 15 July 1914.
11822222761   HALSEY, William Bradley
William was born 15 May 1916. He married **HARRIS**, Elsie Lee 16 April 1944.
118222227611 HALSEY, Sandra Kay
Sandra was born 23 November 1946.
11822222762   HALSEY, Marjorie
Marjorie was born 21 September 1923. She married **WHISNANT**, George Clayton in Sparta, NC, 9 September 1950.
118222227621 WHISNANT, George Clayton, Jr.
George was born 5 June 1959.
118222228   HALSEY, Nancy Jane
Nancy was born 22 November 1865. She married **HASH**, Watson in Sparta, NC, 28 May 1893. Nancy died circa 1939.
1182222281   HASH, Vella Pearl
Vella was born 4 July 1894.
1182222282   HASH, William Fleming
William was born 28 May 1896. William died 1 February 1976.
1182222283   HASH, Flora Mahala
Flora was born 4 February 1899.
1182222284   HASH, Earl
Earl was born 13 February 1902.
1182222285   HASH, Clarence Victor

Clarence was born 30 April 1904.
1182222286   HASH, Greek Garnet
Greek was born in Fox, VA 10 June 1906. He married **HALSEY,**
Polly Madeline 29 June 1927.
11822222861   HASH, Lois Sue
Lois was born 17 June 1929.
11822222862   HASH, Vera Allen
Vera was born 22 April 1932. Vera died 22 April 1932.
11822222863   HASH, Curtis Dale
Curtis was born 18 June 1936. Curtis died 28 September 1937.
1182222287   HASH, Addie Carol
Addie was born 1 October 1908.
118222229   HALSEY, John Hamilton
John was born 8 April 1867. He married **GAMBILL**, Chasa Ellen
'Cora' in Sparta, NC, 9 November 1889. He married **LOVELACE**, Lou Ellen
in Sparta, NC, 20 September 1896. John died 13 June 1949.
1182222291   HALSEY,
He was born 10 November 1890. He died 10 November 1890.
1182222292   HALSEY, Vondon Earl
Vondon was born 5 December 1890. He married **MITCHELL**, Anna
3 October 1913. Vondon died 16 October 1949 at 58 years of age.
11822222921   HALSEY, Wilma Cora
Wilma was born 12 July 1914.
11822222922   HALSEY, Donald
Donald was born 4 November 1915. Donald died 19 March 1945.
11822222923   HALSEY, Delbert
Delbert was born 8 December 1919. Delbert died 4 June 1942 at 22
years of age. Delbert Halsey was a Navy pilot flying dive bombers in the
Pacific Theater under the Command of Admiral William F. Halsey. He was
killed during the early stages of World War II.
1182222293   HALSEY, William Howard
William was born 24 June 1897. He married **HASH**, Mayme Ruth 2
June 1917. He married Virginia 2 September 1949. William died 22 January
1962 at 64 years of age.
11822222931   HALSEY, Evelyn Ruth
She married **LITTLE**, Walter. Evelyn was born 8 April 1919.
11822222932   HALSEY, William Howard, Jr.
William was born 6 November 1951.
11822222933   HALSEY, Jill
Jill was born circa 1954.
1182222294   HALSEY, Conley Bryan
Conley was born 8 July 1898. Conley died 8 March 1967 in
Roanoke, VA, at 68 years of age.
1182222295   HALSEY, James Kyle
James was born 1 May 1908. He married **OSBORNE**, Lizzie Lee 2
March 1926. He married **MURRAY**, Ruby 25 February 1937. James died 29
March 1967 at 58 years of age.

11822222(10)   HALSEY, Ada Selina
Ada was born in Piney Creek, NC 22 March 1869. She married **HALSEY**, George Vance 'Dick' in Ashe Co., NC, 25 March 1885. Ada died 8 March 1948 in Tilden, Nebr., at 78 years of age.

11822222(10)1 HALSEY, Nannie Lee
Nannie was born in Piney Creek, NC 31 March 1889. Nannie died 2 December 1964 at 75 years of age.

11822222(10)2 HALSEY, William Grover
William was born in Piney Creek, NC 3 November 1890.

11822222(10)3 HALSEY, Mary Anice
Mary was born in Piney Creek, NC 6 June 1893. She married **GALYEN**, Thomas Gwyn 5 March 1913.

11822222(10)31   GALYEN, Elmer Leroy
Elmer was born 8 October 1914. He married **SCHUMACHER**, Bernice Mae 14 August 1936. Elmer died circa 1968.

11822222(10)311   GALYEN, Marlene Kay
Marlene was born 8 March 1937.

11822222(10)312   GALYEN, Jimmy Leroy
Jimmy was born 10 February 1939.

11822222(10)313   GALYEN, Gary Dean
Gary was born 7 November 1941.

11822222(10)314   GALYEN, Kermith Lynn
Kermith was born 29 April 1949.

11822222(10)32   GALYEN, Harold Lloyd
Harold was born 7 September 1916. He married **SCHWARTING**, Rose Marie 11 February 1938.

11822222(10)321   GALYEN, Janice Elaine
Janice was born 14 August 1939.

11822222(10)322   GALYEN, Patricia Ann
Patricia was born 23 January 1943.

11822222(10)323   GALYEN, Robert Harold
Robert was born 2 May 1954.

11822222(10)4 HALSEY, Myrtle Mae
She married **FELLOWS**, William. Myrtle was born 25 May 1895. She married **JENNINGS**, Leland 6 December 1922.

11822222(10)41   FELLOWS, Richard
Richard was born 23 July 1928.

11822222(10)5 HALSEY, Cynthia Mahala
Cynthia was born in Piney Creek, NC 11 September 1898. She married **DUNNIVAN**, Charles Vance, Sr. 24 February 1926. Cynthia died September 1951 at 53 years of age.

11822222(10)51   DUNNIVAN, Charles Vance, Jr.
Charles was born 8 January 1927. He married **CROOK**, Marjorie Ruth 1 June 1948.

11822222(10)511   DUNNIVAN, Carolee Jayne
Carolee was born 26 December 1949.

11822222(10)512   DUNNIVAN, Charles Vance, III

Charles was born 20 December 1952.
11822222(10)513   DUNNIVAN, Susan
Susan was born 29 November 1954.
11822222(10)6 HALSEY, Phoebe Ellen
Phoebe was born in Piney Creek, NC 4 August 1900. She married
SHELDON, Kenneth Preston 8 February 1927.
11822222(10)61   SHELDON, Bettie Jean
Bettie was born 29 June 1928. She married **JACKSON**, Clyde
Henry 15 June 1947.
11822222(10)611   JACKSON, Rebecca Diane
Rebecca was born 17 August 1952.
11822222(10)612   JACKSON, Bonnie Joann
Bonnie was born 22 October 1954.
11822222(10)7 HALSEY, Samuel Bruce
He married **FREEMAN**, Elvira. Samuel was born 19 March 1903.
11822222(10)71   HALSEY, Harold Jimmy
Harold was born 29 June 1936.
11822222(10)8 HALSEY, Reeves Dale
Reeves was born in Piney Creek, NC 16 April 1905. Reeves died 24
May 1907 at 2 years of age.
11822222(10)9 HALSEY, Mack Bower
Mack was born in Piney Creek, NC 16 August 1907. He married
CORNET, Ola Virginia 12 December 1928.
11822222(10)91   HALSEY, Katheryn
11822222(10)92   HALSEY, Dean Lloyd
Dean was born 15 May 1930.
11822222(10)93   HALSEY, Delbert Delane
Delbert was born 24 June 1934. Delbert died 3 January 1947.
11822222(10)94   HALSEY, Donald Mack
Donald was born 18 August 1940.
11822222(10)95   HALSEY, Douglas Carl
Douglas was born 12 September 1949.
11822222(10)96   HALSEY, Dwane Lee
Dwane was born 17 August 1950.
11822222(10)(10)   HALSEY, America Alice
America was born in Piney Creek, NC 28 March 1910. She married
DIETZ, Joe 30 October 1934.
11822222(10)(10)1   DIETZ, Mary Alice
Mary was born 10 August 1935.
11822222(10)(10)2   DIETZ, Judianne
Judianne was born 28 October 1939.
11822222(10)(11)   HALSEY, Helen Jaunita
Helen was born in Tilden, Nebr. 16 March 1914. She married
HAWKINS, Gerald 8 March 1937.
11822222(10)(11)1   HAWKINS, Stanley Gene
Stanley was born 15 December 1937.
11822222(10)(11)2   HAWKINS, Jacqueline Jeanell

Jacqueline was born 21 January 1939.

11822222(10)(11)3   HAWKINS, Larry Lee

Larry was born 26 February 1941.

11822222(10)(11)4   HAWKINS, Sharon Marjean

Sharon was born 28 December 1946.

11822222(10)(11)5   HAWKINS, Dennis Craig

Dennis was born 18 July 1950.

11822222(11)   HALSEY, George Washington

George was born 22 June 1871. He married **PENNINGTON**, Victoria 20 December 1896. George died 28 July 1924 at 53 years of age.

11822222(11)1 HALSEY, Helen Mahala

Helen was born 10 November 1897.

11822222(11)2 HALSEY, William Cicero

William was born 6 August 1899. William died 1 June 1901.

11822222(11)3 HALSEY, Hugh Ludrick

Hugh was born 26 April 1901. He married **WARDEN**, Ruth 25 April 1923. He married **HAM**, Carrie (Jones) 24 June 1959. Hugh died 15 October 1963 at 62 years of age.

11822222(11)31   HALSEY, Hugh Warden

Hugh was born 23 November 1939.

11822222(11)4 HALSEY, Ella Mae

Ella was born 5 May 1903. She married **MCMILLAN**, James Vester in Grayson Co., VA, 24 August 1923. She married **BOONE**, Frank Allen 12 October 1940. Ella died 8 August 1977 at 74 years of age.

11822222(11)41   MCMILLAN, Anna Lee Anna was born 14 September 1925. She married **CHILDRESS**, James Kermit 20 September 1940.

11822222(11)411   CHILDRESS, James Kermit, Jr.

James was born 2 April 1943.

11822222(11)412   CHILDRESS, Larry

Larry was born 21 January 1945.

11822222(11)413   CHILDRESS, Harry Joe

Harry was born 6 June 1947.

11822222(11)414   CHILDRESS, Donald

Donald was born 13 January 1949.

11822222(11)415   CHILDRESS, Boyd

Boyd was born 6 May 1955.

11822222(11)42   MCMILLAN, Johnny

Johnny was born 18 November 1927.

11822222(11)43   MCMILLAN, Raymond

Raymond was born 27 April 1929.

11822222(11)44   BOONE, Lewis Allen

Lewis was born 24 February 1941.

11822222(11)5 HALSEY, Joe Henry

Joe was born 27 June 1905. He married **DEHAVEN**, Margaret 29 October 1929. He married **STARK**, Isabella 27 June 1937. Joe died 28 March 1946 at 40 years of age.

11822222(11)6 HALSEY, Almeda
Almeda was born 6 March 1908. She married **COX**, Colonel Edgar 24 May 1925. Almeda died 9 January 1955 at 46 years of age.
11822222(11)61   COX, Kenneth
Kenneth was born in Detroit, MI 11 June 1934.
11822222(11)62   COX, Bettie Joe
Bettie was born in Detroit, MI 10 June 1938.
11822222(11)7 HALSEY, Mary Blanche
She married **WATKINS**, George. Mary was born 14 March 1911. She married **REED**, Joe Bill 20 March 1926.
11822222(11)71   REED, Harold Lawrence
Harold was born 11 February 1928.
11822222(11)72   REED, Bryant Kent
Bryant was born circa 1930. Bryant died circa 1930.
11822222(11)8 HALSEY, Virginia Dale
Virginia was born 27 October 1915. She married **COVEY**, John R. 3 July 1937.
11822222(11)81   COVEY, Johnny R., Jr.
Johnny was born 27 January 1946.
11822222(11)9 HALSEY, Mildred Pennington
Mildred was born 27 June 1918. She married **WINGLER**, Joe 9 March 1946.
11822222(11)91   WINGLER, Janet
11822222(11)92   WINGLER, Sharon
Sharon was born 19 June 1950.
11822222(11)93   WINGLER, Tatsey
Tatsey was born 29 March 1955.
11822222(12)   HALSEY, Malinda Alice
Malinda was born 8 August 1873. She married **HALSEY**, William Cleveland in Ashe Co., NC, 25 July 1894. Malinda died 21 March 1955.
11822222(12)1 HALSEY, Archie
11822222(12)2 HALSEY, Dwight
11822222(12)3 HALSEY, Wallace
11822223   HALSEY, Henry Drury
Henry was born in Mou of Wilson, Virginia 2 May 1832. He married **BUSIC**, Nancy in Ashe County, North Carolina, 10 December 1851. Henry died 3 March 1894 in Pineville, Wyoming Co. W.V., at 61 years of age.
        He arrived upon this earth at a unique time for both his young country and his inherited way of life. Henry was born on Wednesday, May second, Eighteen hundred and thirty two, a leap year. This was the same year that the longest living signer of the Declaration of Independence, Charles Carroll, died. This was also the one hundredth anniversary of George Washington's birth. Ironic, that same Henry Drury would one day join forces, though not in anger, against the same Union that Washington fathered. Drury's birth place and young adult life was spent in and around Grayson County Virginia and Ashe County North Carolina. This was country defined by hills so rugged that hardy frontiersman became mountaineers in

order to survive. Mountains that delineate valleys that provide homes to the same small creeks and runs which cut the valleys in the first place. Dells that are to this day so steep and narrow, with full turns, winding and bending, maze-like in a zig zag pattern, leaning toward the natural drainage of the New River. A natural setting in the headwaters of one of the oldest known river basins in the Americas.

The New River was an ancient river whose lineage began as the Teays River. Within the vee shaped valleys, level ground only existed in the alluvial flood plains. Thus spring high water produced overland flow which would deposit top soil from up river, thus making subsistence farming and an occasional cabin flood all the more tolerable. This was the southern portion of the great Appalachian Highlands. The peneplains in which Henry Drury would one day penetrate deeper to make his mark in the history of Wyoming County, WV.

Like most folk growing up in a pioneer setting, Henry had little choice in culture, religion, and surroundings in general. He was a southern Baptist because his father and his father's father were, and so forth. Being the third sibling in a pioneer family also helps to determine ones personality traits. Henry Drury was soon to become just Drury. During the trip to West Virginia, in 1866, Drury and his family would establish a camp every night for the two-three week trip. As Drury probably would read the bible in the quiet of the evening twilight, as was a common practice after all the chores were done, he could probably hear the songs of many wild creatures with the whip-o-will singing the high notes as well as leading the chorus. He probably began to reflect upon what to say to his good friend David Goode, when they arrived at Bearhole near Pineville, WV.

How Drury and David met is not clear, but I suspect the camaraderie must have begun with a deed of mutual dependence that involved the Confederacy and Baptist. David Goode must have, upon learning that Drury was a fledging Baptist minister with stubborn resolve and great determination, recruited him for the new Mouth of Rockcastle Baptist Church. Drury and his family would live in a log cabin on the Goode farm from 1866 until 1869, at which time they would buy a tract of 129 acres from Ben Short and with the help of neighbors would build a double log house.

The thought of the war must have always been in Drury's mind. Witnessing the dying and suffering, before death, was always expressed vocally in a wail that is never mistaken but for what it was, pure hell on earth for the participants. The Civil War had caused everything to change. All the attitudes and values that one remembered as a teenager were no more. Drury must have longed for an adventure. He surely knew that one-day he would take his family away from his homestead in search of peace, harmony and sanctuary. He knew that once he left he would only return to visit nothing more. Sometime during this healing process must be the time that Drury decided to become a circuit preacher. Drury must have felt that spreading the Gospel was a very important assignment as well as the permanence of planting it in as many different locations as possible.

The Centennial birthday celebration for America was an election

campaign year. Naturally, the old Union soldiers and Republicans joined in
the celebration with the rest of the Pineville community, including a handful of
Confederate veterans. The site chosen for a picnic was the beech grove at
the mouth of Bearhole Fork, and for public speaking, the pine grove near
Castle Rock had been pruned for the occasion. Captain Drury Halsey, a
Baptist Elder, organized a parade from Bearhole grounds to the grove. The
first 60 of the men were mounted on horses, with Captain Halsey and the
Honorable Booker Short leading the way on fine stallions. Circling the Elder
Halsey's big log residence, the parade advanced to Castle Rock, where at
eleven o'clock a large crowed prepared to hear Judge David E. Johnston
deliver the main address of the day.

Drury died from a burst blood vessel in his mouth or throat while
hauling logs out of Gulf Fork, Wyoming County, West Virginia. He had
stopped for a drink of water from a spring, and as he leaned over to sip the
water blood spurted from his mouth. He was taken to the home of LeRoy
Perdew where he died a couple of days later on March 3, 1894.

118222231   HALSEY, Mary
Mary was born in Ashe County, N.C. 8 November 1853. Mary died
circa 1855 in Ashe County, N.C.

118222232   HALSEY, John Troy
John was born in Ashe County, N.C. 2 August 1855. He married
POE, Phoebe Ann 30 August 1876. John died 26 November 1915.

1182222321   HALSEY, Jesse Drury
Jesse was born 23 July 1877. He married **BLANKENSHIP**,
Dendana Eveline 19 March 1896. Jesse died 29 October 1946.

11822223211   HALSEY, Bertie R.
She married **MULLENS**, Neal. Bertie was born 25 January 1898.
Bertie died before 1995.

118222232111   MULLENS, Arlene
She married **BARRETT**, Garnett Ivan.

1182222321111   BARRETT, Jesse Darrell
He married **STEELE**, Carole Faye. Jesse was born 13 December
1939.

11822223211111   BARRETT, Jeffery Darin
Jeffery was born 27 April 1968.

1182222321112   BARRETT, Brenda Sue
She married **PENNINGTON**, John William. Brenda was born 15
June 1944.

11822223211121   PENNINGTON, Garnett Lee
He married Lisa. He married **LAXTON**, Crystal. Garnett was born 6
June 1965.

118222232111211   PENNINGTON, Brandon Lee
Brandon was born 11 January 1985.

118222232111212   PENNINGTON, Jonathan David
Jonathan was born 8 August 1993.

11822223211122   PENNINGTON, Joni Marlene
She married **GOODE**, Cotton. She married **NOVINGER**, Patrick.

Joni was born 26 November 1968.

118222232111221   GOODE, Valerie Arlene

118222232111222   NOVINGER, Amber Renee'
Amber was born 31 December 1993.

11822223211123   PENNINGTON, Amber Louise
Amber was born 25 November 1973.

118222232112 MULLENS, Norma Novella
She married **FORD**, Oley.

1182222321121   FORD, Don
He married **HARVEY**, Nadine.

11822223211211   FORD, Jeannine

11822223211212   FORD, Crystal

1182222321122   FORD, Peggy Ann
She married **SPRECKLEMYER**, Roy. She married **TAYLOR**, Jack.

11822223211221   SPRECKLEMYER, Lisa Michelle
She married **COVERDALE**, Kepp.

118222232113 MULLENS, Ina Ethel
Ina was born 21 March 1915. She married **BROWNING**, Earl Ray
30 December 1933.

1182222321131   BROWNING, Bob

1182222321132   BROWNING, Barbara
She married **MEADOWS**, James.

11822223211321   MEADOWS, Timmy

1182222321133   BROWNING, Forrest Ray
He married Mildred.

11822223211331   BROWNING, Stanley

11822223211332   BROWNING, Kevin

11822223211333   BROWNING, Brian

1182222321134   BROWNING, Ina Mae
She married **FITZGERALD**, Don.

11822223211341   FITZGERALD, Jeff

118222232114 MULLENS, Ivan Dean
He married **GOODE**, Sena Lou. Ivan was born 20 August 1917.

1182222321141   MULLENS, James Roland
James was born 25 September 1948.

118222232115 MULLENS, William Jessie
He married **BRANDENBURG**, Myrtis. William was born 27 March
1931.

1182222321151   MULLENS, Linda Susan
She married **MCTIGUE**, Jerry.

11822223211511   MCTIGUE, Susan

11822223211512   MCTIGUE, Bradley

11822223211513   MCTIGUE, Kimberly

1182222321152   MULLENS, Frederick Eugene
He married **SMART**, Judy. He married **HOLEMAN**, Rita.

11822223211521   MULLENS, Stephanie

11822223211522   MULLENS, Todd

1182222321153   MULLENS, Catherine Marie
She married YIENGST, Randy.
11822223211531   YIENGST, Jason
1182222321154   MULLENS, William Jessie, Jr.
He married LEE, Dixie. He married MILLS, Carole. William was
born 21 September 1951.
11822223211541   MULLENS, Melissa Michelle
Melissa was born 22 August 1973.
11822223211542   MULLENS, Amanda Leigh
Amanda was born 20 March 1983.
118222232116 MULLENS, John
He married JOHNSON, Jean. He married MARSHALL, Betsey.
John was born 2 February 1933.
1182222321161   MULLENS, Jeff
1182222321162   MULLENS, Dana
1182222321163   MULLENS, Sharon
1182222321164   MULLENS, Juddy
118222232117 MULLENS, Vesta Louise
She married JENKS, James. Vesta was born 2 February 1933.
118222232118 MULLENS, Owetta Elizabeth
She married LAXTON, Ronald. Owetta was born 9 November 1935.
1182222321181   LAXTON, Rhonda
11822223212   HALSEY, Virginia
Virginia was born 2 August 1900. She married JEWELL, William
Harrison 17 May 1917. Virginia died circa 1990.
118222232121 JEWELL, Olen James
He married BRISENTINE, Della. He married CONLEY, Evelyn.
Olen was born circa 1918.
1182222321211   JEWELL, William Richard
He married CARTER, Phyllis. William was born circa 1939.
11822223212111   JEWELL, Jimmy
Jimmy was born circa 1959.
11822223212112   JEWELL, Lowell Thomas
Lowell was born circa 1966.
11822223212113   JEWELL, Michael
Michael was born circa 1969.
1182222321212   JEWELL, James Melvin
He married BELCHER, Connie. James was born circa 1943.
11822223212121   JEWELL, Jonathan
He married FRITZ, Sabrina. Jonathan was born circa 1967.
11822223212122   JEWELL, Jessica
Jessica was born circa 1977.
1182222321213   JEWELL, Gerald Lee
He married COOK, Anita. Gerald was born circa 1947. Gerald died
circa 1977.
11822223212131   JEWELL, Fairley
He married BROWN, Melissa. Fairley was born circa 1968.

118222232122   JEWELL, Jesse Verman
He married **SANDERS**, Margaret. Jesse was born circa 1919.
1182222321221   JEWELL, Robert Lee
He married an unknown person. He married **SUMMERS**, Sharon.
Robert was born circa 1940.
11822223212211   JEWELL, Robert Lee, Jr.
He married Barbara. Robert was born circa 1961.
118222232122111   JEWELL, Brian Robert
Brian was born circa 1988.
118222232122112   JEWELL, Staci
Staci was born circa 1990.
11822223212212   JEWELL, Nancy
She married **BEAN**, William. Nancy was born circa 1963.
118222232122121   BEAN, Amber Elizabeth
11822223212213   JEWELL, Susan
She married **CLARK**, Andy. Susan was born circa 1967.
118222232122131   CLARK, Benjamin Robert
Benjamin was born circa 1990.
118222232122132   CLARK, Andrea Sue
Andrea was born circa 1993.
1182222321222   JEWELL, Reginald
He married **FRANCIS**, Karen. Reginald was born circa 1942.
11822223212221   JEWELL, Mark
He married **TAPLIN**, Denise. Mark was born circa 1970.
11822223212222   JEWELL, Timothy
Timothy was born circa 1971.
11822223212223   JEWELL, Rebecca
Rebecca was born circa 1980.
11822223212224   JEWELL, Matthew
Matthew was born circa 1983.
11822223212225   JEWELL, Rachel
Rachel was born circa 1985.
1182222321223   JEWELL, Thomas Eugene
He married **WAGNER**, Sue. Thomas was born circa 1944.
11822223212231   JEWELL, Mary Elizabeth
She married **WELCH**, Joel. Mary was born circa 1966.
118222232122311   WELCH, Katie
Katie was born circa 1988.
118222232122312   WELCH, James Thomas
James was born circa 1991.
11822223212232   JEWELL, Bill
Bill was born circa 1968.
11822223212233   JEWELL, Jeffery
Jeffery was born circa 1970.
11822223212234   JEWELL, Lori
Lori was born circa 1973.
1182222321224   JEWELL, Samuel Harrison

He married **MADARIS**, Patsy. Samuel was born circa 1948.
11822223212241   **JEWELL, Kristen**
Kristen was born circa 1974.
11822223212242   **JEWELL, Paul David**
Paul was born circa 1976.
11822223212243   **JEWELL, Kara**
Kara was born circa 1981.
11822223212244   **JEWELL, Phillip**
Phillip was born circa 1983.
1182222321225   **JEWELL, Victoria Lynn**
She married **BLACKWELL**, Randy. Victoria was born circa 1956.
11822223212251   **BLACKWELL, James Randall**
James was born circa 1979.
11822223212252   **BLACKWELL, David**
David was born circa 1980.
11822223212253   **BLACKWELL, Robert Steven**
Robert was born circa 1985.
118222232123   **JEWELL, William Harrison, Jr.**
He married **SPENCE**, Geneva. William was born circa 1921.
William died circa 1990.
1182222321231   **JEWELL, John Lee**
He married Millicent. John was born circa 1943.
11822223212311   **JEWELL, Tara**
11822223212312   **JEWELL, Teresa**
1182222321232   **JEWELL, William Harrison, III**
He married **SHUMATE**, Donna. William was born circa 1946.
1182222321233   **JEWELL, Darlene**
She married **BROOKS**, Lewis. Darlene was born circa 1947.
11822223212331   **BROOKS, Christopher**
11822223212332   **BROOKS, Mary Lynn**
1182222321234   **JEWELL, Anita (Wood)**
She married an unknown person. Anita was born circa 1949.
11822223212341   **WOOD, Kimberly**
11822223212342   **WOOD, Jennifer**
11822223212343   **WOOD, Drew**
1182222321235   **JEWELL, Kenneth Ray**
Kenneth was born circa 1951.
1182222321236   **JEWELL, Donald**
He married Kathy. Donald was born circa 1953.
11822223212361   **JEWELL, Lindsay**
Lindsay was born circa 1988.
11822223212362   **JEWELL, Justin**
Justin was born circa 1989.
1182222321237   **JEWELL, Ronald**
Ronald was born circa 1953.
118222232124   **JEWELL, Ada Athlene**
She married **BROOKS**, Wiley F., Jr.. Ada was born circa 1925.

1182222321241   BROOKS, Judy
She married **STEWART**, Robert. Judy was born circa 1946.
11822223212411   STEWART, Richard Lon
He married **BALL**, Debra. Richard was born circa 1968.
118222232124111   STEWART, Hannah
Hannah was born circa 1992.
11822223212412   STEWART, Brian
Brian was born circa 1973.
1182222321242   BROOKS, James Steven
James was born circa 1948.
1182222321243   BROOKS, Daniel Raymond
He married an unknown person. Daniel was born circa 1952.
11822223212431   BROOKS, Jonathan
Jonathan was born circa 1979.
11822223212432   BROOKS, Jewel
Jewel was born circa 1983.
118222232125 JEWELL, Mildred Loretta
She married **CANTERBURY**, David Clinton. Mildred was born circa
1927.
1182222321251   CANTERBURY, Larry David
He married **JONES**, Judy. Larry was born circa 1951.
11822223212511   CANTERBURY, Benjamin
Benjamin was born circa 1985.
1182222321252   CANTERBURY, Patricia Ann
She married **TOLER**, Michael. Patricia was born circa 1958.
11822223212521   TOLER, Leslie Ann
Leslie was born circa 1983.
118222232126 JEWELL, Zelma Ruth
She married **STEWART**, D. Homer. Zelma was born circa 1929.
1182222321261   STEWART, Carolyn Ruth
Carolyn was born circa 1950.
1182222321262   STEWART, Marilyn Anita
She married **MCKINNEY**, David. Marilyn was born circa 1954.
11822223212621   MCKINNEY, Kara
Kara was born circa 1978.
11822223212622   MCKINNEY, Brandon
Brandon was born circa 1982.
1182222321263   STEWART, Pamela
She married **BRODERICK**, Richard. Pamela was born circa 1962.
11822223212631   BRODERICK, Amanda
Amanda was born circa 1988.
11822223212632   BRODERICK, Chad
Chad was born circa 1993.
118222232127 JEWELL, Irene
She married **LAXTON**, Alfred. Irene was born circa 1932.
1182222321271   LAXTON, Michael
He married **LOVINS**, Nadine. Michael was born circa 1953.

11822223212711   **LAXTON, Michael, Jr.**
Michael, was born circa 1978.
11822223212712   **LAXTON, Matthew**
Matthew was born circa 1980.
11822223212713   **LAXTON, Thomas**
Thomas was born circa 1984.
11822223212714   **LAXTON, David**
David was born circa 1985.
1182222321272   **LAXTON, Diana**
She married **COOK**, Thomas. Diana was born circa 1955.
11822223212721   **COOK, Randy**
Randy was born circa 1975.
11822223212722   **COOK, Lori**
Lori was born circa 1978.
11822223212723   **COOK, Lisa**
Lisa was born circa 1981.
1182222321273   **LAXTON, Roger Keith**
He married **HALL**, Kimberli. Roger was born circa 1958.
11822223212731   **LAXTON, Jason**
Jason was born circa 1980.
11822223212732   **LAXTON, Melinda**
Melinda was born circa 1988.
1182222321274   **LAXTON, Karen**
She married **ALLEN**, Danny. Karen was born circa 1963.
1182222321275   **LAXTON, Terry**
He married **GOODE**, Lisa. Terry was born circa 1964.
1182222321276   **LAXTON, Kathy**
He married an unknown person. Kathy was born circa 1967.
1182222321277   **LAXTON, Mark**
Mark was born circa 1970.
118222232128 **JEWELL, Barbara**
She married **BROWN**, Horace Lee. Barbara was born circa 1937.
1182222321281   **BROWN, Deborah**
She married **CLARK**, Phillip. Deborah was born circa 1958.
11822223212811   **CLARK, Phillip, Jr. 'Chip'**
Phillip, was born circa 1983.
11822223212812   **CLARK, Jeremy**
Jeremy was born circa 1985.
11822223212813   **CLARK, Olivia**
Olivia was born circa 1991.
1182222321282   **BROWN, Brenda**
She married **WILLIAMS**, Alan. She married **DEARIEN**, Robert.
Brenda was born circa 1960.
11822223212821   **WILLIAMS, Julie**
Julie was born circa 1982.
11822223212822   **DEARIEN, Randall**
Randall was born circa 1989.

1182222321283   BROWN, Timothy Horace
Timothy was born circa 1968.
118222232129 JEWELL, Glenna
She married **GILKESON**, Victor. Glenna was born circa 1940.
1182222321291   GILKESON, Robert Myron
Robert was born circa 1960.
11822223212(10)   JEWELL, Peggy
She married **BLAND**, Thomas Edward. She married **MULLINS**, Aretus J.. Peggy was born circa 1943.
11822223212(10)1   BLAND, Angela
She married **DICKERSON**, Lewis. Angela was born circa 1962.
11822223212(10)2   BLAND, Thomas Edward, Jr.
He married **COOK**, Sherri. Thomas was born circa 1968.
11822223212(10)21   BLAND, Thomas Edward III
11822223212(10)3   BLAND, Charles David
Charles was born circa 1971.
11822223212(11)   JEWELL, David Eugene
He married **HACKNEY**, Vergie. David was born circa 1946.
11822223212(11)1   JEWELL, Robert Eugene
Robert was born circa 1968.
11822223213 HALSEY, Greely
He married **BROOKS**, Lula. Greely was born in Coonfork, WV 20 June 1903. Greely died 3 January 1973 at 69 years of age.
118222232131 HALSEY, Geraldine
118222232132 HALSEY, Trilla Gay
She married **CRAWFORD**, Junior.
118222232133 HALSEY, Immogene
She married **TAYLOR**, Vernon. Immogene was born.
118222232134 HALSEY, Christine
She married **WAMPLER**, Gus.
118222232135 HALSEY, Betty Jane (June?)
She married **KINGREA**, James.
11822223214 HALSEY, Annie Rose
Annie was born in Rockview, WV 22 November 1907. She married **GUNTER**, Dewey George 25 January 1925. Annie died 1 July 1992 in Beckley, WV, at 84 years of age.
118222232141 GUNTER, Neil Dennis
118222232142 GUNTER, Edith Naomi
Edith was born 5 January 1929. She married **STEWART**, Calvert Weldon 18 May 1946.
1182222321421   STEWART, Sheila Louise
Sheila was born 20 April 1947. She married **JONES**, James William circa 1967. She married **MCMILLION**, Donald circa 1975.
11822223214211   MCMILLION, Billie Jean
Billie was born 26 December 1968.
11822223214212   JONES, Barbara Gail
Barbara was born 3 January 1971.

1182222321422   **STEWART, Barbara June**
She married **HEATON**, Robert. She married **DEPRIEST**, Thomas. Barbara was born 17 January 1949.
11822223214221   **DEPRIEST, Elizabeth Ann**
Elizabeth was born 7 December 1967.
11822223214222   **DEPRIEST, Robert Keith**
Robert was born 13 June 1970.
1182222321423   **STEWART, Sandra Gail**
Sandra was born 13 January 1952. She married **BRUNTY**, Davis Gilbert May 1968.
11822223214231   **BRIMTY, John Weldon**
John was born 4 December 1976.
1182222321424   **STEWART, Harvard DeWayne**
Harvard was born 14 August 1955. He married **COMER**, Barbara Lei June 1973. He married **BRAGG**, Patricia Wilson 2 September 1983.
11822223214241   **STEWART, Juanita Dawn**
Juanita was born 18 November 1973.
11822223214242   **STEWART, Janet Leigh**
Janet was born 20 July 1976.
1182222321425   **STEWART, Jeffery Lee**
Jeffery was born 29 August 1958. He married **FRIEND**, Renita Jean circa 1976.
11822223214251   **STEWART, Jeffery Lee, Jr.**
Jeffery was born 21 March 1977.
11822223214252   **STEWART, Jeromie Lyle**
Jeromie was born 3 June 1980.
118222232143   **GUNTER, Virginia Eloise**
She married **STEWART**, Perry Glen. Virginia was born 22 October 1933.
1182222321431   **STEWART, Brenda Joyce**
She married **STEWART**, Kenneth. She married Ed.
11822223214311   **STEWART, April**
11822223214312   **STEWART, Kenneth**
11822223214313   **STEWART, Jason**
1182222321432   **STEWART, Judith**
She married **AKERS**, Curtis.
11822223214321   **AKERS, Rita**
11822223214322   **AKERS, Jennifer**
11822223214323   **AKERS,**
1182222321433   **STEWART, Edward**
He married **BIGGS**, Vicky.
11822223214331   **STEWART, Andrew**
11822223214332   **STEWART,**
11822223214333   **STEWART, Amy**
1182222321434   **STEWART, Dewey**
He married Marsha.
1182222321435   **STEWART, Daniel**

118222232144 GUNTER, James Clarence
He married **BOWMAN**, Cleo. He married **REAPER**, Tina. James was born 16 May 1935.
1182222321441   GUNTER, Clifford
1182222321442   GUNTER, Linda
1182222321443   GUNTER, Sue Ann
Sue was born 18 August 1973.
118222232145 GUNTER, Joseph Edwin
He married **MCMILLION**, Nettie. Joseph was born 4 May 1937.
1182222321451   GUNTER, David
He married **MCMILLION**, Mary.
1182222321452   GUNTER, Joseph
1182222321453   GUNTER, Ricky
He married **HIZER**, Tammy.
1182222321454   GUNTER, Karen
She married **BROWN**, Silas
11822223214541   BROWN, Roscoe
11822223214542   BROWN, Ashley
118222232146 GUNTER, Mary Lou
She married Andy. She married **GURLEY**, George. Mary was born 24 June 1939.
1182222321461   GURLEY, Richard
He married Sue.
1182222321462   GURLEY, Marlene
1182222321463   GURLEY, George, Jr.
118222232147 GUNTER, Bonnie Sue
She married **WAGNER**, Ernest. Bonnie was born 24 June 1939.
1182222321471   WAGNER, Debra Ann
She married **COLEMAN**, Sig. Debra was born 19 July 1956.
1182222321472   WAGNER, Ernestine
She married **BOSNAK**, Peter. Ernestine was born 30 January 1961.
11822223214721   BOSNAK, Angela Lynn
Angela was born 24 February 1984.
11822223214722   BOSNAK, Anthony
Anthony was born 29 December 1987.
118222232148 GUNTER, Charles Vance
He married **MCMILLION**, Linda. Charles was born 4 December 1941. Charles died June 1989 at 47 years of age.
1182222321481   GUNTER, Charles Vance II
1182222321482   GUNTER, Tonya
118222232149 GUNTER, Cora Lee
She married **MCMILLION**, Avery. Cora was born 6 October 1943.
1182222321491   MCMILLION, Tina Marie
She married **LELCY**, Ishnel.
11822223214911   LELCY, James
11822223214912   LELCY, Patrick
1182222321492   MCMILLION, Deana

She married **KNAPP**, David.
11822223214921   **KNAPP, Sharon Kay**
11822223214922   **KNAPP, Amber**
11822223214(10)   **GUNTER, Sharon Kay**
She married **ELLIS**, John. She married **RICHMON**, Carrington. She married **LANE**, Sammy. Sharon was born September 1945. Sharon died 18 October 1988 at 43 years of age.
11822223214(10)1   **ELLIS, Johnny**
He married Gina.
11822223214(10)11   **ELLIS, Ursula Kay**
11822223214(10)2   **ELLIS, Michael**
He married Missy.
11822223214(10)3   **ELLIS, Victor Shane**
He married Lisa.
11822223214(11)   **GUNTER, Wanda Ellen**
She married **HALL**, William. She married **MINTON**, Walter Lee. Wanda was born 6 June 1948.
11822223214(11)1   **MINTON, Michelle Lynn**
Michelle was born 24 October 1971.
11822223214(12)   **GUNTER, George David**
He married Regina. He married Chris. George was born April 1950.
11822223214(12)1   **GUNTER, Michelle**
11822223215   **HALSEY, Troy**
He married **STEWART**, Lela. He married **PHILLIPS**, Louise. Troy was born 4 March 1910. Troy died March 1984 in FL, at 74 years of age.
118222232151   **HALSEY, Clifford**
He married **POWERS**, Naoma.
1182222321511   **HALSEY, Larry**
He married **TANKO**, Mary Linda.
1182222321512   **HALSEY, Aaren**
He married **SIZEMORE**, Donna Michelle.
1182222321513   **HALSEY, Timothy**
He married **COOK**, Andrea.
11822223215131   **HALSEY, Summer LeEtta**
1182222321514   **HALSEY, Viola Lyn**
118222232152   **HALSEY, Shelby Jean**
She married **SHUMATE**, Clyde.
1182222321521   **SHUMATE, Marty**
1182222321522   **SHUMATE,**
11822223216   **HALSEY, Oscar Jay**
Oscar was born in Coonfork, Wyoming Co., WV 6 August 1913. He married **PENDRY**, Vida in New Richmond, Wyoming Co., WV, 3 November 1934. Oscar died 17 October 1995 in Beckley, WV, at 82 years of age.
118222232161   **HALSEY, Beatrice Ruth**
Beatrice was born in Coonfork, Wyoming Co., WV 17 October 1935. She married **ENGLAND**, Boyd Rufus in Matheny, Wyoming Co., WV, 26 December 1950.

1182222321611   ENGLAND, Pamela
1182222321612   ENGLAND, Rodney
1182222321613   ENGLAND, Wendell
118222232162 HALSEY, Kathleen
     Kathleen was born in Coonfork, Wyoming Co., WV 23 October 1937.
She married **ENGLAND**, Douglas Lee in Kimball, McDowell Co., WV, 26
June 1958.
118222232163 HALSEY, Harold Gene
     Harold was born in Jesse, Wyoming Co., WV 10 October 1942. He
married **BAILEY**, Brenda Kay 12 September 1963.
1182222321631   HALSEY, Frances Kay
     Frances was born 12 January 1965. She married **MORGAN**,
Gregory Dean 5 May 1985.
11822223216311   MORGAN, Miranda Kay
     Miranda was born 12 November 1986.
1182222321632   HALSEY, Bobby Gene
     Bobby was born 4 June 1966. He married **BROOKS**, Janet Louise
26 September 1987.
11822223216321   HALSEY, Katelyn Brienna
     Katelyn was born 18 June 1989.
1182222321633   HALSEY, Tammy Lynn
     Tammy was born 15 November 1969. She married **MCMILLION**,
Eugene 22 December 1990.
1182222321634   HALSEY, Harold Jay
     Harold was born 3 July 1974.
118222232164 HALSEY, Juanita Lea
     Juanita was born in Jesse, Wyoming Co., WV 9 February 1945. She
married **SMITH**, Freddie Lawrence in Oceana, Wyoming Co., WV, 15 June
1963. She married **CRANER**, Michael LeRoy in Matheny, Wyoming Co.,
WV, 7 May 1969.
1182222321641   SMITH, Vida Elizabeth
     Vida was born in Newport News, VA 4 June 1964. Vida died 19
September 1964 in Newport News, VA, at less than one year of age.
1182222321642   CRANER, Michael Lane
     Michael was born in Jacksonville, Duval Co., FL 26 September 1970.
1182222321643   CRANER, Constance Renate
     Constance was born in Bountiful, Davis Co., UT 10 January 1976.
1182222321644   CRANER, Jared Anthony
     Jared was born in Salt Lake City, Salt Lake Co., UT 25 September
1978.
1182222321645   CRANER, Deborah Lynette
     Deborah was born in Bountiful, Davis Co., UT 7 October 1980.
11822223217 HALSEY, Irene Gladys
     Irene was born in Rockview, WV 9 June 1916. She married
STEWART, Charles Oley in New Richmond, WV, 16 January 1933.
118222232171 STEWART, Helen
     Helen was born in Rockview, WV 10 March 1934. She married

MOUNTS, Gordon 15 October 1952. She married **HAMBLIN**, Robert 27 December 1972.

1182222321711	MOUNTS, Sherry
1182222321712	MOUNTS, Kim

118222232172 STEWART, Doris

Doris was born 25 January 1936. She married **HALL**, Robert 8 December 1960.

118222232173 STEWART, Rita

Rita was born 23 February 1939. She married **HOWARD**, Morton 17 July 1963.

118222232174 STEWART, Charles

Charles was born 16 September 1940. He married **HOFFMAN**, Kathy 5 April 1963.

1182222321741	STEWART, Charles Andrew
1182222321742	STEWART, Dana Mary
1182222321743	STEWART, Margaret

118222232175 STEWART, Jimmy

Jimmy was born 15 December 1942. He married **ADAMS**, Gloria 27 December 1963.

1182222321751	STEWART, Herbert Weldon
1182222321752	STEWART, Roger Michael
1182222321753	STEWART, Dale Lee

118222232176 STEWART, Jerry

Jerry was born in Jesse, WV 21 October 1945. He married **CHAMBERS**, Pam 12 August 1967.

1182222321761	STEWART, Timothy Damon
1182222321762	STEWART, Gregory Dean
1182222321763	STEWART, Amanda Loucill

118222232177 STEWART, Lacy

Lacy was born in Jesse, WV 14 December 1946.

118222232178 STEWART, Buren

Buren was born in Jesse, WV 31 July 1948. He married **NEAL**, Sharon 25 November 1968.

1182222321781   STEWART, Christopher Buren

118222232179 STEWART, Glenn

Glenn was born in Matheny, WV 5 March 1950. He married **REED**, Eileen 28 December 1974.

11822223218 HALSEY, Woodrow

He married **TILLEY**, Lucy. Woodrow was born in Coonfork, WV 22 May 1919.

118222232181 HALSEY, Carrol

He married **MOODY**, Maxine.

1182222321811	HALSEY, Sheryl
1182222321812	HALSEY, Kimberly
1182222321813	HALSEY, Bret
1182222321814	HALSEY, Brian

Brian was born January 1964.

118222232182   HALSEY, Almeda
  She married **BURKES**, Jerry.
1182222321821   **BURKS, Chris**
1182222321822   **BURKS, Thomas**
118222232183   HALSEY, Gary
  He married **GREENE**, Faye.
1182222321831   **HALSEY, Steven**
1182222321832   **HALSEY, Ray**
11822223219   HALSEY, Avery Carl
  He married **COZORT**, Tressie. Avery was born in Coonfork, WV 21 March 1925.
118222232191   HALSEY, Donald
118222232192   HALSEY,
  He married an unknown person.
1182222321921   **HALSEY, Crystal**
1182222321922   **HALSEY, Adam**
118222232193   HALSEY, Billy
118222232194   HALSEY, Ricky
1182222322   HALSEY, Isaac Jeremiah
  Isaac was born 23 November 1879. He married **TAYLOR**, Laura Etta circa 1899. Isaac died 22 April 1953 at 73 years of age.
11822223221   HALSEY, Lou Vena
  She married **DAMERON**, James. Lou was born 18 October 1900. Lou died 22 March 1940 at 39 years of age.
118222232211   DAMERON, James, Jr.
118222232212   DAMERON, Teddy Mack
118222232213   DAMERON, Ardith
11822223222   HALSEY, Leota
  She married **EARY**, Anthony. Leota was born 6 April 1902.
118222232221   EARY, Edith Mae
118222232222   EARY, Betty
11822223223   HALSEY, Vernie Mae
  She married **BOWERS**, William. Vernie was born 4 May 1904.
118222232231   BOWERS, Louise
118222232232   BOWERS, Ethel
118222232233   BOWERS, Silas
118222232234   BOWERS, Ennis
11822223224   HALSEY, John Vestal
  He married **HASH**, Rosie. John was born 18 June 1906. John died 27 April 1988 in Sophia, WV, at 81 years of age.
118222232241   HALSEY, Gency
118222232242   HALSEY, Karmas
11822223225   HALSEY, Izora B.
  She married **NICHOLS**, Landon W.. Izora was born 6 September 1910.
118222232251   NICHOLS, Landon, Jr.
118222232252   NICHOLS, Julia S.

11822223226   HALSEY, Ora Ann
   She married **TOLLIVER**, Linville. Ora was born 17 May 1912. Ora died 19 March 1992 in Beckley, WV, at 79 years of age.
118222232261   TOLIVER, Genevia
118222232262   TOLIVER, Linda Jane
118222232263   TOLIVER, Jerry
11822223227   HALSEY, Sylvia Marie
   Sylvia was born 23 April 1915. She married **RAYE**, Robert Bruce 7 June 1936. She married **SNUFFER**, William Sherman after 1940.
118222232271   RAYE, Reda
   Reda was born 17 June 1931. She married **PAULEY**, Darrell 11 February 1950.
1182222322711   PAULEY, Darrell Ray
   Darrell was born 18 December 1950. He married **DAVIS**, Barbara 25 May 1974.
11822223227111   PAULEY, Lauren
   Lauren was born 25 March 1980.
11822223227112   PAULEY, Eric
   Eric was born 18 August 1984.
1182222322712   PAULEY, Jeffery Van
   Jeffery was born 21 June 1955. He married **GROVE**, Lisa 17 February 1979.
11822223227121   PAULEY, Jamie
   Jamie was born 24 March 1983.
11822223227122   PAULEY, Dustin
   Dustin was born 6 June 1988.
118222232272   RAYE, Shirley Jean
   Shirley was born 6 January 1937.
118222232273   RAYE, Rachel Deloris
   Rachel was born in Otsego, WV 27 August 1939. She married **CONTI**, Frank John 15 June 1959.
1182222322731   CONTI, Donna Jean
   Donna was born 21 September 1959.
1182222322732   CONTI, Frank John, III
   Frank was born 6 November 1961. He married **PARRISH**, Tina 25 March 1989.
1182222322733   CONTI, Lisa Ann
   Lisa was born 6 May 1967. She married **SMITH**, Philip Jon 29 August 1987.
11822223227331   SMITH, Philip Wesley
   Philip was born 22 January 1987.
118222232274 SNUFFER, Darry Lane
   Darry was born 25 February 1954.
11822223228   HALSEY, Rosella
   Rosella was born 30 October 1919.
11822223229   HALSEY, Geneva
   Geneva was born 2 April 1924.

1182222323   HALSEY, Andrew Albert
Andrew was born 2 March 1882. He married **FARLEY**, Sarah
Elizabeth 21 December 1909. Andrew died 3 September 1960.
11822223231   HALSEY, Earl Carl
Earl was born 12 September 1910. He married **MILLS**, Vertle 28
July 1934. Earl died 16 September 1988 at 78 years of age.
118222232311   HALSEY, Agnes Kay
Agnes was born 25 October 1935. She married **LIVELY**, Paul
James 2 June 1956.
1182222323111   LIVELY, Zachery Earl
Zachery was born 1 April 1958. He married an unknown person 29
July 1988.
1182222323112   LIVELY, Gary Alan
Gary was born 5 February 1961. He married **PRYOR**, Michele Marie
24 March 1979.
11822223231121   LIVELY, Tracy Marie
Tracy was born 22 December 1979.
11822223231122   LIVELY, Lydia Danielle
Lydia was born 25 November 1984.
11822223231123   LIVELY, Pamela Christine
Pamela was born 10 October 1988.
1182222323113   LIVELY, Keith Michael
Keith was born 15 November 1962. Keith died 27 June 1985.
118222232312   HALSEY, Wade Larue
Wade was born 28 January 1938. He married **FLESHMAN**, Linda
Lou 28 October 1959.
1182222323121   HALSEY, Brian Douglas
Brian was born 28 April 1963. He married **OURANT**, Kimberly Sue 9
November 1985.
11822223231211   HALSEY, Jennifer Kay
Jennifer was born 2 April 1990.
11822223231212   HALSEY, Karen Elizabeth
Karen was born 9 May 1993.
1182222323122   HALSEY, Michael Wade
Michael was born 18 August 1964. He married **BURNS**, Cheryl Lynn
26 June 1992.
11822223231221   HALSEY, Michael Kyle
Michael was born 29 December 1992.
1182222323123   HALSEY, Melanie Lynn
Melanie was born 27 September 1967.
118222232313   HALSEY, Teresa Gay
Teresa was born 24 August 1939. She married **GRYGIEL**, Paul, Jr.
28 December 1963.
1182222323131   GRYGIEL, Karen Elizabeth
Karen was born 7 November 1966.
1182222323132   GRYGIEL, Scott Paul
Scott was born 18 April 1972.

11822223232   HALSEY, Ella Mae
Ella was born 18 January 1912. She married **MILLER**, William Al 25 February 1939.
118222232321 MILLER, William Darrell
William was born 8 February 1940. He married **MCNEELY**, Janice Lou 22 February 1968.
1182222323211   MILLER, Shelia Dawn
Shelia was born 16 July 1960. She married **MANN**, Frank Baylor, III 6 June 1987.
118222232322 MILLER, Don Eddie
Don was born 29 April 1941. He married **BURCHETTE**, Joyce Eloise 15 June 1963. He married **HONAKER**, Nellie Brinegar 15 September 1989.
1182222323221   MILLER, Kennith Paul
Kennith was born 29 June 1967.
1182222323222   MILLER, Cynthia Dawn
Cynthia was born 7 November 1969.
11822223233   HALSEY, Carson Dale
Carson was born 19 November 1913. He married **PHILLIPS**, Edna A. 24 August 1946. Carson died 9 October 1997 at 83 years of age.
118222232331 HALSEY, Freddie Carson
Freddie was born 7 July 1948. He married **HALSEY**, Betty Eclantine 26 November 1980.
1182222323311   HALSEY, Andrea Michelle
Andrea was born 22 May 1984.
11822223234   HALSEY, Walter Casha
Walter was born 14 January 1917. He married **BUCHANNAN**, Cora Mae 13 September 1947. Walter died 15 December 1976.
118222232341 HALSEY, Barbara Ann
Barbara was born 10 June 1948. She married **HAGER**, Gerald Edward 9 August 1970.
1182222323411   HAGER, Tammie Lynne
Tammie was born 7 May 1973.
1182222323412   HAGER, Vanessa Ann
Vanessa was born 2 March 1978.
118222232342 HALSEY, Sandra Kay
Sandra was born 30 September 1951. She married **AKERS**, William Howard 25 August 1972.
11822223235   HALSEY, Carrie Elizabeth
Carrie was born 11 February 1919.
11822223236   HALSEY, Harry J.
Harry was born 13 May 1921. He married **ADKINS**, Marie 8 May 1948.
118222232361 HALSEY, Juanita Mae
Juanita was born 3 May 1949. She married **DOOLEY**, Joe Paul 6 June 1970.
1182222323611   DOOLEY, Melinda Lee

Melinda was born 22 December 1972.

1182222323612   DOOLEY, Jodie Marie
Jodie was born 30 April 1975.

1182222323613   DOOLEY, Nikkie Jo
Nikkie was born 11 February 1979.

1182222323614   DOOLEY, Joe Aaron
Joe was born 11 February 1979.

118222232362 HALSEY, Anice Lee
Anice was born 2 May 1951. She married **HATFIELD**, Gregory 28 September 1967.

1182222323621   HATFIELD, Geoffrey Lance
Geoffrey was born 11 July 1968. He married Tammy Lynn 3 November 1989.

1182222323622   HATFIELD, Joshua Lance
Joshua was born 27 December 1989.

118222232363 HALSEY, William Hersey
He married Neil. William was born 30 March 1955.

11822223237 HALSEY, Jeremiah Hersey
Jeremiah was born 12 April 1923. Jeremiah died 3 April 1924.

11822223238 HALSEY, Martha Wanda
Martha was born 8 March 1925. She married **MORGAN**, Willie Gray 2 February 1952.

118222232381 MORGAN, Deborah Ann
She married **DEAN**, William Roger. Deborah was born 29 September 1953.

1182222323811   DEAN, Sarah Beth
Sarah was born 15 March 1980.

118222232382 MORGAN, David Gray
David was born 17 January 1979.

11822223239 HALSEY, Pansy Ann
Pansy was born 14 June 1927.

1182222323(10)   HALSEY, Billy Emerson
Billy was born 24 March 1930. Billy died 20 July 1930.

1182222324 HALSEY, Nancy Ellen
She married **BROOKS**, Kenna. Nancy was born 14 April 1884. Nancy died 5 December 1940 at 56 years of age.

11822223241 BROOKS, Elva Lee
He married **TOLIVER**, Zettie. He married **HASH**, Winnie (Thomas). Elva was born 15 March 1902. Elva died 31 August 1970 at 68 years of age.

118222232411 BROOKS, Kally
118222232412 BROOKS, Roy
118222232413 BROOKS, Audie
118222232414 BROOKS, Donna
118222232415 BROOKS, Edith
118222232416 BROOKS, Ada
118222232417 BROOKS, Faye
118222232418 BROOKS, Woodrow

118222232419 BROOKS, Dee
Dee was born circa 1933. Dee died circa 1972.
11822223242 BROOKS, Kelly Kale
He married **WALKER**, Nona. Kelly was born 15 March 1905.
118222232421 BROOKS, Ira
118222232422 BROOKS, Inez
118222232423 BROOKS, Ida
1182222325 HALSEY, Rachel Victoria
Rachel was born 19 September 1886. She married **ALLEN**,
Sanders 13 December 1905. Rachel died 20 June 1968 at 81 years of age.
11822223251 ALLEN, Essie Mae
She married **CECIL**, Charlie. Essie was born 14 October 1906. She
married **MCMILLAN**, Hobert 19 August 1925.
118222232511 MCMILLAN, Herman
118222232512 MCMILLAN, Nadine
118222232513 MCMILLAN, Sandy Bill
118222232514 CECIL, Audrey
Audrey was born 24 April 1923.
11822223252 ALLEN, Effie
Effie was born 8 May 1909. Effie died 9 May 1909.
1182222326 HALSEY, Dolly
Dolly was born 16 April 1889. Dolly died 19 June 1889.
1182222327 HALSEY, Lou Venia
Lou was born 26 May 1890. Lou died 26 May 1965.
1182222328 HALSEY, Early Lee
Early was born 26 November 1892. Early died 11 September 1901.
1182222329 HALSEY, Ernest B.
Ernest was born in Rockview, WV 19 September 1896. He married
TOLIVER, Lena in Saulsville, WV, 27 August 1919. Ernest died 16
November 1987 in VA Hospital, Beckley, WV, at 91 years of age.
11822223291 HALSEY, Merle Faye
She married **BREEDING**, Johnny. Merle was born 15 July 1920.
118222232911 BREEDING, Donnie Eugene
11822223292 HALSEY, Ivan Dale
Ivan was born in Rockview, WV 19 July 1922. He married
SHREWSBURY, Thelma in Stephenson, WV, 22 December 1948. Ivan was
in the U.S. Navy from September 1942 until March 1946, serving as a
Storekeeper 2nd Class. He was discharged as a V-12 Navy Cadet from the
University of North Carolina.
118222232921 HALSEY, Nancy Ann
Nancy was born 23 October 1949. She married **MOORE**, Dwight 3
August 1974.
1182222329211 MOORE, Robert D.
Robert was born 22 January 1977.
1182222329212 MOORE, Valerie E.
Valerie was born 25 March 1980.
118222232922 HALSEY, Belenda Jane

Belenda was born 14 November 1953. She married **BELL**, Hervie
H. 11 September 1982.
1182222329221   BELL, Andrew Halsey
Andrew was born 5 January 1985.
11822223293   HALSEY, Onnie Lee
He married **RANKIN**, Wanda. Onnie was born 2 February 1925.
118222232931   HALSEY, Howard
118222232932   HALSEY, Steven
118222232933   HALSEY, Connie
11822223294   HALSEY, Luther
Luther was born 10 February 1928. He married **ESTEP**, Lena Opal
29 April 1954.
118222232941   HALSEY, Jeffery Dean
Jeffery was born 30 December 1955. He married **SHUMATE**,
Tammy Jean 23 August 1980.
1182222329411   HALSEY, Kara Nicole
Kara was born 29 July 1983.
1182222329412   HALSEY, Zachary Tyler
Zachary was born 9 July 1987.
118222232942   HALSEY, Terri Lynn
Terri was born 6 March 1959. She married **MUSCARI**, Michael A.
18 June 1983.
1182222329421   MUSCARI, Kyle Michael
Kyle was born 6 April 1987.
1182222329422   MUSCARI, Euan Joseph
Euan was born 5 August 1991.
118222232943   HALSEY, Stacie Denise
Stacie was born 29 December 1970.
118222233   HALSEY, Robert McCoy
Robert was born in Ashe County, N.C. 4 March 1857. He married
SIZEMORE, Cathany in Pineville, West Virginia, 16 November 1879. Robert
died circa 1928 in Pierpoint, West Virginia.
1182222331   HALSEY, Elijah Coy
Elijah was born circa 1881. He married **LAMBERT**, Sarah Elizabeth
circa 1908. Elijah died 24 December 1936 in Pierpoint, West Virginia, at 55
years of age. His body was interred 26 December 1936 in Pierpoint, WV.
OBITUARY- "Elige C. Halsey succumbs Thursday at Pierpoint home. He
was well known throughout central Wyoming County. He will be buried
Saturday. Funeral services for Elige C. Halsey, 55, well known central
Wyoming County citizen and resident of Pierpoint, near Maben, were held
from the Pierpoint church last Saturday afternoon following his sudden death
at his home, likely from a heart attack on Christmas Eve. Apparently in good
health throughout Thursday, Mr. Halsey had walked to the top of the hill
between Pierpoint and Otsego late that afternoon with neighbor companions
but had returned home after complaining of being tired. Found by son He
was found by a son having slumped from his chair to the floor after ten
o'clock Thursday night. State police investigated but reported his death due

entirely to natural causes. Survived by a son and daughter (Editorial note-
there were five daughters and two sons.), the deceased losing his wife
several years ago by death. Mr. Halsey was a former coal miner, having
been employed in the mines near Pierpoint over a number of years and
having lost a leg in a mine accident. A son of Robert L. (Editorial note-
Robert's middle initial was M.) and Cathena (Catherine) Sizemore Halsey,
both dead, Elige Halsey was also the Grandson of the Reverend Drury
Halsey, the pioneer Baptist minister".

11822223311   HALSEY, Ralph Harold
Ralph was born in Pierpoint, West Virginia 6 December 1909. He
married **COOK**, Omeda Ellen in Mullens, West Virginia, 12 May 1934. He
married **HOLT**, Dorothy Charity in Bluefield, WV, 6 December 1973. Ralph
died 26 June 1983 in Beckley-Hosp, West Virginia, at 73 years of age. His
body was interred 28 June 1983 in Sun Set Cem, Beckley, W.V.

118222233111 HALSEY, David Harold
David was born in Pierpoint, West Virginia 1 April 1935. He married
SMITH, Glyn Ellen in Huntington, West Virginia, 10 November 1956. He
married **ABRAHAM**, Ellen Josephine in Florence, Kentucky, 2 May 1974.

1182222331111   HALSEY, Derek David
Derek was born in Huntington, West Virginia 26 May 1959.

1182222331112   HALSEY, Douglas Allen
Douglas was born in Huntington, West Virginia 24 September 1960.
He married **CALKINS**, Colleen Elizabeth in Prisideo Park, San Diego, CA, 30
August 1984. He married **ROSE**, Tamaura Le in Mt. Adams, Cincinnati, OH,
28 June 1997.

11822223311121   HALSEY, Dillon Alexander
Dillon was born in Bethesda Hosp., Cincinnati, OH 14 July 1989.

11822223311122   HALSEY, Devin Patrick
Devin was born 17 July 1992.

11822223311123   HALSEY, Bradley Michael
Bradley was born 28 May 1986. He is the son of Tamaura Le Rose.
He was adopted by Douglas A. Halsey and changed his surname in 1999.

11822223311124   HALSEY, Brian Richard
Brian was born 12 May 1988. He is the son of Tamaura Le Rose. He
was adopted by Douglas A. Halsey and changed his surname in 1999.

1182222331113   HALSEY, Sheridan Lynne
Sheridan was born in Huntington, West Virginia 17 March 1965. She
married **HUTH**, Thomas Casey in Forest Park, Ohio, 30 December 1983.
She married **MILLER**, Gregory in Cincinnati, OH, 25 October 1997.

11822223311131   HUTH, Nicholas Thomas
Nicholas was born in Cincinnati, Ohio 14 October 1983.

1182222331114   HALSEY, Jason David
Jason was born in Covington, Kentucky 2 January 1977.

118222233112 HALSEY, Richard Jerald
Richard was born in Otsego, West Virginia 13 January 1937. He
married **GROSE**, Elva 15 November 1958.

1182222331121   HALSEY, Richard Jerald Jr

He married **FOIT**, Wendy Lea. Richard was born 24 August 1959.
He married **MERCER**, Martha Ann 18 March 1989.
11822223311211   HALSEY, Stephanie Lea
Stephanie was born 31 December 1982.
1182222331122   HALSEY, Ralph John
He married **ADKINS**, Peggy Lynn. Ralph was born 3 September
1961. He married **MCMILLAN**, Kimberlyn 29 March 1994.
11822223311221   HALSEY, Tiffany marie
Tiffany was born 6 August 1982.
11822223311222   HALSEY, Brenton Mathew
Brenton was born 27 February 1986.
1182222331123   HALSEY, Rhonda Jill
Rhonda was born 29 December 1965. She married **JENNINGS**,
Steve 10 November 1990.
118222233113 HALSEY, Edna Louise
Edna was born in Otsego, West Virginia 16 November 1938. She
married **SIEBER**, John Andrew 26 October 1958.
1182222331131   SIEBER, John Curtis
John was born 9 August 1959. He married Elizabeth circa 1978. He
married **SCHAFFER**, Pamela Jean 7 April 1984.
11822223311311   SIEBER, Lisa Marie
Lisa was born 24 January 1979.
118222233113111   NOLAND, Jacob Hamilton
Jacob was born 5 August 1998.
11822223311312   SIEBER, Carrie Jean
Carrie was born 19 March 1985.
11822223311313   SIEBER, Kristi Louise
Kristi was born 18 August 1988.
11822223311314   SIEBER, Emma Lynn
Emma was born 30 October 1993.
11822223311315   SIEBER, John Curtis, Jr.
John was born 12 October 1996.
1182222331132   SIEBER, Anthony Jay
Anthony was born 3 May 1962. He married **FORD**, Barbara Lynn 30
March 1985.
11822223311321   SIEBER, Jessica Megan
Jessica was born 12 January 1986.
11822223311322   SIEBER, Anthony Jay, Jr.
Anthony was born 18 December 1987. Anthony died 28 December
1987.
11822223311323   SIEBER, Brian Caleb
Brian was born in Ft. Campbell, KY 12 February 1989.
11822223311324   SIEBER, Ronald Michael Thomas
Ronald was born 20 March 1993.
1182222331133   SIEBER, Kenneth Ross
Kenneth was born 24 June 1963. He married **VAN NESS**, Debra in
Upperville, VA, 13 September 1986.

11822223311331   SIEBER, Heather Leigh
Heather was born 2 March 1990.
11822223311332   SIEBER, Travis Scott
Travis was born 10 July 1995.
1182222331134   SIEBER, Sondra Kristine
Sondra was born 28 February 1966. She married an unknown person 1 November 1986.
118222233114 HALSEY, Margaret Ann
Margaret was born in Otsego, West Virginia 22 October 1940. She married **PHILLIPS**, Don Ellis in Rockville, MD, 4 March 1966.
1182222331141   PHILLIPS, Don Ellis, Jr
Don was born 10 July 1966. He married **EDMONDS**, Lisa 13 June 1993.
11822223311411   PHILLIPS, Brandon Ellis
Brandon was born 11 December 1994.
11822223311412   PHILLIPS, Kyle Tyler
Kyle was born 14 June 1997.
1182222331142   PHILLIPS, Darrell Ellery
Darrell was born 18 October 1968.
1182222331143   PHILLIPS, Darlene Elise
Darlene was born 10 July 1974.
118222233115 HALSEY, Helen Rebecca
Helen was born in Pierpoint, West Virginia 23 July 1942. She married **VAZQUEZ**, Peter 26 January 1963.
1182222331151   VAZQUEZ, Piper Angela
Piper was born 15 November 1964.
118222233116 HALSEY, Sidney Leon
Sidney was born in Beckley, West Virginia 9 September 1944. He married **LEAVERTON**, Carol 14 June 1966. He married **JOHNSON**, Clare 14 September 1985.
1182222331161   HALSEY, David Scott
David was born 17 March 1971.
1182222331162   HALSEY, Holly Elizabeth
Holly was born 18 December 1974.
11822223312   HALSEY, Delphia
Delphia was born in Pierpoint, West Virginia 2 October 1910. She married **FRANKLIN**, Charles Edgar, Sr. circa 1925. Delphia died 2 June 1971 in Dayton, Ohio, at 60 years of age.
118222233121 FRANKLIN, Geneva Louise
She married **STOOTS**, Ted. She married **RICE**, Homer. She married **MILES**, Bill. Geneva was born 12 March 1926. She married **LONG**, Charles Authur 8 September 1970. Geneva died 20 February 1998.
1182222331211   RICE, Jean
1182222331212   STOOTS, Alice Faye
She married **RICHARDSON**, Conly Delane. Alice was born 13 January 1945.
11822223312121   RICHARDSON, Lisa Gail

Lisa was born 9 December 1964.
1182222331213   STOOTS, Shelby Jean
She married **RICE**, Leon Mack. Shelby was born 6 November 1946.
11822223312131   RICE, Leon Mack, Jr.
Leon was born 23 September 1962.
11822223312132   RICE, Tina Marie
Tina was born 4 June 1966.
11822223312133   RICE, Cindy Kay
Cindy was born 17 October 1970.
11822223312134   RICE, Tony Lee
Tony was born 14 April 1976.
1182222331214   STOOTS, Thomas Ray
He married **MILLS**, Ruby Jean. Thomas was born 25 September
1948.
11822223312141   STOOTS, Shelley Denise
Shelley was born 25 August 1966.
11822223312142   STOOTS, Thomas Ray, Jr.
Thomas was born 18 December 1968.
11822223312143   STOOTS, Sander Lea
Sander was born 26 July 1971.
11822223312144   STOOTS, Tonia Lynn
Tonia was born 2 September 1978.
11822223312145   STOOTS, Christopher Ray
Christopher was born 4 July 1980.
1182222331215   STOOTS, Ronnie Lee
He married **JOHNSON**, Linda Mae. Ronnie was born 9 March 1950.
11822223312151   STOOTS, Ronnie Lee, Jr.
Ronnie was born 2 May 1968.
11822223312152   STOOTS, Richard Shawn
Richard was born 28 July 1970.
11822223312153   STOOTS, Renae Lynn
Renae was born 20 July 1971.
1182222331216   RICE, Larry Dwayne
He married **FRAUEF**, Debra Ann. Larry was born 24 May 1952.
1182222331217   MILES, Randall Kieth
He married **BUSCH**, Glenda Sue. Randall was born 4 October
1960.
11822223312171   MILES, Jamison Ian
Jamison was born 31 January 1978.
118222233122 FRANKLIN, Velma Pearl
Velma was born 2 September 1929. She married **ROUPE**,
Theodore Delaine 16 July 1948.
1182222331221   ROUPE, Dennis Alan
Dennis was born 14 May 1949. He married **FREEDLINE**, Mary
Frances 17 April 1971.
11822223312211   ROUPE, Jennifer Irene
Jennifer was born 16 January 1976.

11822223312212   ROUPE, Dennis Delaine
Dennis was born 17 October 1978.
1182222331222   ROUPE, Donnie Delaine
Donnie was born 22 April 1951. He married **SMITH**, Denise Ann 7 October 1972.
1182222331223   ROUPE, Danny Ray
Danny was born 22 January 1954. He married **THOMPSON**, Helen Marie 15 September 1979.
11822223312231   ROUPE, Jeremy Alan
Jeremy was born 27 July 1976.
1182222331224   ROUPE, Wanda Lee
Wanda was born 24 November 1961.
118222233123 FRANKLIN, Connie Mae
Connie was born 24 November 1932. She married **SIMPSON**, Joseph Jesse 16 July 1948. She married **GRIFFITH**, Harry Lee in New Richmond, WV, 9 September 1952.
1182222331231   SIMPSON, Gary Buzz
Gary was born 25 December 1948. He married **MELODY**, Jean in Flint, MI, 16 May 1971. He married **ANDERSON**, Donna in Dayton, Ohio, 11 July 1975.
11822223312311   SIMPSON, Rhonda Gail
Rhonda was born in Flint, MI 10 May 1971.
11822223312312   SIMPSON, Jennifer Leigh
Jennifer was born in Dayton, Ohio 27 October 1972.
11822223312313   SIMPSON, Gary Lee
Gary was born in Kettering, Ohio 1 January 1978.
1182222331232   SIMPSON, Judith Ann
Judith was born in Caloric, WV 13 February 1950. She married **BERRY**, Charles (Russell) in Dayton, Ohio, 9 May 1970.
11822223312321   BERRY, Jill Renee
Jill was born in Kettering, Ohio 12 May 1972.
11822223312322   BERRY, Stephanie Lynn
Stephanie was born in Kettering, Ohio 13 May 1975.
1182222331233   SIMPSON, Donna Sue
Donna was born 7 October 1951. She married **LONGHWAY**, (Buddy) C. in Dayton, Ohio, June 1977.
1182222331234   GRIFFITH, Harry Lee, Jr.
Harry was born in Beckley, WV 29 August 1953. He married **GONZALEZ**, Tamara 7 December 1972. He married **HARDEMAN**, Bonnie in Atlanta, GA, 3 July 1980.
11822223312341   GRIFFITH, Leslie Lynn
Leslie was born in Riverdale, GA 4 May 1981.
11822223312342   GRIFFITH, Matthew Lee
Matthew was born 3 March 1983.
1182222331235   GRIFFITH, George Edgar (Tim)
George was born in Dayton, Ohio 15 July 1957. He married **PATRICK**, Mary Lillian in Kettering, Ohio, 29 January 1978.

11822223312351   GRIFFITH, Harmony Elizabeth
Harmony was born in Dayton, Ohio 23 May 1978.
118222233124 FRANKLIN, Frances Lillian
She married **VAN BOVEN**, Raymond O.. Frances was born 3 January 1937.
1182222331241   VAN BOVEN, Raymond O.,Jr.
1182222331242   VAN BOVEN, Karen Sue
1182222331243   VAN BOVEN, Ronald
118222233125 FRANKLIN, Reva June
Reva was born in Irquois, WV 12 September 1939. She married **CLARK**, Alex Franklin in Tazeswell, VA, 18 April 1958.
1182222331251   CLARK, Debra Lynn
Debra was born 22 January 1959. She married **POWELL**, John Dayton in Flint, MI, 9 September 1978. She married **RICHMOND**, Don Erwin in Wallahalla, SC, 18 March 1981.
11822223312511   POWELL, Jonathan Jason
Jonathan was born in Flint, MI 5 October 1977.
11822223312512   RICHMOND, Amber Alleen
Amber was born in Monroe, Walton Co., GA 10 February 1981.
1182222331252   CLARK, Alex Franklin, Jr.
Alex was born in Princeton, WV 28 December 1959. He married **WATTS**, Deena in Flint, MI, 28 December 1977.
11822223312521   CLARK, Tiffany Renee
Tiffany was born 25 October 1977.
11822223312522   CLARK, Amanda Gail
Amanda was born 28 February 1980.
1182222331253   CLARK, Susan Marie
Susan was born in Washington, DC 13 November 1961. She married **COOK**, Jeffery Stewart in Athens, GA, May 1981.
11822223312531   COOK, Jeffery Allen
Jeffery was born in Athens, GA 21 April 1982.
11822223312532   COOK, Joshua Adam
Joshua was born in Athens, GA 8 April 1985.
1182222331254   CLARK, Terry Wayne
Terry was born 12 January 1964.
11822223312541   CLARK, Justine Wayne
Justine was born 14 June 1988.
1182222331255   CLARK, Sherry Gail
Sherry was born in Dayton, Ohio 28 January 1966.
11822223312551   MYERS, Tabatha June
Tabatha was born 23 July 1982.
11822223312552   SMITH, Jessica Leann
Jessica was born August 1985.
118222233126 FRANKLIN, Charles Edgar, Jr.
Charles was born 11 February 1947. He married **CASSITY**, Emma Jo in Dayton, Ohio, 30 October 1965. He married **WHITE**, Ruth Ann in Flint, MI, 18 April 1974.

1182222331261   FRANKLIN, Gloria Dawn
Gloria was born in Detroit, MI 6 May 1966. She married **HELTON**, Charles Joseph in Dayton, OH, 7 October 1982. She married **BRANER**, James Michael in Dayton, OH, 15 April 1989.
11822223312611   HELTON, Casey Dawn
Casey was born in Dayton, OH 22 September 1981.
11822223312612   HELTON, Colleen Marie
Colleen was born in Dayton, OH 26 August 1984.
1182222331262   FRANKLIN, Michael Joe
Michael was born in Flint, MI 20 August 1967.
1182222331263   FRANKLIN, Julie Lynn
Julie was born in Flint, MI 6 June 1977.
1182222331264   FRANKLIN, Ann Marie
Ann was born in Nuenberg, Bavaria Germany 5 February 1979.
118222233127 FRANKLIN, Danny Ray
He married **BROWN**, Lois. Danny was born 17 November 1948.
1182222331271   FRANKLIN, Danny Ray, Jr.
1182222331272   FRANKLIN, Donald Montgomery
11822223313 HALSEY, Beatrice
Beatrice was born in Pierpoint, West Virginia circa 1912. She married **COX**, Mason 19 September 1928. Beatrice died circa 1970.
118222233131 COX, Betty Ann
She married **CLAY**, Henry, Jr.. Betty was born 6 April 1929.
1182222331311   CLAY, Sharon Ann
1182222331312   CLAY, Henry Terry
1182222331313   CLAY, Patricia Danese
1182222331314   CLAY, Ray Warden
118222233132 COX, Jackie
Jackie was born 2 May 1931.
118222233133 COX, Mack Dempsey
Mack was born 18 January 1934.
118222233134 COX, Margie L.
Margie was born 26 March 1936.
118222233135 COX, Pauline E.
Pauline was born 13 July 1938. Pauline died circa 1959.
118222233136 COX, Deloris J.
Deloris was born 9 December 1941.
118222233137 COX, Paul Eugene
Paul was born 8 March 1946.
118222233138 COX, John Mace
John was born 9 January 1948.
118222233139 COX, Lettie Sue
Lettie was born 17 June 1950.
11822223313(10)   COX, Kathy L.
Kathy was born 8 March 1954.
11822223314 HALSEY, Woodrow Rolf
Woodrow was born in Pierpoint, West Virginia 31 March 1916. He

married **WOLF**, Helen in Maben, WV, 24 April 1943. Woodrow died 20 May 1962 in Mullens, West Virginia, at 46 years of age.
118222233141 HALSEY, Jimmy Lee
Jimmy was born in Tralee, WV 1 April 1944. He married **PORTER**, Patricia Lee in Rodell, WV, 30 July 1966.
1182222331411   HALSEY, Keith Shawn
Keith was born in Beckley, WV 26 April 1967.
1182222331412   HALSEY, Vanessa Renee
Vanessa was born in Beckley, WV 23 July 1974.
118222233142 HALSEY, Joyce Anne
Joyce was born in Mullens, WV 19 October 1945. She married **MUSTARD**, Thomas Henry in Mullens, WV, 7 May 1964. She married **CLARKE**, Joseph K. Sr in Princeton, WV, 5 December 1981.
1182222331421   MUSTARD, Tonya Rene
Tonya was born in Princeton, WV 1 March 1965.
1182222331422   MUSTARD, Brian Keith
Brian was born in Bluefield, WV 7 August 1969.
1182222331423   MUSTARD, Michael Thomas
Michael was born 22 February 1972.
118222233143 HALSEY, Jarrell Dale
Jarrell was born 19 April 1953. He married **GRAHAM**, Dianna Lynn in Mullens, WV, 18 October 1974.
1182222331431   HALSEY, Jason Dale
Jason was born in Beckley, WV 24 January 1978.
1182222331432   HALSEY, Michelle Lynn
Michelle was born in Beckley, WV 25 February 1981.
1182222331433   HALSEY, Jeremy DeWayne
Jeremy was born in Princeton, WV 27 February 1984.
11822222315 HALSEY, Irene L.
Irene was born in Pierpoint, West Virginia 16 January 1917. She married **THOMPSON**, Dallas Texas 25 September 1937. Irene died 18 December 1990 in Sanford, FL, at 73 years of age. Her body was interred 21 December 1990 in Sunset Cem, Beckley, WV. **OBITUARY** "Mrs. Irene L. Thompson, 73, of Second Street, Shady Spring, died Tuesday, December 18, 1990, at 3:45 a.m., in Sanford, FL. hospital following a long illness. Born January 16, 1917, at Pierpoint (Wyoming Co., WV) she was the daughter of the late Elige and Elizabeth Lambert Halsey. Mrs. Thompson was a homemaker and had lived the greater part of her adult life in Michigan (? Painsville, OH?) and had been a resident of Shady Spring since 1979. Her husband, Dallas Texas Thompson in 1983; two brothers, Woodrow and Ralph Halsey and three sisters; Delphie Franklin, Beatrice Cox, and Nellie Perdue preceded her in death. Survivors include her devoted sister, Athleen Thomas and brother-in-law, William H. Thomas of Orange City, FL., and numerous nieces and nephews and many friends. Services will be Friday at 11 a.m. at the Rose and Quesenberry Peace Chapel in Beckley. Burial will be in the Sunset Memorial Park in Beckley. Friends may call today from 5 p.m. to 9 p.m. at the Rose and Quesenberry Funeral Home in Beckley.

Nephews will serve as pallbearers.
11822223316   HALSEY, Nellie
She married **PERDUE**, Frank. Nellie was born in Pierpoint, West Virginia 20 December 1920. Nellie died 19 February 1975 in Sabine, WV.
11822223317   HALSEY, Athleen
Athleen was born in Pierpoint, West virginia 1 March 1922. She married **THOMAS**, William H. 13 July 1942. Athleen died 15 October 1993 in Orange City, FL, at 71 years of age.
118222233171   HALSEY, Kenneth L.
Kenneth was born 16 May 1939. He married **KIRKUM**, Joann August 1961. He married **HARMER**, Susan 23 December 1979.
1182222331711   HALSEY, Penny E.
Penny was born 31 May 1962.
1182222331712   HALSEY, Debra D.
Debra was born 27 May 1963.
1182222331713   HALSEY, Betsey Ann
Betsey was born 12 July 1980.
1182222331714   HALSEY, Katherine Irene
Katherine was born 31 March 1983.
1182222332   HALSEY, Isaac Jackson
He married **LAMBERT**, Minta. Isaac was born in Wyoming County, West Virginia 22 January 1883. Isaac died circa 1958 in Otsego, West Virginia. **OBITUARY- MULLENS-** "Funeral arrangements are incomplete for Isaac Jackson Halsey, retired Otsego miner and carpenter, who died at 8:20 a. m. Saturday in the Raleigh General Hospital, Beckley. He was 66. He had entered the hospital the hospital Monday when his condition became serious following a heart attack he suffered Sunday, two weeks ago, while returning home in a car from church. A resident of the Otsego- Pierpoint vicinity for over forty years, he formerly lived in McDowell County. He leaves as survivors his widow, Mrs. Minnie Halsey; four sons, Aubrey, of near Caloric, Orville, of Itmann, Hershey and Jack, at home; three daughters, Mrs. Carl Harmon, of Baltimore, MD. Mrs. Ralph Cole, of Corinne and Mrs. Roy Preston, Gary, Ind. A sister, Mrs. Lake Morgan, of Pierpoint, also survives. The body is at the Robertson and Foglesong mortuary, Mullens" (WV).
11822223321   HALSEY, Vada (Virdie)
She married **BAILEY**, Dock. Vada was born circa 1906.
118222233211   BAILEY, Mable
118222233212   BAILEY, Bill
118222233213   BAILEY, Jimie
11822223322   HALSEY, Sada May (Sadie)
She married **BRATCHER**, Gilliam Austeen. Sada was born circa 1907. Sada died 7 April 1969 at 61 years of age.
118222233221   BRATCHER, Gilliam Austeen, Jr.
He married **HUSKA**, Anneliese Juliana. Gilliam was born 10 April 1927.
1182222332211   BRATCHER, Gilly Ann
Gilly was born 25 July 1952.

1182222332212   BRATCHER, John Austeen
John was born 21 June 1958.
1182222332213   BRATCHER, Barbara Sue
Barbara was born 11 October 1959.
118222233222 BRATCHER, Amos Marvin 'Red'
He married **GRAHAM**, Bertha Peral. Amos was born 18 September 1929.
1182222332221   BRATCHER, Marvin Amos
1182222332222   BRATCHER, Gerald Jeffery
1182222332223   BRATCHER, Sherel
1182222332224   BRATCHER, William Lee
1182222332225   BRATCHER, Sandra Kay
11822223323   HALSEY, Aubrey Mack
He married **ENGLAND**, Elizabeth. Aubrey was born in Pierpoint, Wyoming County, WV 16 December 1910. Aubrey died 13 June 1993 in Beckley, WV, at 82 years of age. Aubrey was an Elder of the Cabin Creek Primitive Baptist Church, Pierpoint, Wyoming County, WV. He was a coal miner, retired from the Winding Gulf Coal Company at Maben, WV.
118222233231 HALSEY, Vivian Lee
118222233232 HALSEY, Norma Jean
She married **JENSEN**, John.
118222233233 HALSEY, Sharon Gail
She married **HARTSOG**, James Keith.
118222233234 HALSEY, Debra Lynn
She married **TRAIL**, Rocky.
118222233235 HALSEY, Lenora Dawn
She married **MCGHEE**, Dan.
118222233236 HALSEY, David Wayne
He married Donna.
118222233237 HALSEY, Raben
He married **ANN**, Joyce.
118222233238 HALSEY, Randall
He married Jesse.
118222233239 HALSEY, Shannon Dean
11822223323(10)   HALSEY, Charles Buck
He married Virginia.
11822223323(11)   HALSEY, Rodney
Rodney was born 9 March 1933. Rodney died 17 November 1988.
11822223324   HALSEY, Orvil Jackson "Preacher"
Orvil was born circa 1914.
11822223325   HALSEY, Ada (Adie)
She married **COLE**, Ralph. Ada was born circa 1916.
118222233251 COLE, Margaret
118222233252 COLE, Phyllis
118222233253 COLE, Janet
118222233254 COLE, Wriston
118222233255 COLE, William D.

He married **FLACH**, Alice. William was born circa 1938. William died 8 January 1991 at 52 years of age.

1182222332551	**COLE, Tina**
1182222332552	**COLE, Tammy**
1182222332553	**COLE, Christie**
1182222332554	**COLE, Tracey**
1182222332555	**COLE, Jeff**
1182222332556	**COLE, Steven**

11822223326   HALSEY, Ethel

Ethel was born circa 1919.

11822223327   HALSEY, Hersey Evert

Hersey was born after 1920.

11822223328   HALSEY, Andrew Jack

Andrew was born in Otsego, Wyoming Co., WV circa 1924. He married **HOUSTON**, Nellie K. in Amigo, WV, 3 May 1947. Andrew died 31 May 1994 in Damascus, VA, at 69 years of age. Jack & Nellie started their married life in Otsego, WV, living with his parents, Isaac & Mintie Halsey. Eventually they moved into their very own home, built by Tom Houston, in Allen Junction, WV. After exhausting all of his employment opportunities in Wyoming County, WV, Jack & Nellie moved to Gary, IN, where Jack's brother, Hershel, lived. They raised five children while Jack was employed in the construction industry. After the five children graduated from High school and were married and settled, Jack & Nellie moved, in 1974, to Damascus, VA. near Nellie's parents, Tom & Ethel Houston. Jack & Nellie have 14 grandchildren & 2 great-grandchildren, as of 1992.

118222233281   HALSEY, Penny Oleen

She married **BANKS**, Dennis M.

1182222332811   BANKS, Bruce Wayne

He married **BURKE**, Lisa.

1182222332812   BANKS, Janet Eleen

She married **DOANE**, Michael A..

1182222332813   BANKS, Kathy Jean

She married **BLEVINS**, Charles L. Jr.

11822223328131   BLEVINS, Isaac James

118222233282   HALSEY, Tennis Lee

He married **GORMAN**, Cheryl. He married Debbie. He married Shelia. He married Barbara.

1182222332821   HALSEY, Dawn Marie

She married **NORRELL**, John.

1182222332822   HALSEY, Randy

1182222332823   HALSEY, Stephen

118222233283   HALSEY, Judy Kay

She married **ELLER**, Gregory L..

1182222332831	**ELLER, Chad Eric**
1182222332832	**ELLER, Laura Leigh**
1182222332833	**ELLER, Jeanette Marie**
1182222332834	**ELLER, Jennifer Lynn**

118222233284 HALSEY, Vicky Lynn
    She married RALPH, Marvin W.
1182222332841   RALPH, Michael Wayne
1182222332842   RALPH, Stacy Lavada
118222233285 HALSEY, Kenneth Wayne
    He married SIERRA, Elsa.
1182222332851   HALSEY, Adam J.
1182222332852   HALSEY, Andrea Nickole
1182222332853   HALSEY, Tennis Lee
1182222333 HALSEY, Lake
    She married MORGAN, James. Lake was born in Wyoming County,
West Virginia 16 August 1886. Lake died 16 May 1959 in Pierpoint, WV.
11822223331   MORGAN, Carl
11822223332   MORGAN, Rosco
11822223333   MORGAN, Leona
    She married TONY
11822223334   MORGAN, Orion
11822223335   MORGAN, Willie
11822223336   MORGAN, Evertt
11822223337   MORGAN, Clarence
    Clarence was born circa 1903.
11822223338   MORGAN, Laurence "Ted"
    Laurence was born circa 1905.
11822223339   MORGAN, Herbert
    He married SPARKS, Luticia. Herbert was born circa 1908.
1182222333(10)   MORGAN, Aaron
    He married ELIZABETH, Josephine. Aaron was born in Pierpoint,
Wyoming Co., WV 2 February 1924. Aaron died 14 September 1998 in
Pierpoint, Wyoming Co., WV, at 74 years of age. His body was interred 18
September 1998 Dowdy Cemetery, Summers Co., WV.
1182222333(10)1   MORGAN, James
    He married Ena.
1182222333(10)11   MORGAN, Cassie
1182222333(10)12   MORGAN, Dustin
1182222333(10)13   MORGAN, Jordan
1182222333(10)2   MORGAN, Billy
    He married Donna.
1182222333(10)21   MORGAN, Brian
1182222333(10)3   MORGAN, Regina
    She married SIZEMORE, Robert.
1182222333(10)31   SIZEMORE, Holly
1182222333(10)32   SIZEMORE, Aaron
1182222333(10)4   MORGAN, Mona
    She married TILLEY, Ricky.
1182222333(10)41   TILLEY, April
1182222333(10)42   TILLEY, Sierra
1182222334   HALSEY, Roscoe

He married **SIZEMORE**, Hattie. Roscoe was born in Wyoming County, West Virginia circa 1896. Roscoe died circa 1960 in Maben, WV.

118222234　　HALSEY, Stephen Grigg

Stephen was born in Ashe County, N.C. 8 January 1859. He married **SIZEMORE**, Evaline 14 April 1873. He married **PENDRY**, Belle 10 October 1878. He married **PRIVETT**, Eunice (Weaver) 2 February 1900. Stephen died 14 November 1950 at 91 years of age.

1182222341　　HALSEY, Harrison
1182222342　　HALSEY, Mary Jane
1182222343　　HALSEY, Jane
1182222344　　HALSEY, Robert Lee
1182222345　　HALSEY, Drury 'Dock'
1182222346　　HALSEY, Senter
1182222347　　HALSEY, William
1182222348　　HALSEY, Carrie
1182222349　　HALSEY, Mabel
118222234(10)　HALSEY, Lois
118222234(11)　HALSEY, Jack
118222234(12)　HALSEY, Arnold
118222234(13)　HALSEY, Nancy Rebecca "Nannie"

Nancy was born 26 March 1880. She married **GOODE**, Thomas Jefferson 20 January 1898. Nancy died 21 September 1953.

118222234(13)1　　GOODE, Zetta

She married **MCDANIEL**, Phil A.

118222234(13)2　　GOODE, Mabel

She married **REYNOLDS**, J. Max.

118222234(13)3　　GOODE, B. Max

He married **BONDS**, Julia.

118222234(13)4　　GOODE, Gladys

She married **SHIPMAN**, Jack.

118222234(13)5　　GOODE, Paul

He married **BAILEY**, Kathleen.

118222234(13)6　　GOODE, Hersie Lee

Hersie was born Newfound, WV 20 December 1899. He married **BOYES**, Ethel Elizabeth in Wayne Co., WV, 6 May 1925. Hersie died 8 January 1977 Huntington, WV, at 77 years of age.

118222234(13)61　　GOODE, James Jefferson

James was born Echo, WV 6 February 1926. He married **FRAMPTON**, Lois Jane Huntington, WV, 3 September 1948.

118222234(13)7　　GOODE, Thomas Jackson

He married **HARMAN**, Mary Lou. Thomas was born 11 April 1917. Thomas died 15 October 1971 at 54 years of age.

118222234(13)71　　GOODE, Linda Lee

She married **PHILLIPS**, Ronnie Dean. Linda was born 21 October 1952.

118222234(13)711　　PHILLIPS, Katherine A.

Katherine was born 22 November 1980.

118222234(13)712   PHILLIPS, John Paul
John was born 2 September 1983.
118222234(13)713   PHILLIPS, Justin
Justin was born 10 February 1987.
118222235   HALSEY, Susan Victoria
Susan was born in Ashe County, N.C. 4 March 1861. She married
MEADOWS, Joseph in Wyoming County, WV, 29 January 1880. She
married **COX**, Alven A. in Summers County, WV, 9 September 1880. Susan
died circa 1930.
1182222351   COX, Miles
1182222352   COX, Cleveland
He married Maude.
11822223521   COX, Leonard
11822223522   COX, Versie (Bertha?)
1182222353   COX, Robert Lee
He married **MEADOWS**, Alice.
11822223531   COX, Phoebe
11822223532   COX, Ruby
11822223533   COX, Boyd
11822223534   COX, David
11822223535   COX, Milton
11822223536   COX, Leona
11822223537   COX, Susie
11822223538   COX, Macie
11822223539   COX, Dewey
1182222353(10)   COX, Lemuel
1182222354   COX, Martha Victoria
She married **HATCHER**, Simon.
11822223541   HATCHER, Belle
She married **WILLS**, Howard.
1182222355   COX, Mary
She married **CADLE**, Lige.
11822223551   CADLE, Wilma
11822223552   CADLE, Juluis
11822223553   CADLE, John
He married **WILLS**, June.
1182222356   COX, Nancy S. I.
Her body was interred in Pack Cemetery, Summers County, WV.
Nancy was born in Dunn, WV 9 November 1884. She married **WILLS**,
Charles Leland circa 1900. Nancy died 22 April 1965 in Beckley, WV.
11822223561   WILLS, Robert
11822223562   WILLS, Rosie
11822223563   WILLS, Emma
11822223564   WILLS, Zina
11822223565   WILLS, William Coy
He married **HYLTON**, Tiny. He married **SMITH**, Barbara. William
was born in Summers County, WV 10 September 1902. William died 15

October 1981 in CA, at 79 years of age.
11822223566   WILLS, Arthur Earl
He married **SOUTHALL**, Ruby. Arthur was born in Summers County, WV 24 December 1904. Arthur died 25 April 1989 in DL.
118222235661 WILLS, Josephine Ennis
She married **PRICE**, W.
1182222356611   PRICE, Andrew Wesley
Andrew was born 8 November 1946.
1182222356612   PRICE, Donald Raymond
Donald was born 20 January 1949.
1182222356613   PRICE, Robert Lee
Robert was born 26 February 1955.
1182222356614   PRICE, Virginia Susan
She married **CLARKSON**, . Virginia was born 24 May 1957.
118222235662 WILLS, Cecil Junior
118222235663 WILLS, Charles Edward
118222235664 WILLS, Lloyd Carlos
118222235665 WILLS, Eugene Franklin
118222235666 WILLS, Earl Dean
118222235667 WILLS, Pauline Juanita
118222235668 WILLS, Melvin Ray
118222235669 WILLS, William Douglas
11822223567   WILLS, Daisy Lillian
She married **WILLS**, Auther. Daisy was born in Summers County, WV 29 May 1907. Daisy died 22 March 1984 in Raleigh County, WV.
118222235671 WILLS, Donald Lee
He married JoAnn. Donald was born in Raleigh County, WV circa 1935.
1182222356711 WILLS, Betty
1182222356712 WILLS, Nancy
1182222356713 WILLS, Donna
1182222356714 WILLS, Sherril
1182222356715 WILLS, Brenda
118222235672   WILLS, Ronald
He married Cathy. Ronald was born in Raleigh County, WV 18 July 1941.
1182222356721   WILLS, Katie
1182222356722 WILLS,
118222235673 WILLS, Mary
She married **KELLER**, William. Mary was born in Raleigh County, WV 18 February 1943.
1182222356731   Lea Ann
118222235674 WILLS, Harry
He married Sharon. Harry was born in Raleigh County, WV circa 1945.
11822223568   WILLS, Etta Pearl
She married **PRINCE**, Frank. Etta was born 22 August 1909.

118222235681 PRINCE, Anna Lee
118222235682 PRINCE, James
118222235683 PRINCE, Robert
118222235684 PRINCE, Isabel
118222235685 PRINCE, Mary
11822223569   WILLS, Effie Arzonia
     Effie was born in Summers County, WV 2 December 1911. She married **SMITH**, William Arthur 13 October 1932. She married **ARMS**, Edward in Lorain, OH, 21 February 1970.
118222235691 SMITH, Dora Belle
     Dora was born in Raleigh County, WV 3 December 1933. She married **SMITH**, Verlan Ruff in Raleigh County, WV, 19 February 1952.
1182222356911   SMITH, Michael Ray
     Michael was born in Raleigh County, WV 26 February 1953. He married **ANDERSON**, Robin Gail in Lorain, OH, 8 November 1975.
1182222356912   SMITH, Catherine Paulette
     Catherine was born in Raleigh County, WV 28 October 1954. She married **DUMNEY**, Marcel in PA, 29 April 1979.
1182222356913   SMITH, Dorothy Alice
     Dorothy was born in Baltimore, MD 18 January 1956. She married **SCHENFIELD**, Robert in Kanawha, VA, 6 May 1975.
1182222356914   SMITH, Verian Dale
     Verian was born in Lorain, OH 28 March 1957. He married **WHITAKER**, Roberta L. in Lorain, OH, 23 August 1980.
1182222356915   SMITH, Shirley Diane
     Shirley was born in Nashville, TN 26 December 1959. She married **SOPKO**, Charles Albert in Lorain, OH, 28 March 1981.
1182222356916   SMITH, Arthur Ruff
     Arthur was born in Nashville, TN 11 February 1961. He married **FECHKO**, Ilene in Elyria, OH, 10 November 1979.
1182222356917   SMITH, Laura Leigh
     Laura was born in Nashville, TN 16 November 1962. She married **GUS**, Robert 23 October 1980. She married **MOORE**, Garry in Lorain, OH, 22 August 1987.
118222235692 SMITH, Billie Jean
     She married **WADDELL**, Norman. Billie was born in Fireco, Raleigh Co., WV 13 October 1935. She married **KLINE**, Michael before 1953. She married **HYLTON**, James T. in Raleigh County, WV, 28 July 1953. Billie died 16 September 1990 in New London, OH, at 54 years of age.
1182222356921   HYLTON, James Arthur
     James was born in Raleigh County, WV. James died in Lorain, OH.
1182222356922   KLINE, Sherry
1182222356923   WADDELL, Linda Sue
     She married **KLINE**, Mickey. Linda was born in Raleigh County, WV 28 June 1953.
1182222356924   HYLTON, Sandra Kaye
     She married **HUGHES**, Larry. Sandra was born in Lorain, OH 11

March 1956.

11822223569241	**HUGHES, Eugene**
11822223569242	**HUGHES, Tracy Tate**
1182222356925	**HYLTON, Danny Ray**

He married Teresa. Danny was born in Lorain, OH 28 May 1957.

11822223569251	**HYLTON, Melissa**
11822223569252	**HYLTON, Kara**
11822223569253	**HYLTON, Matthew**
11822223569254	**HYLTON, Danny**
1182222356926	**HYLTON, Mary Ann**

She married **MCGANNON**, Daniel. Mary was born in Lorain, OH 10 September 1960.

11822223569261	**MCGANNON, Lisa**
11822223569262	**MCGANNON, Daniel**
11822223569263	**MCGANNON, Brian**
1182222356927	**HYLTON, Rebecca Jean**

Rebecca was born in Lorain, OH 1 November 1961. She married **JIMENEZ**, M.. She married **HERNANDEZ**, Salvador.

11822223569271	**JIMENEZ, Miguel**
11822223569272	**JIMENEZ, Eric**
11822223569273	**HERNANDEZ, Salvador**
11822223569274	**HERNANDEZ, Linda**
1182222356928	**HYLTON, Rose Marie**

She married **PEREZ**, Ruben. Rose was born in Lorain, OH 31 May 1964.

11822223569281	**PEREZ, Crystal**
11822223569282	**PEREZ, Ruben**
11822223569283	**PEREZ, Vincent**
1182222356929	**HYLTON, Chrystal Thersa**

Chrystal was born in Lorain, OH 3 February 1972. She married **MYERS**, Michæl circa 1990.

11822223569291	**MYERS, Michæl J.**

Michæl was born circa 1991.

118222235693	**SMITH, Doris Jacqueline**

She married **ELLISON**, James E.. Doris was born in Raleigh County, WV 28 July 1941. She married **DEDMAN**, Charles Owen in Winchester, VA, 31 May 1979.

1182222356931	**ELLISON, Ricky Alan**

Ricky was born in Lorain, OH 31 January 1959. He married **HODGES**, Drema Faye 28 October 1978.

11822223569311	**ELLISON, Angela Dawn**

Angela was born in Raleigh County, WV 30 November 1982.

1182222356932	**ELLISON, William James**

He married **BEATTY**, Darlene. William was born in Lorain, OH 4 May 1961.

11822223569321	**ELLISON, Cory William**

Cory was born in Ft. Myers, FL 29 January 1988.

11822223569322   ELLISON, Amber Lynn
Amber was born in Ft. Myers, FL 27 October 1989.
1182222356933   ELLISON, Drema Lynn
Drema was born in Lorain, OH 19 February 1964. She married
BAKER, Clarence 22 February 1981.
11822223569331   BAKER, Christina Lynn
Christina was born 16 December 1982.
11822223569332   BAKER, Joshua Emmanuel
Joshua was born 3 September 1984.
11822223569333   BAKER, Nicholas Jermiah
Nicholas was born 27 August 1986.
1182222356934   ELLISON, Timothy Lee
Timothy was born in Lorain, OH 2 September 1965.
1182222356(10)   WILLS, Richard Sterling
Richard was born 26 February 1920. Richard died 6 January 1986.
1182222356(11)   WILLS, Thelma Mae
She married **WILLS**, A.. She married **MCINTOSH**, Charles. She
married **FOWLER**, James. Thelma was born 20 March 1927.
118222236   HALSEY, Isaac Jackson
Isaac was born in Ashe County, N.C. 4 June 1863. He married
PRIVETT, Alice 14 June 1883. He married **VANHOY**, Liza Jane circa 1900.
Isaac died 7 May 1915 at 51 years of age.
1182222361   HALSEY, Elsie
Elsie was born in Pierpoint, WV. She married **BROWNING**, Jasper.
1182222362   HALSEY, Lelia
1182222363   HALSEY, General Lee
He married **MEYER**, Euginia Alice. General was born 2 September
1888. General died 8 October 1960 in Saulsville, WV, at 72 years of age.
11822223631   HALSEY, Wilton
He married **CAMPBELL**, Ada. Wilton died 13 October 1988 in
Richmond, VA.
11822223632   HALSEY, Sylvia
11822223633   HALSEY, Thelma
Thelma was born in Itmann, WV 15 October 1910. She married
TEETS, Frederick in Oakland, MD, 28 February 1933.
118222236331 TEETS, Janet Elane
She married **MARTIN**, John Taylor. Janet was born in Terra Alta,
WV 1 January 1934.
118222236332 TEETS, Forest Lee
He married an unknown person. He married **HOWARD**, Beverly.
Forest was born in Williamson, WV 1 January 1936.
11822223634 HALSEY, Rupert Lee
He married **MARINE**, Verna. Rupert was born in Itmann, WV 22
September 1914. Rupert died 15 June 1949 in Welch, WV.
11822223635 HALSEY, Winford J.
He married **STATUM**, Eleanor. Winford was born in Itmann, WV 1
January 1918. Winford died 25 December 1971 in Welch, WV.

118222236351 HALSEY, Deborah
She married **SIZEMORE**, Stewart.
118222236352 HALSEY, Winford J., Jr.
118222236353 HALSEY, Claudia
She married **COOK**, Wilson.
118222236354 HALSEY, Stephen Douglas
He married **HAMILTON**, Linda.
1182222363541   HALSEY, Kimberly Lynn
She married **COOKE**, Hugh Shannon in Emory, VA, 31 August 1991.
118222236355 HALSEY, Nathan Dale II
Nathan was born 1 January 1957. Nathan died 1 January 1976.
11822223636 HALSEY, Edith A.
Edith was born in Itmann, WV 16 February 1921. She married
BROOKS, Kelly W. in Bluefield, WV, 11 March 1939.
118222236361 BROOKS, Billy Eugine
Billy was born 15 January 1940. Billy died 1 January 1947.
118222236362 BROOKS, Dweight Lee
Dweight was born 18 August 1941. He married **ASBURY**, Carol 25
July 1964.
118222236363 BROOKS, Christine
Christine was born 18 November 1943. She married **BEYMER**, Ray
8 June 1963.
118222236364 BROOKS, Myron
Myron was born 27 September 1947. He married **HAYNES**,
Dorathea 20 February 1970.
118222236365 BROOKS, David
David was born 8 April 1952. He married **TOLLIVER**, Patricia 28
December 1970.
118222236366 BROOKS, Barbara
Barbara was born 28 February 1956. She married **MULLINS**,
Dennis 25 September 1976.
118222236367 BROOKS, Cheryl
Cheryl was born 29 February 1956. She married **MORGAN**, Woody
21 September 1979.
11822223637 HALSEY, Ray
Ray was born in Itmann, WV 1 January 1923. Ray died 1 January
1926 in Itmann, WV, at 3 years of age.
11822223638 HALSEY, Euginia 'June'
She married **BALDWIN**, Raymond. Euginia was born in Itmann, WV
18 April 1923.
118222236381 BALDWIN, Byron
He married **WILLIAMS**, Dorcus.
118222236382 BALDWIN, Hilda
She married **KENNEDY**, Micky.
118222236383 BALDWIN, Alice Euginia
She married **MEADOWS**, Dayton.
118222236384 BALDWIN, Sandra

She married **WILLIAMS**, Eldon.

11822223639   HALSEY, Rene'

Rene' was born in Itmann, WV 9 May 1925. She married **GREEN**, Calvin in Welch, WV, 8 May 1948.

118222236391 GREEN, Susan

Susan was born in Maitland, WV 11 March 1949.

118222236392 GREEN, Linda

Linda was born 5 October 1952. She married **UHL**, Zachery 16 December 1972.

118222236393 GREEN, Patricia

Patricia was born 14 May 1955. She married **STAGGERS**, Allen 8 November 1980.

1182222363931   STAGGERS, Ashley

Ashley was born in Gassaway, WV 28 April 1983.

1182222363(10)   HALSEY, James

He married **TRUMP**, Betty. James was born in Itmann, WV 22 January 1931.

1182222363(10)1   HALSEY, Stephany

1182222363(10)2   HALSEY, Gary Lee

1182222363(10)3   HALSEY, Barry

1182222363(10)4   HALSEY, Michael

1182222363(10)5   HALSEY, Jamie

1182222363(10)6   HALSEY, Ricky Carl

Ricky was born in Bluefield, WV 10 February 1956. Ricky died 11 July 1985 in Bluewell, WV, at 29 years of age.

1182222363(11)   HALSEY, Drewie

He married Betsey. Drewie was born in Itmann, WV 2 February 1933.

1182222363(11)1   HALSEY, Brenda

1182222363(11)2   HALSEY, Linda

1182222363(12)   HALSEY, Phyllis Ann

She married **HODSON**, Earnest Randall. Phyllis was born in Itmann, WV 5 September 1935. She married **HIGHTOWER**, Roger in Salem, VA, 5 May 1984.

1182222363(12)1   HODSON, Diana

Diana was born 13 January 1954. She married **BISHOP**, John in Salem, VA, 20 October 1974.

1182222363(12)11   BISHOP, Joshua

Joshua was born in Roanoke, VA 20 April 1977.

1182222363(12)12   BISHOP, Jeremy

Jeremy was born in Roanoke, VA 23 October 1980.

1182222363(12)2   HODSON, Randall Alan

Randall was born in Roanoke, VA 30 November 1959. He married **WEST**, Joan Marie 30 June 1982.

1182222363(12)21   HODSON, Randall Alan II

Randall was born in Washington, DC 25 December 1986.

1182222364   HALSEY, Charles McCoy, Sr.

Charles was born 21 February 1890. He married **KEADLE**, Virgie E. 13 August 1920. Charles died 23 August 1944 at 54 years of age.

11822223641 HALSEY, Newasta

She married **BLANKENSHIP**, Woodrow. Newasta was born in Pierpoint, WV 1 October 1921.

11822223642 HALSEY, Charles McCoy, Jr.

Charles was born in Pierpoint, Wyoming County, WV 13 April 1923. He married **TOLLIVER**, Ruby in Columbia, SC, 2 October 1944. Charles died 16 May 1997 in Beckley, WV, at 74 years of age.

118222236421 HALSEY, Barbara Jean

Barbara was born 17 October 1946. She married **CRING**, Richard 11 June 1965.

118222236422 HALSEY, Janet Lea

Janet was born 30 May 1948. She married **FRANK**, Jim 1 March 1969.

118222236423 HALSEY, Mary Ann

Mary was born 14 January 1950. She married **PRIVETT**, James 30 August 1974. Mary died 27 March 1985 at 35 years of age.

1182222364231 PRIVETT, Julie

Julie was born 18 August 1975.

1182222364232 PRIVETT, Paula Jo

Paula was born 22 December 1976.

118222236424 HALSEY, Richard Allen

Richard was born 6 November 1953. He married **BARTLEY**, Rita 17 August 1973.

1182222364241 HALSEY, Rhonda Gail

Rhonda was born 3 April 1974.

1182222364242 HALSEY, Richard Allen

Richard was born 16 February 1979.

118222236425 HALSEY, Robin Lynn

Robin was born 28 May 1957. She married **BARKER**, Leanord 2 July 1980.

1182222364251 BARKER, Leanord Shane

Leanord was born 13 August 1981.

118222236426 HALSEY, Thomas Charles

Thomas was born 11 April 1961. He married **STOVER**, Rebecca 1 August 1987.

11822223643 HALSEY, Louise

She married **WOODRUFF**, P.B.. Louise was born in Pierpoint, WV September 1925.

11822223644 HALSEY, James Stewart

He married **KELLY**, Betty. James was born 23 December 1927.

11822223645 HALSEY, Jack

He married **UNDERWOOD**, Joan. Jack was born 22 July 1929. Jack died September 1984 in Beckley, WV, at 55 years of age. **OBITUARY** "BECKLEY- Jack Halsey, 55, of 305 Circle St., Beckley, WV, died Saturday in a Washington, D.C., VA hospital after a long illness. He was born in

Pierpoint, Wyoming County, and was a 10 year resident of Beckley. He was an Army veteran. Surviving: wife, Joanne Underwood; mother, Virgie Keadle Halsey of Beckley; brothers, Charles Jr. of Pierpoint, Stewart of Los Angeles, CA., Dorse of Bossier City, LA.; sisters, Mrs. T.W. Blankenship of Beckley, Mrs. P.B. Woodruff of Charleston, Mrs. George Patterson of Fairfax, VA. Service will be at 1 p.m. Wednesday in Melton Mortuary, Beckley, with the Rev. Robert Henson officiating. Burial will be in Blue Ridge Memorial Gardens, Prosperity. Friends may call from 6 to 9 p.m. today at the funeral home".

11822223646   HALSEY, Jill
She married **PATTERSON**, George. Jill was born in Pierpoint, WV 22 July 1929.

118222236461   PATTERSON, Craig Charles
Craig was born 18 December 1952.

118222236462   PATTERSON, Jay Kieth
He married **DOWN**, Heidi. Jay was born 4 November 1960.

1182222364621   PATTERSON, Ashley Nichole
Ashley was born 27 March 1988.

118222236463   PATTERSON, Scott Aliken
Scott was born 29 January 1966.

11822223647   HALSEY, Dorse Lee
He married **MILAN**, Easter. He married **JOHNSON**, Elizabeth. Dorse was born in Pierpoint, WV 15 January 1932.

1182222365   HALSEY, Walter Watson
Walter was born 22 November 1891. He married **SARVER**, Mary Elizabeth 30 October 1912. Walter died 3 August 1922 in Otsego, WV.

11822223651   HALSEY, Violet Auldine
She married **STEWART**, Raymond V.. Violet was born 13 October 1913.

118222236511   STEWART, Raymond V. Jr.
118222236512   STEWART, William Dewayne
118222236513   STEWART, Gerald
118222236514   STEWART, Danese
118222236515   STEWART, Sue Ann
118222236516   STEWART, Sandra
118222236517   STEWART, Larry
118222236518   STEWART, Eldon
118222236519   STEWART, Judy
11822223651(10)   STEWART, Patsey Gail
11822223651(11)   STEWART, Sherry
11822223651(12)   STEWART, Philip
11822223652   HALSEY, Romie Jackson
He married **SIZEMORE**, Helen. Romie was born in Pierpoint, Wyoming Co., WV 26 January 1916. Romie died 21 February 1994 in Glen Burnie, MD, at 78 years of age.

118222236521   HALSEY, Mary Ellen
118222236522   HALSEY, Karen Lee

118222236523   HALSEY, Viola Imogene
11822223653   HALSEY, Wanda Ethel
Wanda was born 29 January 1918. She married **PHILLIPS**, Garland Thomas 12 September 1936.
118222236531   PHILLIPS, Ronald William
Ronald was born in Herndon, WV 27 January 1938. He married **CORTHINE**, Lillian Margaret in Harrow Middlesex, England, 30 October 1964.
118222236532   PHILLIPS, Marilyn Jean
Marilyn was born in Allen Junction, WV 20 October 1939. She married **MCKINNEY**, William Thomas in Allen Junction, WV, 30 May 1958.
1182222365321   MCKINNEY, Mary Elizabeth
Mary was born in Abington, PA 14 June 1959. She married **DAVIS**, Randall Lee in Savannah, GA, 4 March 1978.
11822223653211   DAVIS, Justin Lee
Justin was born in Savannah, GA 26 September 1978.
11822223653212   DAVIS, James Matthew
James was born in Savannah, GA 5 November 1980.
11822223653213   DAVIS, Elizabeth Ashley
Elizabeth was born in Savannah, GA 26 March 1984.
1182222365322   MCKINNEY, William Thomas, Jr.
William was born in Millington, TN 27 December 1960. He married **MOSLEY**, Freda Marie in CA, 21 May 1980.
11822223653221   MCKINNEY, William Thomas, III
William was born in CA 8 May 1981.
11822223653222   MCKINNEY, Christopher Andrew
Christopher was born in CA 22 April 1987.
(18222236533) SPENCER, Belinda Kay
Belinda was born 2 October 1949. She married **MULLINS**, James Eugene in Parisburg, VA, 15 October 1970. She is the daughter of Joy Phillips (sister to Garland) and Willard Spencer, raised by Wanda H.Phillips.
1182222365331   MULLINS, Joy Lynn
Joy was born in Beckley, WV 19 December 1972.
1182222365332   MULLINS, Jason Ellery
Jason was born in Beckley, WV 30 March 1977.
1182222365333   MULLINS, Joshua Aaron
Joshua was born in Beckley, WV 14 October 1978.
11822223654   HALSEY, Robert Vaughn
Robert was born 23 February 1920. Robert died 8 September 1958.
11822223655   HALSEY, Alma Ruth
Alma was born 8 January 1921. Alma died 16 April 1924.
1182222366   HALSEY, Effie
Effie was born 19 March 1894. She married **SIZEMORE**, Emmett April 1916.
11822223661   SIZEMORE, Mildred
She married **MERCER**, Grant. Mildred was born in Pierpoint, WV 17 January 1917.

11822223662   SIZEMORE, Garland
He married **SPEARS**, Ruby. Garland was born 12 August 1918.
Garland died 2 September 1967 at 49 years of age.
11822223663   SIZEMORE, Erma
She married **JUSTICE**, Cecil. Erma was born 13 July 1920.
11822223664   SIZEMORE, Margie
She married **MCGRAW**, Kyle. She married **SPEARS**, Willie. Margie
was born in Pierpoint, WV 17 August 1922.
11822223665   SIZEMORE, Mary Lee
She married **SPENCER**, James. Mary was born in Pierpoint, WV 2
January 1924.
11822223666   SIZEMORE, Glenn
He married **PETTY**, Garnet. He married **BLEVINS**, Mary. Glenn
was born 6 April 1927.
11822223667   SIZEMORE, Vivian
She married **FARRNGGIA**, Tony. Vivian was born 25 November
1929.
11822223668   SIZEMORE, Wilma
She married **STEWART**, Ray. Wilma was born in Pierpoint, WV 22
December 1932.
11822223669   SIZEMORE, Kethel
She married **JONES**, George. Kethel was born 15 June 1935.
1182222366(10)   SIZEMORE, Lela Mae
She married **SMITH**, Gene. Lela was born 31 March 1937.
1182222367   HALSEY, Okey Jennings
Okey was born 30 September 1896. He married **HOUCK**, Mary 4
June 1918. Okey died May 1989 at 92 years of age.
11822223671   HALSEY, Lorene
She married **WORKMAN**, Roy B. Jr.,. Lorene was born 31 March
1919.
11822223672   HALSEY, Aldeen
She married **WORKMAN**, Earl Carson. Aldeen was born 10 March
1920.
118222236721 WORKMAN, Okey
He married Jewel.
118222236722 WORKMAN, Earl Ann
She married **MATICS**, Frank.
118222236723 WORKMAN, Valinda
She married **BAILEY**, Michael.
11822223673   HALSEY, Okey Jennings, Jr.
Okey was born 7 October 1921. Okey died August 1922.
11822223674   HALSEY, Orion
He married **MCKINNEY**, Jo Ellen. Orion was born 23 June 1923.
118222236741 HALSEY, Orion J., Jr.
118222236742 HALSEY, Jerry
11822223675   HALSEY, Herman Jackson (Pete)
He married **HENLY**, Betty. He married **MOTO**, Eutemio. Herman

was born 20 April 1926.

11822223676 HALSEY, Emma Lee
She married **REED**, Orbin. Emma was born 1 April 1928.

11822223677 HALSEY, Lorna Helen
She married **CARTER**, James Noble. Lorna was born 26 March 1930. She married **WYATT**, Greeley Andrew in Roanoke, VA, 28 May 1983.

118222236771 CARTER, James Noble, Jr.
James was born 12 May 1952. He married **MARLIN**, Lynn 22 September 1973.

118222236772 CARTER, Joy L.
Joy was born 25 January 1955. She married **PARRISH**, William M. 29 September 1973.

1182222367721 PARRISH, Joy Carter
118222236773 CARTER, Julie L.
Julie was born in Norfolk, VA 18 November 1960. She married **BERRY**, Richard 2 April 1983.

1182222367731 BERRY, Julie Carter
11822223678 HALSEY, Carroll Dewayne
He married **PAITSEL**, Frieda. Carroll was born 28 February 1932.

11822223679 HALSEY, Norma
She married **BOLT**, Paul. Norma was born 8 October 1933.

1182222367(10) HALSEY, Martin
He married **REED**, Sue. Martin was born 7 October 1935.

1182222367(11) HALSEY, Ronnie
He married **MORGAN**, Peggy. Ronnie was born 12 April 1937.

1182222367(12) HALSEY, Michael Steven
He married **BELCHER**, Betty. Michael was born 21 May 1941.

1182222368 HALSEY, Winnie
Winnie was born in Pierpoint, WV 28 July 1899. She married **HOUCK**, Sam 4 July 1914. She married **PHILLIPS**, Gilbert 24 December 1928. Winnie died 21 November 1971 at 72 years of age.

11822223681 PHILLIPS, Bonnie
She married **BELL**, Vernon. Bonnie was born 24 September 1928.

11822223682 PHILLIPS, Mary Alice
She married **BELL**, Charles. She married **LESTER**, Harold. Mary was born 25 August 1931.

11822223683 PHILLIPS, Joan
She married **GRATION**, Sam. Joan was born 23 March 1933.

11822223684 PHILLIPS, Frances
She married **COALSON**, Charles, Jr.. Frances was born 31 December 1938.

118222237 HALSEY, William Hamilton
William was born in Ashe County, N.C. 6 September 1865. William died 27 September 1882 at 17 years of age.

118222238 HALSEY, Fields Lee
Fields was born 4 March 1868. He married **GOODE**, Mary Frances in Pineville, WV, 10 May 1892. Fields died 20 March 1950.

1182222381   HALSEY, Bertie Peral
Bertie was born in Pineville, WV 5 April 1893. Bertie died 3 August 1896 in Pineville, WV, at 3 years of age.
1182222382   HALSEY, Everette McCoy
Everette was born 14 November 1894. He married **TILLEY**, Mahala Brookie 14 March 1920. Everette died October 1981 at 86 years of age.
11822223821   HALSEY, Mary Garnet
She married **CROTTY**, Edward. Mary was born in Princeton, WV 30 December 1920.
118222238211   CROTTY, Darlene
118222238212   CROTTY, Carolyn
11822223822   HALSEY, Leona
She married **ALVIS**, Billy Joe. Leona was born in Princeton, WV 29 November 1922.
118222238221   ALVIS, Russel Joe
11822223823   HALSEY, Eldon McCoy
Eldon was born 20 October 1924. Eldon died 22 April 1945 in So Pacific, at 20 years of age.
11822223824   HALSEY, Dennie D
He married **COOK**, Elizabeth. Dennie was born 11 September 1926. Dennie died November 1976 in Wayne, MI, at 50 years of age.
118222238241   HALSEY, Scott
118222238242   HALSEY, Kieth
118222238243   HALSEY, Mark
118222238244   HALSEY, Denise
118222238245   HALSEY, Scyntha
118222238246   HALSEY, John
11822223825   HALSEY, Albin Thomas
Albin was born in Princeton, WV 4 December 1928. He married **FARLEY**, Cleo 27 June 1953.
118222238251   HALSEY, Deborah Jean
Deborah was born 20 May 1954.
118222238252   HALSEY, Therisa Dawn
Therisa was born in Princeton, WV 6 October 1956.
118222238253   HALSEY, Timothy Lane
Timothy was born 22 February 1962.
1182222383   HALSEY, Thomas Lee
Thomas was born in Pineville, WV circa 1895.
1182222384   HALSEY, Hattie Evaline
Hattie was born in Pineville, WV 9 December 1896. She married **TILLEY**, Freely Cleveland 17 September 1908.
11822223841   TILLEY, Lucy
11822223842   TILLEY, Verlie Ward
Verlie was born 19 December 1911.
11822223843   TILLEY, Edward Edison
Edward was born 13 August 1917.
11822223844   TILLEY, Evelyn Evaline

Evelyn was born 30 September 1919. Evelyn died 17 May 1958.
11822223845   TILLEY, William Jennings
William was born 5 October 1920.
1182222385   HALSEY, Lacey Herbert
Lacey was born in Pineville, WV 14 April 1899. He married
BUCHANAN, Eva 1 November 1931. Lacey died 28 January 1972.
1182222386   HALSEY, Sadie Gay
Sadie was born in Pineville, WV 22 July 1901. She married
PERDUE, Frank 18 June 1918. Sadie died 17 June 1937 at 35 years of age.
1182222387   HALSEY, Vada May
Vada was born 22 July 1901.
1182222388   HALSEY, Della Frances
Della was born in Pineville, WV 8 April 1903. Della died 13 February
1907 at 3 years of age.
1182222389   HALSEY, Lemuel
Lemuel was born in Pineville, WV 20 April 1905. Lemuel died 17
February 1907 in Pineville, WV, at 1 year of age.
118222238(10)   HALSEY, George Carson
George was born in Pineville, WV 2 March 1907. He married
CLINE, Lake 6 February 1931.
118222238(11)   HALSEY, Eva Ann
Eva was born in Pineville, WV 25 March 1909. She married **COOK,**
Edward Lee 16 November 1927.
118222238(12)   HALSEY, Lula Rose
Lula was born in Pineville, WV 9 June 1911. Lula died January 1951
118222238(13)   HALSEY, Ida Verona
Ida was born 16 August 1913. She married **GUNTER**, Estel 20
August 1929. Ida died 19 May 1990 in Beckley, WV, at 76 years of age.
118222238(13)1   GUNTER, Betty Jo
Betty was born 10 June 1934.
118222238(13)2   GUNTER, Nancy Louise
Nancy was born in Mullensville, WV 20 April 1939. She married
STOUTAMYER, Raymond Edward in Gassaway, WV, 26 August 1958.
118222238(13)21   STOUTAMYER, Richard Wayne
He married **BIAS**, Kimberly. Richard was born in Sutton, WV 14
August 1959.
118222238(13)211   STOUTAMYER, Kelsie Louise
Kelsie was born in Warrenton, VA 28 June 1990.
118222238(13)22   STOUTAMYER, Chris Ann
Chris was born in Beckley, WV 21 October 1970.
118222238(13)3   GUNTER, Daisy Mae
Daisy was born in Marrianna, WV 27 March 1941. She married
PHELPS, John Richard 24 June 1961.
118222238(13)31   PHELPS, Nancy Jo
She married **INGE**, John Thomas. Nancy was born in Newport
News, VA 11 August 1966.
118222238(13)32   PHELPS, Daniel Wayne

Daniel was born in Newport News, VA 17 August 1969.

118222238(13)4   GUNTER, Robert Lee

He married **HOOD**, Sandra. Robert was born in Barrett, WV 10 January 1951.

118222238(13)41   GUNTER, Robert Lee, Jr.

Robert was born in Beckley, WV 14 June 1981.

118222238(14) HALSEY, Ethel Tabitha

She married **MORGAN**, Henry. Ethel was born 23 April 1916. Ethel died 26 June 1961 at 45 years of age.

118222238(15) HALSEY, Harry

Harry was born 18 December 1917. He married **LESTER**, Cletus 6 November 1942. Harry died 12 September 1984 in Summers Co., WV.

118222239   HALSEY, Martha Victoria

Martha was born 10 April 1869. She married **STEWART**, William H.H. in Pineville, WV, circa 1886. Martha died 12 August 1936 in Wyoming County, West Virginia, at 67 years of age.

1182222391   STEWART, Lillie Ann

She married **ELLISON**, Chester A.

1182222392   STEWART, Walter O.

1182222393   STEWART, Ocie

1182222394   STEWART, Shelfy

1182222395   STEWART, Mattie A.

1182222396   STEWART, Corbra

1182222397   STEWART, Jay E.

1182222398   STEWART, Forest D.

1182222399   STEWART, Sylvia

118222239(10) STEWART, Alberta A.

Alberta was born 20 August 1887. Alberta died 13 April 1981.

11822223(10) HALSEY, Sena

Sena was born 11 September 1874. She married **GOODE**, George Washington in Pineville, WV, 26 March 1892. Sena died 16 December 1946.

11822223(10)1 GOODE, William Clarence

William died circa 1944.

11822223(10)2 GOODE, Hillery Hobert

Hillery died March 1970 in Beckley, WV.

11822223(10)3 GOODE, S. Scott

11822223(10)4 GOODE, Ted

11822223(10)5 GOODE, Vida

11822223(10)6 GOODE, Hazel

11822223(10)7 GOODE, Walter Quenton

Walter was born 31 January 1892. Walter died circa 1972.

11822223(10)8 GOODE, Leland Dearmond

Leland was born 2 February 1897. Leland died 8 May 1986 in Beckley, WV, at 89 years of age.

11822223(10)9 GOODE, Rose

Rose was born 8 September 1903. Rose died 5 November 1954.

11822223(10)(10)   GOODE, Oscar

Oscar was born 18 October 1911. He married **ADAMS**, Opal 25 August 1935.

11822223(10)(10)1   GOODE, Harold Michael
He married **ELKINS**, Dora Sue. Harold was born 19 July 1939.
11822223(10)(10)11   GOODE, Chris
11822223(10)(10)12   GOODE, Shannon
11822223(11)   HALSEY, Drury Miles
Drury was born 7 April 1878. He married **PHILLIPS**, Ollie Mae in Pineville, WV, 6 May 1897. Drury died 13 November 1956.
11822223(11)1   HALSEY, Florence
11822223(11)2   HALSEY, Nancy
11822223(11)3   HALSEY, Zetta
11822223(11)4   HALSEY, Ennice
11822223(11)5   HALSEY, Hester
11822223(11)6   HALSEY, Pearl
11822223(11)7   HALSEY, Alice
11822223(11)8   HALSEY, Herbert
Herbert died after 1998.
11822223(11)9   HALSEY, Woodrow
11822223(11)(10)   HALSEY, Otis
11822223(11)(11)   HALSEY, William Howard
William was born 30 June 1905. William died circa 1950.
11822223(11)(12)   HALSEY, Nola
She married **COOK**, Orville. Nola was born in New Richmond, WV 5 August 1912. Nola died 1 October 1998 in Otsego, WV, at 86 years of age.
11822223(11)(12)1   COOK, Odell
He married **LOU**, Mary.
11822223(11)(12)11   COOK, Mike
He married Linda.
11822223(11)(13)   HALSEY, Ruth
She married **GREEN**, Wesley. Ruth was born 18 May 1921. Ruth died after 1998.
11822223(12)   HALSEY, Elijah Coy
Elijah was born 30 September 1880. Elijah died circa 1910 in Wyoming County, West Virginia.
11822224   HALSEY, Dilphia S.
Dilphia was born in Mou of Wilson, Virginia 3 November 1837. She married **HACKLER**, Garfield in Ashe Co., NC, 26 May 1855. Dilphia died 3 January 1903 at 65 years of age.
118222241   HACKLER, Rosan
118222242   HACKLER, Thomas
118222243   HACKLER, Coy
118222244   HACKLER, Frank
118222245   HACKLER, Mary
118222246   HACKLER, Griggs
118222247   HACKLER, Linney
118222248   HACKLER, Robert Halsey

He married **DAUGHTON**, Bessie. He married **HARDIN**, Lura. Robert was born 5 November 1859. Robert died 22 January 1933.

1182222481   HACKLER, Frank

1182222482   HACKLER, Robert Halsey, Jr.

1182222483   HACKLER, Vance Bain

Vance was born 19 November 1892. Vance died 6 December 1892.

1182222484   HACKLER, Lewis W.

Lewis was born 16 December 1904. Lewis died 22 September 1925.

1182222485   HACKLER, Doris

Doris was born 4 April 1914.

11822225   HALSEY, Fidella Ann 'Dilla'

Fidella was born 3 April 1840. She married **HALSEY**, Ezekial 19 September 1856. She married **DELP**, John Marshall 26 January 1871. Fidella died 24 April 1903 at 63 years of age.

118222251   HALSEY, Polly J. Ann

Polly was born. She married **HALSEY**, J. Emmett in Grayson Co., VA, 12 January 1890.

1182222511   HALSEY, Celia B

1182222512   HALSEY, William Clay

1182222513   HALSEY, Ada B.

1182222514   HALSEY, Charles B.

118222252   HALSEY, Rosa J.

She married **HASH**, Thomas M. in Grayson Co., VA, 16 December 1884.

1182222521   HASH, John

1182222522   HASH, Eugene

Eugene was born 27 February 1886. He married **HALSEY**, Oma Pearl in Grayson Co., VA, 31 December 1913. Eugene died 4 November 1941 in Chase City, VA, at 55 years of age.

11822225221   HASH, Etta

Etta was born 12 November 1914. Etta died circa 1942 in Chase City, VA.

11822225222   HASH, Thomas

Thomas was born 12 November 1914.

11822225223   HASH, Ella Mae

Ella was born 21 September 1917.

118222253   HALSEY, Fishie

She married **DIXON**, James Wiley 18 July 1886.

118222254   HALSEY, Ada Ann

Ada was born 28 May 1869. She married **HALSEY**, James Jackson in Grayson Co., VA, 2 January 1890. Ada died circa 1941.

1182222541   HALSEY, Lewis Bruce

Lewis was born 3 December 1890. He married **ANDERSON**, Mintie in Grayson Co., VA, 27 October 1917.

11822225411   HALSEY, Clara

She married **YOUNG**, Ralph.

118222254111 YOUNG, Bessie Carol

118222254112 YOUNG, Jeanie La Yvonne
118222254113 YOUNG, Lonnie
118222254114 YOUNG, Joseph
118222254115 YOUNG, Debra K.
11822225412 HALSEY, Louise
11822225413 HALSEY, Maxine
11822225414 HALSEY, Bettie Joe
11822225415 HALSEY, Clifford
11822225416 HALSEY, Patsey
11822225417 HALSEY, Gale
11822225418 HALSEY, Cecil H.
    Cecil was born 10 June 1918.
1182222542 HALSEY, Oma Pearl
    Oma was born 1 December 1892. She married HASH, Eugene in Grayson Co., VA, 31 December 1913.
1182222543 HALSEY, Bessie Mae
    Bessie was born 14 April 1895. She married HASH, Herschell 8 January 1914.
11822225431 HASH, Floyd Wilborn
    Floyd was born 27 August 1915.
11822225432 HASH, Ada Lucille
    Ada was born 5 October 1917.
11822225433 HASH, Electia Kate
    Electia was born circa 1919. Electia died circa 1921.
11822225434 HASH, Raymond
    Raymond was born 23 September 1921.
11822225435 HASH, Richard
    Richard was born 25 February 1924.
11822225436 HASH, Ardith Adell
    Ardith was born 23 October 1926.
1182222544 HALSEY, Ezekial
    Ezekial was born 18 August 1898.
1182222545 HALSEY, Dilla Ann
    Her body was interred in Fox Creek, VA. Dilla was born 7 April 1900. Dilla died 21 August 1991 at 91 years of age.
1182222546 HALSEY, Polly Madeline
    Polly was born 12 December 1902. She married HASH, Greek Garnet 29 June 1927. Polly died 2 January 1971 at 68 years of age.
1182222547 HALSEY, Vivian Carr
    Vivian was born in Mouth of Wilson, Grayson Co., VA 10 May 1907. He married BOYER, Louise 14 May 1938.
11822225471 HALSEY, Sammy
    Sammy was born 7 October 1947.
1182222548 HALSEY, Ella McKee
    Ella was born 4 May 1910.
118222255 DELP, Robert Washington
    Robert was born circa 1872. He married HALSEY, Callie 6 January

1895.

1182222551   DELP, Troy

118222256   DELP, Nannie Solina

Nannie was born 24 March 1875. Nannie died 5 September 1924.

118222257   DELP, Charles Alexander

Charles was born 28 March 1877. Charles died 15 December 1952.

118222258   DELP, Lucy Caroline

Lucy was born 6 July 1879. She married **HALSEY**, Troy Fielden 28 August 1897. Lucy died 12 February 1965 at 85 years of age.

1182222581   HALSEY, Annie

Annie was born 21 May 1900.

1182222582   HALSEY, John Wiley

John was born 6 July 1902. He married **YOUNG**, Ola Mae in Grayson Co., VA, 13 September 1922.

11822225821   HALSEY, Audrey Alleta

Audrey was born 28 July 1923. Audrey died 20 August 1925.

11822225822   HALSEY, Armond Harold

Armond was born 8 April 1925. Armond died 27 February 1959 in Grassy Creek, (NC?) at 33 years of age.

11822225823   HALSEY, Richard Glenden

Richard was born 10 January 1931. Richard died 8 September 1967 in Lenor, NC, at 36 years of age.

11822225824   HALSEY, Ronald Dean

Ronald was born 11 July 1935.

11822225825   HALSEY, Lloyd Lowell

Lloyd was born 9 September 1945.

1182222583   HALSEY, Lessie

Lessie was born 18 February 1905. Lessie died 15 June 1965.

1182222584   HALSEY, Fannie

She married **OSBORNE**, Reeves. Fannie was born 12 February 1907.

11822225841   OSBORNE, William

11822225842   OSBORNE, Fielden

11822225843   OSBORNE, Reeves, Jr.

11822225844   OSBORNE, Betty Lou

1182222585   HALSEY, Bayard Albert

Bayard was born 4 May 1909. He married **WADDELL**, Zenna 30 August 1930.

11822225851   HALSEY, Alden

Alden was born 4 June 1931.

11822225852   HALSEY, Carson Rhudy

Carson was born in Colora, MD 2 May 1934. He married **YOUNG**, Linda Taylor in Grayson Co., VA, 1 June 1957.

118222258521   HALSEY, Gregory Stephen

Gregory was born in Marion, VA 22 May 1958.

118222258522   HALSEY, Pamelia J.

Pamelia was born in Boone, NC 17 November 1959.

118222258523   HALSEY, Christopher David
Christopher was born in Jefferson, NC 9 June 1962.
11822225853   HALSEY, Carolyn
Carolyn was born in Grayson Co., VA 25 December 1939.
1182222586   HALSEY, Walter F.
Walter was born 2 May 1911.
118222259   DELP, Bertie Florence
Bertie was born circa 1881. Bertie died 26 January 1966.
11822225(10)   DELP, William McCoy
William was born circa 1883. William died 17 April 1948.
11822226   HALSEY, Adah Ann
Adah was born in Mou of Wilson, Virginia 12 June 1841. She
married **BUSIC**, John 25 October 1857. Adah died 3 November 1922.
118222261   BUSIC, Nannie
118222262   BUSIC, Mary Ann 'Polly'
She married **RICHARDSON**, Martin.
1182222621   RICHARDSON, Elizabeth
1182222622   RICHARDSON, Ada
1182222623   RICHARDSON, Cora
1182222624   RICHARDSON, Martha Jane
1182222625   RICHARDSON, Robert Burl
1182222626   RICHARDSON, Lillie Mae
1182222627   RICHARDSON, John Franklin
John was born 23 June 1893.
118222263   BUSIC, Troy
118222264   BUSIC, Mary Ann
She married **DELP**, William G. in Sparta, NC, 11 August 1878.
1182222641   DELP,
He was born 5 September 1879. He died 5 September 1879.
1182222642   DELP,
He was born 5 September 1879. He died 5 September 1879.
11822227   HALSEY, Robert McCoy
Robert was born in Mou of Wilson, Virginia 10 June 1844. He
married **YOUNG**, Lucy Jane 15 October 1865. Robert died 2 March 1909.
118222271   HALSEY, John Reed
John was born 7 September 1866. John died 18 January 1926.
118222272   HALSEY, Victoria I.
Victoria was born 18 March 1868. Victoria died 11 November 1950.
118222273   HALSEY, William Cleveland
William was born 13 November 1869. He married **HALSEY**, Malinda
Alice in Ashe Co., NC, 25 July 1894. William died 29 June 1935.
118222274   HALSEY, Fields McMillan 'Colonel'
Fields was born 30 September 1871. He married **PARSONS**, Ida in
Sparta, NC, 31 October 1891. Fields died 9 September 1920 in Asotin, WA.
1182222741   HALSEY, Walter Lester
Walter was born 8 August 1892. Walter died 3 May 1979.
1182222742   HALSEY, Lonnie C.

Lonnie was born 17 July 1894. Lonnie died 13 September 1967.

1182222743   HALSEY, McCoy

McCoy was born circa 1897. McCoy died circa 1954.

1182222744   HALSEY, Nancy L.

Nancy was born 3 December 1900. Nancy died circa 1967.

1182222745   HALSEY, Lola I.

Lola was born 25 December 1906.

1182222746   HALSEY, Robert Gwyn

Robert was born circa 1913. Robert died circa 1976.

118222275   HALSEY, Howard

Howard was born 15 April 1874.

118222276   HALSEY, Alice E.

Alice was born 7 October 1875. She married **PARSONS**, Charles T. 20 July 1893. Alice died 29 June 1902 at 26 years of age.

1182222761   PARSONS, Edgar Eugene

Edgar was born 7 July 1894.

1182222762   PARSONS, Albert G.

He married **WEAVER**, Luna. Albert was born 23 April 1896.

11822227621   PARSONS, Marguerite

11822227622   PARSONS, Weldon Thomas

11822227623   PARSONS, Dell Watson

11822227624   PARSONS, Jaunita

11822227625   PARSONS, Reba Mae

1182222763   PARSONS, Lloyd Britain

Lloyd was born 30 July 1898.

1182222764   PARSONS, John McCoy

John was born 1 July 1900.

118222277   HALSEY, Robert Jesse

Robert was born 24 March 1878. He married **LIVESAY**, Lura 10 February 1904. Robert died 30 October 1942 at 64 years of age.

1182222771   HALSEY, Pauline G.

Pauline was born 7 February 1905. She married **WEISS**, Bronson H, 29 May 1931.

11822227711   WEISS, James Hershel

James was born in Clarkston, ID 3 December 1935. James died 2 November 1973 in Lewston, ID, at 37 years of age.

1182222772   HALSEY, A. Leota

A. was born 22 March 1907.

1182222773   HALSEY, Hurley M.

Hurley was born 28 July 1923. He married **JACOBSON**, Wanda 15 May 1941.

11822227731   HALSEY, Dennis

Dennis was born 26 January 1942.

11822227732   HALSEY, Gerald

Gerald was born 10 February 1944.

1182222774   HALSEY, Donald

Donald was born 20 February 1924. Donald died 20 February 1924.

118222278   HALSEY, Mary Ann
Mary was born 17 September 1880. She married **PARSONS,** Joseph Volney in Grayson Co., VA, 24 December 1902. Mary died 28 February 1915 at 34 years of age.
1182222781   PARSONS, Isaac
Isaac was born 23 September 1903. Isaac died circa 1946.
1182222782   PARSONS, William
William was born 12 February 1907.
1182222783   PARSONS, Lucy
Lucy was born 21 July 1908.
1182222784   PARSONS, Evaline
Evaline was born 10 March 1910.
1182222785   PARSONS, Joseph Waddell V.
Joseph was born 17 October 1912.
1182222786   PARSONS, Mazie
Mazie was born 26 February 1915.
118222279   HALSEY, Dilphia A.
She married **GAMBILL,** James William. Dilphia was born 25 December 1883.
1182222791   GAMBILL, James Gwyn
James was born 2 February 1906. He married **POOLE,** Edna 19 January 1940.
11822227911   GAMBILL, Emma Jane
Emma was born 7 December 1940.
11822227912   GAMBILL, James Gwyn, Jr.
James was born 8 July 1944.
1182222792   GAMBILL, Lucille Elizabeth
Lucille was born 11 August 1907.
1182222793   GAMBILL, Willie Irene
Willie was born 29 June 1909.
1182222794   GAMBILL, Donna Howard
Donna was born 2 February 1912. Donna died 10 February 1912.
1182222795   GAMBILL, Virginia Halsey
Virginia was born 6 May 1917.
11822227(10)   HALSEY, Isaac Lester
Isaac was born 7 January 1885. He married **GRAHAM,** Winnie Belle 28 April 1911. Isaac died 18 October 1948 at 63 years of age.
11822227(10)1 HALSEY, Anna Graham
Anna was born 2 April 1912. She married **FIELDS,** John Cam 18 September 1937.
11822227(10)11   FIELDS, Nancy Rosamond
Nancy was born 9 July 1941. She married **HALSEY,** James Clinton in Mouth Of Wilson, VA, 26 June 1965. Nancy died 23 August 1976.
11822227(10)2 HALSEY, Carolyn
Carolyn was born 19 March 1915.
11822227(10)3 HALSEY, Dorothy Winnifred
Dorothy was born 7 July 1916.

11822227(10)4 HALSEY, Lester Howard
Lester was born 19 September 1920.
11822227(10)5 HALSEY, Hardin Graham
Hardin was born 19 September 1920. Hardin died 2 June 1942 in
Norfolk, VA, at 21 years of age.
11822227(10)6 HALSEY, Donald Augustus
Donald was born 26 March 1923.
11822228   HALSEY, Rosamond E.
She married **POOLE**, John F.. Rosamond was born in Mou of
Wilson, Virginia circa 1846. Rosamond died circa 1910. Her body was
interred circa 1910 in Rock Creek Cem.
118222281   POOLE, Robert Henderson 'Bud'
118222282   POOLE, John C.
118222283   POOLE, Drury
118222284   POOLE, Mattie
118222285   POOLE, Sarah
118222286   POOLE, Mary
118222287   POOLE, George
118222288   POOLE, James McCoy
James was born 19 September 1860. He married **PHILLIPS**,
Margaret 24 December 1884. James died 16 September 1928.
1182222881   POOLE, Leonidas Ernest
Leonidas was born 10 April 1886. Leonidas died 24 December 1942
1182222882   POOLE, Drwie Price
Drwie was born 7 December 1887. Drwie died 9 April 1962.
1182222883   POOLE, Robert Kyle
Robert was born 10 June 1888. Robert died 19 February 1961.
1182222884   POOLE, James Claudy
James was born 18 March 1892. James died 4 September 1962.
1182222885   POOLE, Sarah Almertie
Sarah was born 20 July 1894. She married **WINGATE**, Troy William
in Grayson, VA, 17 April 1921.
11822228851   WINGATE, Raymond Claude
Raymond was born 7 December 1922.
11822228852   WINGATE, James Richard
James was born 6 April 1924.
11822229   HALSEY, Elvira Dacia
She married **WYATT**, Eli E.. Elvira was born in Mou of Wilson,
Virginia circa 1850. Elvira died circa 1910.
118222291   WYATT, Monroe
118222292   WYATT, Miles
Miles was born circa 1841.
118222293   WYATT, Riley
Riley was born circa 1846.
118222294   WYATT, John
John was born circa 1848
118222295   WYATT, James Monroe

James was born circa 1850.

118222296   WYATT, D. F.
D. was born circa 1852.

118222297   WYATT, Evander Eli
Evander was born 30 March 1855. He married **STURGILL**, Sarah M. 20 July 1877. Evander died 6 May 1946 at 91 years of age.

1182222971   WYATT, William Justus
William was born 16 July 1878. William died 23 August 1972.

1182222972   WYATT, Becky Ann
Becky was born circa 1880.

1182222973   WYATT, J. Everette
J. was born 17 March 1882.

1182222974   WYATT, Cordia E.
Cordia was born circa 1883.

1182222975   WYATT, Eli Freely
Eli was born 28 March 1886. Eli died 2 July 1968 at 82 years of age.

1182222976   WYATT, Robert N.
Robert was born circa 1887. Robert died circa 1911.

1182222977   WYATT, John S.
John was born circa 1891.

1182222978   WYATT, Dora D.
Dora was born 2 May 1893. Dora died 30 August 1966.

118222298   WYATT, G. Lee Ander
G. was born circa 1856.

118222299   WYATT, Mary A.
Mary was born circa 1860.

1182223   HALSEY, Eli
Eli was born in Mou of Wilson, Virginia 15 April 1815. Eli died 19 January 1892 at 76 years of age.

118223 HALSEY, Mehetable
Mehetable was born circa 1761. Mehetable died circa 1830.

118224 HALSEY, Sarah
Sarah was born circa 1763. Sarah died circa 1835.

118225 HALSEY, Jason
Jason was born circa 1768. Jason died 11 March 1835 in Bridgehampton, NY, at 66 years of age.

11823   HALSEY, Theophilus
Theophilus was born circa 1733. Theophilus died circa 1800.

1183   HALSEY, William
William was born June 1703. He married **STANTON**, Sarah 19 June 1738. William died 6 December 1783 at 80 years of age. His body was interred 7 December 1783 in Preston, Conn.

11831   HALSEY, William
William was born in Stonington, CT circa 1739.

11832   HALSEY, Sarah
Sarah died in Preston, CT. Sarah was born in Stonington, CT circa 1741.

11833   HALSEY, Jeremiah

Jeremiah was born in Stonington, CT circa 1743. He married **PARK**, Esther 1 January 1769. Jeremiah died 25 August 1829 in Preston, CT, at 86 years of age. He took an active part in the Revolutionary War. Jeremiah spent more money and time than any other man in Connecticut except Gov. Trumbell and General Putnam. On May 1, 1775, he was commissioned as a Lieutenant in Captain Mott's Co., Colonel Edward's Regiment, and joined the Northern Department. In the preparations to capture Ticonderoga he went from Hartford with others as far as Sheffield, Mass., when with Captain John Stevens he was sent to Albany to discover the temper of the people. They thought it hazardous. He was with Ethan Allen in the capture of the fort which he, with seven others, had planned and carried out at their own expense. He was one of the men sent to Congress with his "present of a major, a captain, two lieutenants and 16 regulars".

Jeremiah was commissioned by Colonel Hinman in command of the forces as captain of the armed sloop "Enterprise," and to command the fleet of vessels in the lake, and was thus the first naval commander of the U.S. He was present at the siege and capture of St. Johns as an engineer. In December 1776, he was commissioned a captain in the Continental line. In January 1780, he was commissioned as Lieutenant Colonel of the 27th Regiment for Preston.

He was a man of tall and commanding presence, sanguine temperament and great force and energy of character.

1184   HALSEY, Elijah

Elijah was born circa 1704. Elijah died circa 1776.

1185   HALSEY, Silas (Jerusha)

Silas was born in Bridgehampton, NY circa 1704. He married **HOWELL**, Abigail 19 June 1750. Silas died 4 February 1777 in Morristown, NJ, at 72 years of age.

11851   HALSEY, Silas

Silas was born circa 1751.

11852   HALSEY, Luther

Luther was born 10 May 1758.

11853   HALSEY, Abigail

Abigail was born circa 1760. She married **LINDSLEY**, Aaron 19 August 1771.

118531 LINDSLEY, Abigail

Abigail was born in NJ. Abigail died in Central Ohio.

118532 LINDSLEY, Polly (Mary)

Polly was born in New Jersey 5 August 1775. Polly died 27 February 1857 in Phelps, Ontario Co., NY, at 81 years of age.

118533 LINDSLEY, Silas Halsey

Silas was born in NJ 27 December 1777. Silas died 27 July 1864 in Schenectady, NY, at 86 years of age.

118534 LINDSLEY, Aaron, Jr.

Aaron, was born in Morristown, NJ 20 July 1786. He married **TAYLOR**, Dorcus in Amsterdam, NY, 12 April 1810. Aaron, died 14 October

1825 in Troy, NY, at 39 years of age.
1185341   LINDSLEY, Abigail Halsey
Abigail was born in Amsterdam, NY 5 January 1811. Abigail died 23 November 1884 in Ft. Wrangle, AK, at 73 years of age.
1185342   LINDSLEY, Joseph Taylor
Joseph was born in Saratoga Co., NY 16 December 1812. Joseph died 13 August 1819 in Troy, NY, at 6 years of age.
1185343   LINDSLEY, Nancy Maria
Nancy was born in Saratoga Co., NY 2 December 1814. Nancy died after 1895 in Los Angeles, CA.
1185344   LINDSLEY, Aaron Ladner
Aaron was born in Troy, NY 4 March 1817. Aaron died 12 August 1891 in Portland, OR, at 74 years of age.
1185345   LINDSLEY, Charles Henry
Charles was born in Troy, NY 17 July 1820. Charles died August 1898 in New York, NY, at 78 years of age.
1185346   LINDSLEY, George Halsey
George was born in Troy, NY 10 May 1822. He married **ASH-JONES**, Louisa (Harriet) in Neenah, WI, 30 August 1852. George died 2 December 1895 in Neenah, Winnebago Co., WI, at 73 years of age.
11853461   LINDSLEY, Aaron Llewellyn
Aaron was born in Neenah, WI 1 August 1854. Aaron died 20 October 1905 in Menominee, MI, at 51 years of age.
11853462   LINDSLEY, George
George was born in WI circa 1856.
11853463   LINDSLEY, Asa Herbert
Asa was born in WI circa 1858.
11853464   LINDSLEY, Edward Ashburton
Edward was born in MO circa 1860.
11853465   LINDSLEY, Charles Perry
Charles was born in Neenah, WI 18 July 1866. He married **BARNES**, Josephine in Neenah, WI, 23 June 1891. Charles died 22 December 1922 in Hot Lake, OR, at 56 years of age.
118534651   LINDSLEY, Howarth B.
Howarth was born in Neenah, WI 22 March 1892. Howarth died 29 October 1906 in Spokane, WA, at 14 years of age.
118534652   LINDSLEY, Daniel Leslie
Daniel was born in Neenah, WI 15 June 1892. Daniel died 26 April 1990 in Orange, CA, at 97 years of age.
118534653   LINDSLEY, Marjorie
Her body was interred. Marjorie was born in Neenah, WI 22 February 1897. She married **MORGAN**, Ray Seth in San Francisco, CA, 22 April 1927. Marjorie died 5 December 1988 in Walnut Creek, CA.
1185346531   MORGAN, Mary Lynn
Mary was born in Hollywood Hos., Los Angeles, CA 14 July 1928. She married **AHLGREN**, George Lewis in Albuquerque, NM, 20 June 1949.
11853465311   AHLGREN, Diane Christine

Diane was born in Berkeley, CA 28 January 1950. She married **MCADAMS**, John in Oakland, CA, 6 October 1979.

11853465312   AHLGREN, George Lewis, Jr.
George was born in Hamilton AFB, Novato, CA 8 March 1952. He married **OTTUM**, Nancy in Davis, CA, 22 July 1978.

1185346532   MORGAN, Jo Ann
Jo was born in Los Angeles, CA 18 March 1933.

1185347   LINDSLEY, Margaret Elizabeth
Margaret was born in Troy, NY 14 May 1826.

118535 LINDSLEY, Luther
Luther was born in New Windsor Town, NY 23 May 1791. Luther died circa 1828 in Troy, NY.

118536 LINDSLEY, Phebe
Phebe was born in New Windsor Town, NY 16 February 1794. Phebe died before 1798 in NY.

118537 LINDSLEY, Eliza
Eliza was born in NY 17 April 1796. Eliza died circa 1870.

11854   HALSEY, Sarah
Sarah was born circa 1762.

1187   HALSEY, Experience
Experience was born in Bridgehampton, NY circa 1705. She married **HOWELL**, Samuel, Sr. circa 1739. Experience died circa 1777. Some sources list Experience's birth date as circa 1705, and the daughter of Ruth, Jeremiah first wife. The footnoted sources list her birth as about 1720 which is after Ruth's death.

11871   HOWELL, Samuel, Jr.
Samuel, was born circa 1740. He married Phebe about 1765. Samuel, died 20 Jul 1820 Bridgehampton, Suffolk Co., NY.

11872   HOWELL, Walter
Walter was born in NY circa 1741. Walter died 20 Jan 1820.

11873   HOWELL, Benjamin
Benjamin was born in NY about 1744.

11874   HOWELL, Jeremiah
His body was interred Presbyterian Church Cementery, Morris, NJ. Jeremiah was born in Southampton, NY 25 September 1747. He married Mary about 1770. Jeremiah died 17 Feb 1846 Parsippany, Morris Co., NJ, at 98 years of age. Jeremiah enlisted as a private in the Morris County militia and served as a sargeant at the Mounmouth, NJ, battle. In 1835 the New Jersey military pension records list Sargeant Jeremiah Howell, age 87, living in Morris County and receiving an annual allowance of $45.00.

118741 HOWELL, Abraham
Abraham was born circa 1773. He married Mary about 1792. Abraham died 13 April 1815 in NJ, at 41 years of age. Abraham's will, Book F, page 97, mentions his wife Mary, and daughter Amanda. The will of his father Jeremiah, who outlived him, mentions his granddaughter, Amanda.

1187411   HOWELL, Charles H.
Charles was born 30 April 1794.

1187412   HOWELL, Merit
Merit was born 11 July 1795. He married Sarah about 1810. Merit died 1 Jan 1818 at 22 years of age.

1187413   HOWELL, Jeremiah
Jeremiah was born about 1800. He married **SHARP**, Margaret Morris Co., NJ, 23 March 1820.

11874131   HOWELL, Aaron
Aaron was born Morris County, NJ January 1823. He married **SMITH**, Margaret in OH, about 1845. Aaron Howell and his bride moved to Cosochton County, OH where he was a farmer until 1849, when they moved to Madison County, IA, settling on a timber claim of 120 acres. At the time of his death he owned 2500 acres of land. Aaron Howell appeared in the census of 1850 in Madison County, IA. He was listed as a farmer, age 27 and born in NJ. He again appeared in the 3 August 1860 census in Crawford Twp., Madison County, IA, listed as a farmer, age 37, worth $3,500 in real estate and $1,000 in personal estate, and born in NJ. He appeared in the 3 August 1870 census for Crawford Twp., Madison County, IA, as a farmer, age 47, worth $33,275 in real estate and $4,284 in personal estate, and born in NJ. Aaron also appeared in the 26 July 1880 census in Crawford Twp., as a 57 year old farmer born in NJ. He became blind at age 55.

118741311   HOWELL, Emerson Goodrich
His body was interred Concordia Cemetery, El Paso, TX. Emerson was born Coshocton Co., OH 26 June 1846. He married **ARNOLD**, Ellen Elizabeth Madison Co., IA, 1 December 1872. Emerson died 6 January 1916 at 69 years of age. He appeared in the 1850 and 1860 census in Madison Co., IA as being age 4 and 14 born in OH.

118741312   HOWELL, Lanson
His body was interred Patterson, Madison Co., IA. Lanson was born Coshocton Co., OH 23 September 1847. He married **HUGHART**, Melvina E. Madison Co., IA, 24 April 1873. He married **WILLIAMS**, Mary E. about 1886. Lanson died 29 December 1918 in Los Angeles, CA, at 71 years of age. Lanson appeared on the census of 1850, 3 August 1860, 3 August 1870, 26 July 1880 of Crawford Twp., Madison Co., IA, as ages 3, 13, 23, and 33, respectively, and born in OH. In 1880 he was listed as a farm laborer living with his parents. A grandson Charles, age 6 and a granddaughter Emma, age 13, both born in IA, were also shown living with Aaron in the 1880 census. These were possibly Lanson's children.

118741313   HOWELL, Martha Angeline
Her body was interred Winterset, Madison Co., IA. Martha was born Coshocton Co., OH 18 February 1849. She married **EVERLY**, George W. about 1865. Martha died 24 October 1892 at 43 years of age. She appeared in the 1850 and 1860 census for Madison Co., IA. She was listed as being 2 and 11 years old, respectively, and born in OH.

118741314   HOWELL, Nelson Sharp
His body was interred Norwalk, Warren Co., IA. Nelson was born in IA 30 July 1851. He married **THRASHER**, Sarah Jane Madison Co., IA, 27 February 1873. He married **BIRD**, May about 1900. Nelson died 12 October

1908 at 57 years of age. He was listed in the Crawford Twp., Madison Co., IA census of 1860 and 1870 as being born in IA, ages 9 and a farm laborer at 18, respectively.

118741315   HOWELL, Ellen Amanda

Her body was interred Winterset, Madison Co., IA. Ellen was born Madison Co., IA 27 November 1853. She married **DABNEY**, John Wesley Madison Co., IA, 21 September 1872. Ellen died 29 Julyn 1931 at 77 years of age. She appeared in the 3 August 1860 and 1870 censes for Madison Co., IA as a 7 and 16 year old born in IA.

118741316   HOWELL, John Wilson

His body was interred Patterson, Madison Co., IA. John was born Madison Co., IA 22 August1856. John died 27 September 1859.

118741317   HOWELL, Eva Alice Matilda

Her body was interred Pasedena, CA, Mountain View. Eva was born Patterson, Madison Co., IA 7 March 1858. She married **GRIMES**, Leander Reed Patterson, Madison Co., IA, 31 December 1877. Eva died 5 March 1924 at 65 years of age. She was listed in the Crawford Twp., Madison Co., IA census for 1860 and 1870 as being 2 and12 years old, respectively, being born in IA.

1187413171   GRIMES, Lillian

1187413172   GRIMES, Robert Howell

11874132   HOWELL, Nelson

Nelson was born in NJ 4 August 1825. He married Margaret about 1855. He appeared on the 26 July 1880 census as a 54 year old farmer born in NJ.

11874133   HOWELL, Morris Sharp

Morris was born 12 February 1829.

11874134   HOWELL, David

David was born 17 February 1834.

11874135   HOWELL, Calab

Calab was born about 1838.

1187414   HOWELL, Amanda

Amanda was born about 1805. She married **HARRISON**, John about 1825.

118742 HOWELL, Burnet

Burnet was born about 1775.

118743 HOWELL, Jared

Jared was born circa 1781. Jared died 27 Apr 1855.

118744 HOWELL, Samuel

His body was interred Parsippany, Morris Co., NJ. He married **CAMPFIELD**, Matilda. Samuel was born circa 1787. Samuel died 11 June 1853 at 65 years of age.

118745 HOWELL, Mary

Mary was born circa 1792. Mary died 20 May 1868.

11875 HOWELL, Elizabeth

Elizabeth was born in NY about 1750.

11876 HOWELL, Abigail

Abigail was born in NY about 1752.

119   HALSEY, Johnathan
Johnathan was born 22 December 1669. Johnathan died before 1699.

11(10)   HALSEY, Phebe
Her body was interred in Old South g.y., LI. Phebe was born 29 December 1671. She married **HOWELL**, Hezekiah 10 September 1702. Phebe died 17 July 1732 in Southampton, LI, NY, at 60 years of age. **11(10)1 HOWELL, Phebe**
She married **WHITE**, Sylvanus. Phebe was born 11 January 1704/5.

11(10)2 HOWELL, Experience
Experience was born 28 August 1706.

11(10)3 HOWELL, Hezekiah
Hezekiah was born 6 May 1709. He married **SAYRE**, Susanna 11 December 1735.

11(10)4 HOWELL, Jedidiah
He married **BREWSTER**, Elizabeth in Catchoque, LI, NY. Jedidiah was born 28 June 1713. Jedidiah died circa 1795 in Blooming Grove, NY.

11(11)   HALSEY, Abigail
Her body was interred in Southampton g.y., LI. Abigail was born 19 April 1673. Abigail died 10 October 1696 at 23 years of age. She married **HOWELL**, Theophilus before 1699. The will of Abigail's mother, Mary, dated 18 December 1699, mentioned her as Abigail Howell.

11(11)1 HOWELL, Deborah
She married **COOPER**, Ananis. She married Ananias Cooper.

11(11)11   COOPER, Phebe
She married Jeremiah.

11(11)12   COOPER, Eunice
She married Charles Cooper.

11(11)13   COOPER, Abigail
Abigail was born in Bridgehampton 20 January 1750/1. She married Elias Cook.

11(11)14   COOPER, Prudence
Prudence was born 15 May 1754. She married James Sayre.

11(11)15   COOPER, Matthew
Matthew was born 14 May 1757. He married Lucretia Havens.

11(11)2 HOWELL, Prudence
Prudence was born circa 1702.

11(12)   HALSEY, Nathaniel
Nathaniel was born 1 June 1675. He married **STANSBOROUGH**, Anna 15 December 1697. He married an unknown person 15 December 1697. Nathaniel died circa 1746.

11(12)1 HALSEY, Elisha
Elisha was born 3 September 1699. Elisha died circa 1770.

11(12)11   HALSEY, Naomi
11(12)12   HALSEY, Jerusha
11(12)13   HALSEY, Anna Paine

11(12)14   HALSEY, Elizabeth
11(12)15   HALSEY, Elisha
He married **CLARK**, Esther in Southampton, LI, NY. Elisha was born in Southampton, LI. NY circa 1753. Elisha died circa 1820.
11(12)151   HALSEY, Silas Sayres
Silas was born 9 February 1779.
11(12)152   HALSEY, Hannah
Hannah was born 2 October 1781.
11(12)153   HALSEY, Catherine
Catherine was born 14 August 1784.
11(12)154   HALSEY, John
John was born 29 September 1787.
11(12)155   HALSEY, Samuel
Samuel was born circa 1791.
11(12)156   HALSEY, Eunice Maria
Eunice was born circa 1794.
11(12)157   HALSEY, Sarah S. B. H.
Sarah was born 1 May 1795.
11(12)158   HALSEY, Lindsley
Lindsley was born circa 1797.
11(12)159   HALSEY, Elisha Lindsley
His body was interred in Liverpool. Elisha was born in Long Island, NY circa 1800. He married **LOPEZ**, Leonora before 1830. He married **PERRYCLEAR**, Elizabeth Gray after 1830. Elisha died 8 August 1844 in Bay of Biscay, at 44 years of age.
11(12)1591   HALSEY, Leonora Sarah
Leonora was born in Charleston, SC 4 May 1823. She married **FINN**, Philander G. in Long Island, NY, 5 December 1841. Leonora died 23 December 1920 in Merchantville, NJ, at 97 years of age.
11(12)15911   FINN, Lois E.
She married **BUTCHER**, William 18 January 1869.
11(12)15912   FINN, Leonora H. 'Nora'
She married **BODAMER**, LT. John A. 12 January 1871.
11(12)15913   FINN, Lillian Estelle
She married **WILLIAMS**, Jacob I. 14 October 1880.
11(12)159131   WILLIAMS, Maude W.
She married **SAILER**, Randolph.
11(12)15914   FINN, Robert W.
Robert was born in NY circa 1843. Robert died 3 January 1863.
11(12)15915   FINN, Henry E.
Henry was born in PA circa 1845. Henry died 24 February 1857 in Erie, PA, at 11 years of age.
11(12)15916   FINN, Mary Evelyn
Mary was born May 1849. Mary died 4 September 1849.
11(12)15917   FINN, Charles Wilbur
Charles was born May 1851. Charles died 2 September 1851.
11(12)15918   FINN,

He was born 30 July 1859. He died 31 July 1859.

11(12)15919   FINN, Mabelle Maud
Mabelle was born in Erie, PA 10 November 1860. She married **MILLER**, Albert in Erie, PA, 3 December 1885. Mabelle died 15 January 1937 in Merchantville, NJ, at 76 years of age.

11(12)159191   MILLER, (Infant)
(Infant) was born. (Infant) died circa 1886 in Erie, PA.

11(12)159192   MILLER, Maud
Maud was born circa 1887. Maud died circa 1888.

11(12)159193   MILLER, Granville Gould
Granville was born in Philadelphia, PA 19 March 1896. He married **TRUSCOTT**, Katharine Frances in Merchantville, NJ, 15 September 1923. He married **COGHILL**, Isabel Margaret 13 June 1936. Granville died 16 April 1971 in Merchantville, NJ, at 75 years of age.

11(12)1591931   MILLER, Barbara Innes
Barbara was born. She married **JACKSON**, Warren Roger, Jr. in Merchantville, NJ, 30 March 1963.

11(12)15919311   JACKSON, Lori Anne
Lori was born in Marlton, NJ 16 April 1964. She married **DIPASCALE**, Paul Eugene in Merchantville, NJ, September 1984. She married **PURDY**, Edward Donald III in Merchantville, NJ, 4 November 1989.

11(12)159193111   DIPASCALE, Danielle Rose
Danielle was born 5 November 1985.

11(12)15919312   JACKSON, Deborah Lynn
Deborah was born 4 November 1968. She married **CASEY**, Frank Nelson III in Merchantville, NJ, 9 October 1993.

11(12)15919313   JACKSON, Michael Roger
Michael was born in Camden, NJ 30 May 1971.

11(12)15919314   JACKSON, Michele Faith
Michele was born in Camden, NJ 9 May 1975.

11(12)1591932   MILLER, Joyce Truscott
Joyce was born in Camden, NJ 6 December 1929. She married **PERRY**, Harold Francis, Jr. in Merchantville, NJ, 6 June 1951.

11(12)15919321   PERRY, William Harold
William was born in Philadelphia, PA 23 August 1952. He married **GREENE**, Jennifer Sue in Ft. Lauderdale, FL, 3 May 1980.

11(12)159193211   PERRY, Brian William
Brian was born in Ft. Lauderdale, FL 22 July 1982.

11(12)159193212   PERRY, Rachel Joy
Rachel was born 8 July 1985.

11(12)159193213   PERRY, Linda Marian
Linda was born in Ft. Lauderdale, FL 7 February 1987.

11(12)159193214   PERRY, Christine Faith
Christine was born in Ft. Lauderdale, FL 10 October 1989.

11(12)159193215   PERRY, Stephanie Grace
Stephanie was born in Ft. Lauderdale, FL 20 June 1991.

11(12)159193216   PERRY, Jessica Hope

Jessica was born in Ft. Lauderdale, FL 22 June 1994.

11(12)15919322   PERRY, Richard Alan

Richard was born in Camden, NJ 5 August 1953. He married **CHAFFON**, Annette in Pittsburgh, PA, 27 December 1980.

11(12)159193221   PERRY, Ezra Alan

Ezra was born in Miami, FL 5 February 1996.

11(12)15919323   PERRY, Kathryn Lynne

Kathryn was born in Ft. Lauderdale, FL 28 June 1963. She married **BUDD**, Craig Russel in Ft. Lauderdale, FL, 26 May 1984.

11(12)1591933 MILLER, Douglas Alan, Sr.

He married **GAMBLE**, Lynne. Douglas was born in Camden, NJ 30 October 1943. He married **BERTHEL**, Francina Susanna in Merchantville, NJ, 5 May 1970.

11(12)15919331   MILLER, Douglas Allan, Jr.

Douglas was born 18 March 1977.

11(12)15919332   MILLER, Dana Susanne

Dana was born in Marlton, NJ 7 August 1978.

11(12)159194   MILLER, Halsey Wilkinson, Sr.

Halsey was born in Philadelphia, PA 6 September 1897. He married **BORDEN**, Caroline Mulford circa 1929. Halsey died 8 May 1964 in Asheville, NC, at 66 years of age.

11(12)1591941 MILLER, Halsey Wilkerson, Jr.

Halsey was born 1 July 1930. He married **RODENBECK**, Mary H. 16 June 1951.

11(12)15919411   MILLER, Diana Lynn

Diana was born 22 January 1956. She married **SUSYKO**, Mark May 1980.

11(12)159194111   SUSYKO, Erik

11(12)159194112   SUSYKO, Stephen Christopher

Stephen was born 24 December 1985.

11(12)15919412   MILLER, Susan Linda

Susan was born 12 February 1965.

11(12)1592   HALSEY, Anna Maria

Anna was born January 1836. She married **O'NEALE**, Thomas P. 11 June 1856.

11(12)15921   O'NEALE, Robert Gourdin

Robert was born 1 January 1858.

11(12)1593   HALSEY, Stephen Ellis

Stephen was born March 1838.

11(12)1594   HALSEY, Edwin Lindsley

Edwin was born 29 May 1840. He married **THERESA**, Maria 14 September 1870. Edwin died circa 1903.

Edwin Lindsley Halsey was an artillery officer in the Confederate Army. General Wade Hampton in an article in the October 1887 "Century Magazine" describing the battle of Bentonville mentioned Captain Edwin Halsey's battery. He wrote "This absence of Hardee let a gap between Bragg and Stewart, and in order to hold this gap until the arrival of Hardee, I had two batteries of horse artillery, Captains Halsey and Earle, placed in the vacant space. Captain Halsey's battery had constituted a part of the Hampton Legion; it served with me during all the campaigns in Virginia, making an honorable and brilliant record, and it joined me at Bentonville just in time to render efficient service in the last battle in which we fought together. All gun of both batteries were admirably served, and their fire held the enemy in their front until Hardee reached his allotted position." A member of the same artillery company in an article written for the "Charleston News and Courier" of August 25, 1893, thus speaks of Captain Halsey: "At the promotion of Hart to First Lieutenant, E.L. Halsey became Captain. Halsey had been elected first lieutenant at the reorganization in April 1862. He was cool, calm, fearless and as firm as a rock in battle. He loaded the gun that threw the first ball fired on by the Confederacy, (the Star of the West was fired on by State troops) against the United States flag, and he commanded the battery that fired the last shot." The article continues: "Some of your readers will remember that on the morning of the 8th of March, 1861, a shot was fired accidentally from the Iron Battery at Cumming's Point that struck Fort Sumter. Few know the history of that ball. The Washington Artillery was stationed on Morris Island and had charge of the Iron Battery, the three guns of which were trailed on Fort Sumter. The men drilled at these guns every morning and evening, hoping that each day would bring orders to open fire. At last it became monotonous and the evening of the 7th Of March, while marching from the battery to camp after drill, Private Halsey said, "He was tired of this nonsense, and that there would be some fun in the harbor the next morning." When drilling at the guns on the following morning, to the astonishment of everybody, one of them was found to be loaded, the shot from which hit Fort Sumter. Of course no one knew anything about it. Col. Maxcy Gregg in his report to Gen. Beauregard says, "he does not suspect that it was put in by any man intentionally." General Hampton in an address to Hart's Battery said, "that they were literally the last guns fired in defense of Southern liberty," in a skirmish near Raleigh, NC, just before the surrender of Johnson's army. The battery on that occasion was commanded by Captain Halsey."

11(12)1595   HALSEY, Michael Perryclear
Michael was born in Beaufort, SC 3 July 1842. He married **MAULL**, Cecilia Bassellieu circa 1864. Michael died January 1881 in Memphis, TN.

11(12)2 HALSEY, Recompense
Recompense was born 19 August 1700. He married **JAGGERS**, Hannah circa 1721. Recompense died circa 1771 in Afton, NJ.

11(12)21   HALSEY, Ruth
She married **HOWELL**, Silas. Ruth was born circa 1722.

11(12)22   HALSEY, William, Sr.
William, was born circa 1723. He married an unknown person circa 1743.

11(12)221   HALSEY, John
John died in Weybridge, VT. He married **SANDFORD**, Jemima (Stanford?).

11(12)2211   HALSEY, Silas
His body was interred in Clinton Grove, Cem., Macomb Co., MI. Silas was born in Middlebury, VT 7 February 1789. He married **CADY**, Lucy M. in MI, 1 May 1825. Silas died 11 June 1862 in Lennox Township, MI.
11(12)22111   HALSEY, Sarah Caroline
11(12)22112   HALSEY, Eliza Maria
11(12)22113   HALSEY, Henry Hutchins
11(12)22114   HALSEY, David Knight
11(12)22115   HALSEY, Mary louisa
11(12)22116   HALSEY, Anne R.
11(12)22117   HALSEY, Chauncey Jordon
11(12)22118   HALSEY, Joseph
Joseph was born circa 1821. Joseph died circa 1864.
11(12)22119   HALSEY, Georgianna
Georgianna was born circa 1826. Georgianna died circa 1828.
11(12)2211(10) HALSEY, William Halleck
William was born 20 March 1830. He married **LAMPHERE**, Charlotte 25 September 1853. He married **DRYER**, Martha (Shattuck) 13 May 1875. He lived in Richmond Village, MI., was in business with his brother, Joseph, and brother-in-law, James M. Hicks, running a stage line from Ridgeway Station to Romio (MI?). On 13 August 1861, William enlisted in the 9th MI Infantry as a sergeant. He was discharged in 1862, and served as a recruiting officer until 1864, when he reenlisted in the 5th Infantry. He served until the close of the Civil War.
11(12)2211(10)1   HALSEY, Silas Herbert
Silas was born in New Haven, MI December 1854. He married **WOODRUFF**, Harriett 19 October 1875.
11(12)2211(10)11   HALSEY, Homer Archie
Homer was born in New Haven, MI 15 August 1880. He married **SNYDER**, Ethel Theids in Ritzville, WA, circa 1912. Homer died August 1936 in Spirit Lake, ID, at 56 years of age.
11(12)2211(10)111   HALSEY, Milfred Benjamin
Milfred was born in Cariwood, ID 4 January 1929. He married **LAMBOURNE**, Patricia Maria 24 October 1949.
11(12)2211(10)1111   HALSEY, Scott J.
Scott was born in Salt Lake City, UT 20 July 1960. He married **SMITH**, Nora 6 October 1984.
11(12)222   HALSEY, John
He married **STANFORD**, Jemima. John was born in Columbia, NJ circa 1750.
11(12)223   HALSEY, Phoebe
Phoebe was born in Columbia, NJ circa 1750.
11(12)224   HALSEY, William, Jr.
William, was born in Columbia, NJ 23 March 1760. He married **COBB**, Rachel in Columbia, NJ, 3 November 1780. William, died 21 February 1832 at 71 years of age. During the War for Independence, William served under Captain Emily, who was commanded by General Dayton.

William enlisted on May 9, 1778 and joined the Continential Army at Mount Holly, NJ., on June 5, 1778. He was involved in several conflicts, namely; the battles of Brandywine, Bunker Hill, Ash Swamp, and Cowpens. He was one of George Washington's life guards at Morristown, NJ., for three years. He returned to Columbia, NJ., about 1782 and was married by the Revervened Joseph Graves, at the Presbyterian Church.

11(12)2241   HALSEY, James
He married **PEAK**, Pattie in Mo of Wilson, VA, circa 1814.

11(12)22411   HALSEY, Troy
He married **HASH**, Polly Jane in Ashe Co., NC, circa 1849.

11(12)224111   HALSEY, J. Emmett
He married **HALSEY**, Polly J. Ann in Grayson Co., VA, 12 January 1890.

11(12)224112   HALSEY, Newton
Newton was born circa 1849. He married **HALSEY**, Polly Ann 23 September 1872. Newton died 1 April 1881 at 31 years of age.

11(12)2241121 HALSEY, Kelly

11(12)2241122 HALSEY, James G
James was born circa 1868. James died circa 1937.

11(12)2241123 HALSEY, John N.
John was born 24 February 1874. He married **HASH**, Polly Jane 8 February 1895. John died 5 August 1958 at 84 years of age.

11(12)22411231   HALSEY, Paul James
Paul was born 7 November 1895. Paul died 24 January 1955.

11(12)22411232   HALSEY, Maggie
Maggie was born 30 July 1897. Maggie died 9 February 1912.

11(12)22411233   HALSEY, Isom
Isom was born 7 September 1899.

11(12)22411234   HALSEY, Ben
Ben was born 10 September 1901. Ben died 1 August 1919.

11(12)22411235   HALSEY, Thomas
Thomas was born 17 September 1903.

11(12)22411236   HALSEY, Edna
She married **CORNETT**, Bryan. Edna was born 15 August 1907.

11(12)224112361   CORNETT, Ernest
11(12)224112362   CORNETT, Joseph
11(12)224112363   CORNETT, Shirley
11(12)22411237   HALSEY, Gracie
Gracie was born 10 August 1910. She married **HOLDAWAY**, Dean 1 January 1930.

11(12)224112371   HOLDAWAY, Edgar
11(12)224112372   HOLDAWAY, Gaile
11(12)224112373   HOLDAWAY, Rex
11(12)224112374   HOLDAWAY, Curtis
11(12)224112375   HOLDAWAY, Guy
11(12)224112376   HOLDAWAY, Mary Jane
11(12)22411238   HALSEY, Lena

She married **SUMMERS**, Bayne. Lena was born 8 August 1912.

11(12)224112381   SUMMERS, Roy

11(12)224112382   SUMMERS, Johnny

11(12)224112383   SUMMERS, Sidney

11(12)22411239   HALSEY, Reba

Reba was born 14 October 1914. She married **HOLDAWAY**, Willard Crockett in Grayson Co., VA, December 1933.

11(12)224112391   HOLDAWAY, James

James was born 27 April 1934.

11(12)224112392   HOLDAWAY, Robert R.

Robert was born 8 May 1935.

11(12)224112393   HOLDAWAY, Rebecca

Rebecca was born 1 September 1936.

11(12)224112394   HOLDAWAY, William Crockett, Jr.

William was born 7 June 1944.

11(12)2241123(10)   HALSEY, Virgie

Virgie was born 18 August 1916. She married **HOLDAWAY**, Vance 31 August 1935.

11(12)2241123(10)1   HOLDAWAY, Muncie

Muncie was born 16 November 1936.

11(12)2241123(10)2   HOLDAWAY, Susie

Susie was born 12 February 1940.

11(12)2241123(10)3   HOLDAWAY, Donna Lee

Donna was born 20 January 1943. She married **DOWELL**, Scott E. circa 1958.

11(12)2241123(10)31   DOWELL, Donna Sue

11(12)2241123(10)4   HOLDAWAY, Johnny

Johnny was born 9 September 1944.

11(12)2241123(10)5   HOLDAWAY, Blanche

Blanche was born 17 June 1946.

11(12)2241123(10)6   HOLDAWAY, Emma

Emma was born 12 August 1948.

11(12)2241123(11)   HALSEY, William

William was born 15 October 1919. William died 14 May 1937.

11(12)2241124 HALSEY, Callie

Callie was born circa 1882. She married **DELP**, Robert Washington 6 January 1895.

11(12)224113 HALSEY, Benjamin Franklin

Benjamin was born 1 December 1851. He married **HALSEY**, Virginia Florence 2 September 1881. Benjamin died 12 September 1937.

11(12)2241131 HALSEY, Missouri Kansas

Missouri was born 22 August 1871. Missouri died 29 April 1947.

11(12)2241132 HALSEY, Daniel Eugene   Daniel was born 7 September 1875. Daniel died 28 July 1939 at 63 years of age.

11(12)2241133 HALSEY, Ellis Conley

Ellis was born in Mouth Of Wilson, Grayson Co., VA 29 July 1882. Ellis died 3 January 1955 in Meadow Grove, Nebr, at 72 years of age.

11(12)2241134 HALSEY, Walter McTier
Walter was born in Mouth of Wilson, Grayson Co., VA 4 September 1884. Walter died 6 August 1950 in Madison, Nebr, at 65 years of age.
11(12)2241135 HALSEY, Emmette Breckenridge
Emmette was born in Mouth of Wilson, VA 11 May 1886. Emmette died 8 February 1946 at 59 years of age.
11(12)2241136 HALSEY, William Oscar
William was born in Mouth of Wilson, VA 7 September 1888. William died 11 February 1920 at 31 years of age.
11(12)2241137 HALSEY, Cynthia Irene
Cynthia was born in Mouth of Wilson, VA 29 December 1890. Cynthia died 22 October 1963 at 72 years of age.
11(12)2241138 HALSEY, Polly Jane
Polly was born in Mouth of Wilson, VA 30 November 1892. Polly died 15 July 1960 at 67 years of age.
11(12)2241139 HALSEY, Laura Alice
Laura was born in Mouth of Wilson, VA 18 February 1895.
11(12)224113(10)   HALSEY, Loy Otto
Loy was born 12 March 1897. Loy died 19 January 1961.
11(12)224113(11)   HALSEY, Minnie Leata
Minnie was born 16 April 1899.
11(12)224113(12)   HALSEY, Doctor Earl 'Jack'
Earl was born 5 June 1901. He died 21 December 1932.
11(12)224113(13)   HALSEY, Zettie Victoria
Zettie was born 15 July 1903.
11(12)224113(14)   HALSEY, Leonard Franklin
His body was interred in Emerich Cemetery, Norfolk, Nebr. Leonard was born 23 December 1906.
11(12)224113(15)   HALSEY, Eula Lois
Eula was born 25 February 1908. Eula died 7 December 1957.
11(12)224113(16)   HALSEY, Fannie 'Leola'
Fannie was born 18 February 1910.
11(12)224114 HALSEY, William
William was born circa 1853. William died circa 1860.
11(12)224115 HALSEY, Loucinda Jane
Loucinda was born 30 June 1854. She married **HASH**, Isom 2 August 1872. Loucinda died 2 February 1947 at 92 years of age.
11(12)2241151 HASH, Emmett
He married **HALSEY**, Florence 5 January 1904.
11(12)22411511   HASH, Earl McKey
Earl was born 8 February 1904.
11(12)22411512   HASH, Mammie Rose
Mammie was born 4 December 1906.
11(12)22411513   HASH, Eva Loucinda
Eva was born 29 March 1909.
11(12)22411514   HASH, William Hillery
William was born 25 May 1912.

11(12)22411515   HASH, Troy Leeter
Troy was born 7 September 1914.
11(12)22411516   HASH, Annie Belle
Annie was born 7 December 1916.
11(12)22411517   HASH, Hazel Virginia
Hazel was born 15 October 1919.
11(12)22411518   HASH, Emmett, Jr.
Emmett, was born 8 April 1922. Emmett, died 10 March 1946.
11(12)22411519   HASH, Clayton
Clayton was born 19 February 1925.
11(12)2241151(10)   HASH, Tommy Edwin
Tommy was born 18 May 1929.
11(12)2241152 HASH, Polly Jane
She married **HALSEY**, John N. 8 February 1895.
11(12)2241153 HASH, Cleveland, Dr.
His body was interred in William Halsey, Cemetery. Cleveland, died
5 May 1898.
11(12)2241154 HASH, Rush
11(12)2241155 HASH, (Unnamed Infant)
(Unnamed died 27 December 1896.
11(12)2241156 HASH, Maggie Robena
Maggie was born 23 November 1873. She married **HALSEY**, John
Ander in Ashe Co., NC, 25 December 1891. Maggie died 17 July 1966.
11(12)2241157 HASH, Tommy H.
Tommy was born 22 May 1885. Tommy died 17 July 1949.
11(12)2241158 HASH, Sena
Sena was born 31 May 1890. She married **HALSEY**, Andrew
Jackson 23 December 1910. Sena died 7 March 1965 at 74 years of age.
11(12)22411581   HALSEY, Bradley
11(12)22411582   HALSEY, Nina Rose
She married **TAYLOR**, Norman. Nina was born 1 November 1913.
Nina died 27 October 1960 at 46 years of age.
11(12)224115821   TAYLOR, Kyle Conrad
11(12)224115822   TAYLOR, Norma Jean
11(12)22411583   HALSEY, Lessie Lee
Lessie was born 13 April 1916. She married **HALSEY**, James Rhoa
in Grayson Co., VA, 24 December 1946.
11(12)224115831   HALSEY, Ronnie Lee
Ronnie was born in Jefferson, NC 31 December 1949.
11(12)224115832   HALSEY, Joyce Ann
Joyce was born 3 December 1950.
11(12)224115833   HALSEY, Danny Franklin
Danny was born 3 March 1955. Danny died 24 September 1955.
11(12)224115834   HALSEY, James Ronald
James was born 12 July 1959.
11(12)22411584   HALSEY, Kyle J.
Kyle was born 8 October 1918. Kyle died 18 July 1944.

11(12)22411585   HALSEY, Mae
Mae was born 20 January 1921.
11(12)22411586   HALSEY, Ossie Faye
Ossie was born 4 March 1923. She married **MABE**, Claude Wayne
9 April 1943.
11(12)224115861   MABE, Gerald Dean
Gerald was born 2 June 1944.
11(12)224115862   MABE, James
James was born 21 March 1947.
11(12)22411587   HALSEY, Ira Isom
Ira was born 8 May 1927.
11(12)224116   HALSEY, Polly Jane 'Molly'
Her body was interred in Oak Hill, Cemetery. Polly was born circa
1858. She married **PASLEY**, Drury Calvin 22 July 1877. Polly died circa
1935.
11(12)2241161 PASLEY, Samuel Emmitt
11(12)2241162 PASLEY, Lou
11(12)2241163 PASLEY, Myrtle
11(12)2241164 PASLEY, Grover Cleveland
Grover was born 10 July 1884. Grover died 8 February 1960.
11(12)2241165 PASLEY, Lelia Minta
Lelia was born circa 1888. Lelia died 25 October 1972.
11(12)2241166 PASLEY, Reece Calvin
Reece was born 28 August 1892. Reece died 19 April 1933.
11(12)2241167 PASLEY, Bryan
Bryan was born 16 May 1896. Bryan died 30 May 1976.
11(12)22412   HALSEY, Malinda
Malinda was born. She married **DAUGHERTY**, Daniel 20 February
1856.
11(12)224121   HALSEY, Mastin
His body was interred in Fox Creek, VA. Mastin was born 15 March
1843. He married **HALSEY**, Rosamond J. 21 March 1867.
Mastin died 16 September 1934 at 91 years of age. He was a
Confederate soldier. A Sergeant in Company I, 51st Virginia Infantry,
enlisting on 24 June 1861 from Fox Creek in Grayson County. He went from
Private to Sergeant between 31 October 1861 and 1 November 1862. Mastin
was captured at Waynesboro on 2 March 1865 and taken from Harpers Ferry
to Winchester to Fort Delaware on 12 March 1865. He was released at Fort
Delaware on 20 June 1865. He returned to Grayson County. Mastin had a
fair complexion with dark hair and gray eyes. He was five feet ten inches tall.
11(12)2241211 HALSEY, Lee Jackson
Lee was born 13 October 1868. He married **HASH**, Polly Ann 26
September 1892. Lee died 1 May 1952 at 83 years of age.
11(12)22412111   HALSEY, Carrie
11(12)22412112   HALSEY, Ora
11(12)22412113   HALSEY, Virginia
11(12)22412114   HALSEY, John Curtis

John was born 30 July 1897. John died 14 August 1899.

11(12)22412115   HALSEY, Drucie

Drucie was born 9 May 1906. She married **BRYANT**, James Blair 22 May 1929.

11(12)2241212 HALSEY, Lettie Beatrice

Lettie was born 15 April 1870. She married **WINGATE**, Wright 28 September 1895.

11(12)22412121   WINGATE, Hurley

Hurley was born 29 July 1896. Hurley died 21 July 1962.

11(12)22412122   WINGATE, Lester

Lester was born 29 October 1897. Lester died 29 September 1969.

11(12)22412123   WINGATE, Lessa

Lessa was born 11 November 1898. Lessa died May 1900.

11(12)22412124   WINGATE, Lelia

Lelia was born 8 March 1900.

11(12)22412125   WINGATE, Horner

Horner was born 17 May 1901.

11(12)22412126   WINGATE, Curtis

Curtis was born 12 November 1902. Curtis died 16 January 1971.

11(12)22412127   WINGATE, Claude

Claude was born 10 August 1904.

11(12)22412128   WINGATE, Stella

Stella was born 17 August 1906.

11(12)22412129   WINGATE, Ruth

Ruth was born 8 February 1909.

11(12)2241212(10)   WINGATE, Charlie

Charlie was born 3 April 1910.

11(12)2241212(11)   WINGATE, Robert W.

He married **HOLMES**, Majol. Robert was born 14 April 1914.

11(12)2241212(11)1   WINGATE, Barbara Jean

Barbara was born 2 November 1938.

11(12)2241212(11)2   WINGATE, Wayne Robert

Wayne was born 1 September 1946.

11(12)2241213 HALSEY, Therissa Caroline

Therissa was born 13 January 1872. She married **WINGATE**, R. Verdigan 'Dock' 6 December 1890.

11(12)22412131   WINGATE, Harmon

He married **PHIPPS**, Ruth. Harmon was born 7 September 1892.

11(12)224121311   WINGATE, Ben

11(12)224121312   WINGATE, Ernest

11(12)224121313   WINGATE, Bays

11(12)224121314   WINGATE, Edgar

11(12)22412132   WINGATE, Myrtle

Myrtle was born 3 May 1894. She married **WAGONER**, Fred 13 November 1913.

11(12)224121321   WAGONER, Neal

Neal was born 31 October 1914.

11(12)22412133   WINGATE, Walter Lee
Walter was born 6 February 1896. He married **COX**, Faye 20 May 1922. Walter died 15 April 1965 at 69 years of age.
11(12)224121331   WINGATE, Jerry
Jerry was born 22 November 1933.
11(12)22412134   WINGATE, Geneva
She married **STURDIVANT**, Fielden L.. Geneva was born 20 March 1898. Geneva died 21 November 1932 at 34 years of age.
11(12)224121341   STURDIVANT, Paul
11(12)224121342   STURDIVANT, Reba
Reba was born 29 February 1916.
11(12)224121343   STURDIVANT, Clifford
Clifford was born 4 February 1919.
11(12)224121344   STURDIVANT, Mary
Mary was born 21 December 1921.
11(12)22412135   WINGATE, Zollie Virginia
She married **TOMLINSON**, Paul. Zollie was born 2 May 1899.
11(12)224121351   TOMLINSON, Pauline
11(12)224121352   TOMLINSON, Ruby
11(12)224121353   TOMLINSON, Alice
11(12)224121354   TOMLINSON, Grace
11(12)22412136   WINGATE, Lillie Rose
She married **RECTOR**, Hurst. Lillie was born 19 June 1900.
11(12)224121361   RECTOR, Eugene
Eugene was born 12 January 1922.
11(12)224121362   RECTOR, Ralph
Ralph was born 26 January 1923.
11(12)22412137   WINGATE, Vilace
Vilace was born 10 April 1905. He married **HOLLAND**, Jessie circa 1941.
11(12)22412138   WINGATE, Eugene Mitchell
Eugene was born 24 May 1907. Eugene died 23 December 1907.
11(12)22412139   WINGATE, Ina Jane
She married **COX**, Carl. She married **ROLLINS**, Bill. Ina was born 17 October 1912.
11(12)224121391   COX,
11(12)2241214 HALSEY, America Virginia
America was born 28 February 1873. She married **WINGATE**, Richard Elmore in Grayson County, VA, 2 April 1893. America died 11 January 1952 at 78 years of age.
11(12)22412141   WINGATE, Troy William
Troy was born 24 March 1894. He married **POOLE**, Sarah Almertie in Grayson, VA, 17 April 1921. Troy died 16 December 1969.
11(12)22412142   WINGATE, Cora Lee
Cora was born 10 January 1896. She married **CARR**, Boyd 5 July 1916.
11(12)224121421   CARR, Donald Bryan

Donald was born 29 November 1917. Donald died 4 October 1948.

11(12)224121422   CARR, Glenn Paul
Glenn was born 8 February 1920.

11(12)224121423   CARR, Mabel Louise
Mabel was born 26 March 1921.

11(12)224121424   CARR, Guyda Faye
Guyda was born 27 October 1923.

11(12)224121425   CARR, Mildred
Mildred was born 29 August 1925.

11(12)224121426   CARR, Dorothy Lee
Dorothy was born 3 June 1928.

11(12)224121427   CARR, Edith Rosamond
Edith was born 18 July 1931.

11(12)22412143   WINGATE, Letcher Carlisle
Letcher was born 4 October 1898. He married **BOYER**, Ada Mae 28 December 1921.

11(12)224121431   WINGATE, Frances Irene   Frances was born in Akron, OH 3 November 1922. She married **OGLESBY**, Richard Bowen in Drapes, VA, 9 June 1944.

11(12)224121432   WINGATE, Garnett Smith
He married **THAWLEY**, Mary Ellen. Garnett was born 8 May 1924.

11(12)2241214321   WINGATE, Suzanne
She married **HAMM**, Charles. She married **HARRIS**, Bill.

11(12)22412143211   HAMM, Gregory Allen
11(12)22412143212   HAMM, Marty Allen
11(12)22412143213   HARRIS, Keena
11(12)2241214322   WINGATE, Geneva Louise
She married **TULLIUM**, Steve.

11(12)2241214323   WINGATE, Danny
Danny was born 19 May 1951. He married **HARRIS**, Clevie Ellen 19 May 1973.

11(12)224121433   WINGATE, Mary Lucille
Mary was born in Independence, VA 28 December 1925. She married **RICHARDSON**, Argie Cecil 30 June 1944.

11(12)224121434   WINGATE, Charles Curtis
Charles was born in Independence, VA 30 July 1928. He married **ROARK**, Edna 7 April 1955.

11(12)224121435   WINGATE, Margaret Ann
Margaret was born in Independence, VA 6 July 1931. She married **HAMPTON**, Hale 30 June 1951.

11(12)22412144   WINGATE, Wright McCamant
Wright was born 29 April 1900. He married **MORTON**, Vera 21 October 1928.

11(12)224121441   WINGATE, Josephine
Josephine was born 13 January 1930.

11(12)224121442   WINGATE, Gordon
Gordon was born 3 November 1932.

11(12)22412145   WINGATE, Lettie Rosmond
Lettie was born 6 May 1903.
11(12)22412146   WINGATE, Lillian Virginia
Lillian was born 4 November 1904. Lillian died 4 November 1904.
11(12)22412147   WINGATE, Lura Marie
Lura was born 1 November 1905. She married **RING**, Roy 15 June 1930.
11(12)224121471   RING, Nancy
11(12)224121472   RING, Julia
11(12)224121473   RING, R. J.
11(12)22412148   WINGATE, Alexander Mitchell
Alexander was born 14 March 1908. He married **DUBBS**, Gertrude 24 September 1932.
11(12)224121481   WINGATE, Connie
11(12)224121482   WINGATE, Jean
11(12)22412149   WINGATE, Hobert Banks
Hobert was born 28 November 1909.
11(12)2241214(10)   WINGATE, Paul Jones
Paul was born 1 September 1911. He married **MCKNIGHT**, Virginia 15 April 1939. He married **STONE**, Edna 15 February 1948.
11(12)2241214(10)1   WINGATE, Emily
Emily was born 5 February 1941.
11(12)2241214(10)2   WINGATE, Mava
Mava was born 5 January 1949.
11(12)2241214(11)   WINGATE, Myrtle Carolyn
She married **COUNTS**, Charles. Myrtle was born 25 November 1914. She married **GUNTHIE**, Hobert 18 January 1937.
11(12)2241215 HALSEY, Annie Belle
Annie was born 26 March 1874. Annie died 15 February 1962.
11(12)2241216 HALSEY, Cora Dell
She married **JONES**, Mitchell. Cora was born 1 June 1878.
11(12)22412161   JONES, Grace
11(12)22412162   JONES, Vivian
11(12)22412163   .   JONES, Paul
11(12)22412164   JONES, Gladys
11(12)2241217 HALSEY, Myrtle Florence
Myrtle was born circa 1880. She married **WINGATE**, Rush 25 September 1904.
11(12)22412171   WINGATE, Gwyn
Gwyn was born 24 March 1906.
11(12)22412172   WINGATE, Kyle
Kyle was born 31 March 1907.
11(12)22412173   WINGATE, Eugene
Eugene was born circa 1910.
11(12)22412174   WINGATE, Lenna
Lenna was born circa 1913.
11(12)22412175   WINGATE, James

James was born circa 1917.
11(12)22412176   WINGATE, Cecelia
Cecelia was born circa 1922.
11(12)2241218 HALSEY, Vilas Manning
Vilas was born 12 November 1884. He married **HALSEY**, Celia
Clyde 31 December 1914. Vilas died circa 1967.
11(12)2241219 HALSEY, Leesa Mae
Leesa was born 26 October 1892. Leesa died 20 June 1968.
11(12)224122   HALSEY, Loudema
She married **HALE**, John. Loudema was born 18 January 1850.
Loudema died 11 April 1943 at 93 years of age.
11(12)2241221 HALE, Robert
11(12)2241222 HALE, William
11(12)224123   HALSEY, Polly Jane
Polly was born circa 1853. She married **PASLEY**, Marshall Gerome
'Gee' 14 September 1881. Polly died circa 1940.
11(12)2241231 PASLEY, William Mastin
William was born 15 November 1882.
11(12)2241232 PASLEY, John Isom
John was born 30 May 1885.
11(12)2241233 PASLEY, Edwin Lee
Edwin was born 25 November 1886.
11(12)2241234 PASLEY, Maude Leota
Maude was born 14 June 1890.
11(12)2241235 PASLEY, Annie
Annie was born 24 May 1895. Annie died 17 July 1935.
11(12)2241236 PASLEY, Lou Ann
Lou was born 24 May 1895. Lou died 24 May 1895.
11(12)22413   HALSEY, Olive
Olive was born. She married **HASH**, Enoch D. in Ashe Co., NC, 30
September 1852. Olive died 21 July 1909.
11(12)224131   HASH, Jeston
11(12)224132   HASH, Ellen
She married **PHIPPS**, Larkin 23 January 1876.
11(12)224133   HASH, Thomas
He married **PICKLE**, Lura.
11(12)224134   HASH, Carrie or Caroline (Halsey)
She married **HASH**, Andrew Jackson. Carrie was born 7 February
1847.
11(12)2241341 HASH, Jennie 'Virginia'
Jennie was born 1 December 1866.
11(12)2241342 HASH, James Marion
James was born 17 October 1868. James died 22 May 1937.
11(12)2241343 HASH, Polly Jane
Polly was born 17 July 1870.
11(12)2241344 HASH, William
William was born 23 March 1873.

11(12)224135   HASH, 'Fronie' Sophronie
She married **ANDERSON**, John W.. 'Fronie' was born 3 January 1863. 'Fronie' died 12 October 1944 at 81 years of age.
11(12)224136   HASH, Alice
Her body was interred in Gold Hill Cem., Grayson Co., VA. Alice was born 8 May 1866. She married **COX**, Lafayette in Grayson Co., VA, circa 1885. Alice died 10 May 1926 at 60 years of age.
11(12)224137   HASH, J. Alex
J. was born 20 October 1868. He married **ANDERSON**, Minnie in Grayson Co., VA, 11 October 1885. He married **DALTON**, Jincy in Grayson Co., VA, 30 December 1895. J. died 24 November 1948 at 80 years of age.
11(12)22414   HALSEY, Adah
11(12)22415   HALSEY, Ahart
He married **COX**, Elizabeth. Ahart was born in Mou of Wilson, VA 18 December 1814. Ahart died 20 May 1887 at 72 years of age.
11(12)224151   HALSEY, Jackson
11(12)224152   HALSEY, Catherine
She married **PASLEY**, William in Sparta, N.C., 2 May 1876.
11(12)2241521 PASLEY, Gertrude
11(12)2241522 PASLEY, Hershell
His body was interred in Pomeroy, WA.
11(12)2241523 PASLEY, Cleo
11(12)2241524 PASLEY, Loucinda
Loucinda was born circa 1876.
11(12)2241525 PASLEY, John F.
John was born 27 January 1881. John died 9 January 1884.
11(12)2241526 PASLEY, Carlia J.
Carlia was born 25 December 1882. Carlia died 10 January 1884.
11(12)2241527 PASLEY, Ahart
Ahart was born 31 December 1884. Ahart died 10 January 1968 in Grassy Creek, NC, at 83 years of age.
11(12)2241528 PASLEY, Jimmy J.
Jimmy was born 20 October 1886. Jimmy died 31 December 1889.
11(12)2241529 PASLEY, Annie B.
Annie was born 9 May 1887. Annie died 26 December 1889.
11(12)224152(10)   PASLEY, Maudie Mae
Maudie was born circa 1891. Maudie died circa 1891.
11(12)224152(11)   PASLEY, Jincy F.
Jincy was born circa 1898. Jincy died circa 1914.
11(12)224153   HALSEY, James (Big Jim)
He married **HALSEY**, Rena. James was born 20 January 1837. James died 23 November 1928 at 91 years of age.
11(12)2241531 HALSEY, Isom
He married **SENTER**, Martha Virginia. Isom was born 24 November 1861. Isom died 17 July 1951 at 89 years of age.
11(12)22415311   HALSEY, Phoebe
11(12)22415312   HALSEY, Ada Virginia

Ada was born 4 November 1882. Ada died 7 July 1889.
11(12)22415313   HALSEY, Samuel
Samuel was born 2 September 1884. He married **COX**, Nancy Jane in Grayson Co., VA, 1 April 1905. Samuel died 14 October 1945.
11(12)224153131   HALSEY, I. L.
I. was born 25 June 1906. I. died 30 September 1909.
11(12)224153132   .   HALSEY, R. F.
R. was born 27 January 1908. R. died 25 September 1909.
11(12)224153133   HALSEY, Mattie E.
Mattie was born 23 March 1909.
11(12)224153134   HALSEY, Norman
Norman was born 18 November 1911.
11(12)224153135   HALSEY, James Fred
James was born 21 December 1914.
11(12)22415314   HALSEY, Zollie Mae
Zollie was born 21 May 1887. Zollie died 18 January 1888.
11(12)22415315   HALSEY, Roye
She married **RUTHERFORD**, Andrew McCoy. Roye was born 16 March 1889.
11(12)224153151   RUTHERFORD, Brack McKennly
Brack was born 28 September 1907. Brack died 6 June 1974.
11(12)224153152   RUTHERFORD, Zack
Zack was born 14 January 1909.
11(12)224153153   RUTHERFORD, Izetta
Izetta was born 27 February 1912.
11(12)224153154   RUTHERFORD, Claude
Claude was born 14 March 1913.
11(12)224153155   RUTHERFORD, Zona Mae
Zona was born 14 July 1914.
11(12)224153156   RUTHERFORD, Ruth
Ruth was born 10 February 1916. Ruth died 26 February 1932.
11(12)224153157   RUTHERFORD, Max
Max was born 28 November 1917.
11(12)224153158   RUTHERFORD, Clyde
Clyde was born 4 November 1919.
11(12)224153159   RUTHERFORD, Marie
Marie was born 22 April 1922.
11(12)22415315(10)   RUTHERFORD, Myrtle
Myrtle was born 9 June 1923.
11(12)22415315(11)   RUTHERFORD, Albert
Albert was born 4 February 1925.
11(12)22415315(12)   RUTHERFORD, Marvin Ruth
Marvin was born 10 November 1926. Marvin died 29 November 1926 at less than one year of age.
11(12)22415315(13)   RUTHERFORD, Edna Hazel
Edna was born 6 November 1927. Edna died 6 November 1927.
11(12)22415315(14)   RUTHERFORD, Russell

Russell was born 30 October 1928.
11(12)22415315(15)   RUTHERFORD, Helen Irene (Lee)
Helen was born 12 April 1931.
11(12)22415316   HALSEY, Nannie Lee Nannie was born 25
October 1890. She married **HOLLAND**, Grant in Oak Hill, FL, 10 January
1912.
11(12)224153161   HOLLAND, Edna
11(12)224153162   HOLLAND, Helen
Helen was born 17 November 1914. Helen died 9 September 1964.
11(12)224153163   HOLLAND, Mildred Margaret
Mildred was born 3 September 1918.
11(12)224153164   HOLLAND, Bettie Ruth
Bettie was born 25 September 1927.
11(12)224153165   HOLLAND, Joseph Buren
Joseph was born 17 September 1931.
11(12)22415317   HALSEY, Annie Bell
Annie was born 25 June 1896. Annie died 3 April 1966.
11(12)22415318   HALSEY, Walter James
Walter was born 2 January 1899. He married **DIXON**, Bina in
Grayson Co., VA, 4 June 1919.
11(12)224153181   HALSEY, Mabel Edith
Mabel was born 6 May 1920. She married **GRIFFITH**, Robert O'Neil,
Sr. 5 May 1946.
11(12)2241531811   GRIFFITH, Robert O'Neil, Jr.
Robert was born 4 February 1948.
11(12)2241531812   GRIFFITH, Gary Alan
Gary was born 31 July 1953.
11(12)224153182   HALSEY, Henry Ford
Henry was born 12 October 1922. He married **TRAVIS**, Louise 9
May 1944.
11(12)2241531821   HALSEY, Ronald Ford
Ronald was born 28 April 1945.
11(12)2241531822   HALSEY, Jerald Lee
Jerald was born 8 April 1947.
11(12)2241531823   HALSEY, Walter James
Walter was born 12 October 1951.
11(12)22415319   HALSEY, Clarence
Clarence was born 11 March 1900. Clarence died 21 January 1913.
11(12)224154   HALSEY, Peggy Ann
Her body was interred in Potato Creek, Church Cemetery. Peggy
was born 15 September 1837. Peggy died 28 April 1916 at 78 years of age.
11(12)224155   HALSEY, John C.
His body was interred in Potato Creek, Church Cemetery. John was
born 15 February 1840. John died 15 February 1862 at 22 years of age.
11(12)224156   HALSEY, Polly Adaline
Her body was interred in Potato Creek, Church Cemetery. Polly was
born 8 May 1845. Polly died 8 December 1845 at less than one year of age.

11(12)224157   HALSEY, Joseph AB
His body was interred in Potato Creek, Church Cemetery. Joseph was born 27 June 1849. Joseph died 27 October 1849.

11(12)224158   HALSEY, Ira Franklin
He married **HASH**, Cansada. Ira was born 1 November 1850. Ira died 11 August 1940 at 89 years of age.

11(12)2241581 HALSEY, Florence
Florence was born. She married **HASH**, Emmett 5 January 1904.

11(12)2241582 HALSEY, Loudora
Loudora was born 31 August 1868. She married **HALSEY**, William 15 January 1887. Loudora died 20 January 1888 at 19 years of age.

11(12)2241583 HALSEY, Granville Stuard
Granville was born circa 1873.

11(12)2241584 HALSEY, Verdie Elizabeth
Her body was interred in Potato Creek, Cemetery, Grayson Co., VA. Verdie was born 8 July 1874. She married **HALSEY**, William Terry 21 October 1899. Verdie died 16 May 1963 at 88 years of age.

11(12)2241585 HALSEY, Henry
Henry was born 7 April 1877. Henry died 7 April 1877.

11(12)2241586 HALSEY, Mary
Mary was born 6 November 1878. Mary died 6 November 1878.

11(12)2241587 HALSEY, L. E.
L. was born 6 November 1878. L. died 15 May 1891.

11(12)2241588 HALSEY, Ennice
Ennice was born 22 February 1881. She married **KIRK**, Jones in Grayson Co., VA, 8 October 1898. She married **HALSEY**, Sylvester 18 January 1905. Ennice died 8 June 1970 at 89 years of age.

11(12)2241589 HALSEY, Andrew Jackson
Andrew was born 1 April 1889. He married **HASH**, Sena 23 December 1910.

11(12)224158(10)   HALSEY, Blair F.
Blair was born 10 April 1902. Blair died 25 June 1932.

11(12)224159   HALSEY, Isaac Richard
Isaac was born 6 October 1857. He married **PASLEY**, Mary Evaline in Sparta, N.C., 19 March 1876. Isaac died 3 November 1903.

11(12)2241591 HALSEY, Sally

11(12)2241592 HALSEY, James Isaac
James was born 14 April 1878. He married **DELP**, Minnie Ellen 24 September 1899. James died 12 April 1948 at 69 years of age.

11(12)22415921   HALSEY, Earl McKee
Earl was born 21 July 1900. Earl died 22 December 1900.

11(12)22415922   HALSEY, Garnet Edison
Garnet was born 13 February 1902. He married **COX**, De Ette in Grayson Co., VA, 6 March 1923. He married **BUMGARDNER**, Ethel in Sparta, NC, 23 July 1937.

11(12)224159221   HALSEY, Harold Edison
Harold was born 24 December 1923. Harold died 24 December

1923 at less than one year of age.
11(12)224159222   HALSEY, James Boyden
James was born 9 February 1927. James died 6 February 1975.
11(12)224159223   HALSEY, Robert James
Robert was born 21 February 1931.
11(12)224159224   HALSEY, Garnet Edison, Jr.
Garnet was born 13 April 1937.
11(12)224159225   HALSEY, Bettie Joe
Bettie was born 6 November 1939.
11(12)224159226   HALSEY, James Wayne
James was born 12 February 1941.
11(12)224159227   HALSEY, Edwin Carlyle
Edwin was born 10 March 1942.
11(12)22415923   HALSEY, Stanley
Stanley was born 13 March 1905. Stanley died 15 February 1911.
11(12)22415924   HALSEY, Charles
Charles was born 13 February 1909. Charles died 13 February 1909
11(12)22415925   HALSEY, Opal Curtis
Opal was born 24 January 1910. She married **ANDERSON**, Dare 26
October 1929.
11(12)224159251   ANDERSON, Opal Curtis, Jr.
Opal was born in Mouth of Wilson, VA circa 1932. Opal died circa
1934.
11(12)2241593 HALSEY, Rosa Belle
Rosa was born 5 October 1880. She married **TRENT**, Joseph 15
February 1901. Rosa died 16 April 1960 at 79 years of age.
11(12)22415931   TRENT, Mary Elizabeth
Mary was born 5 March 1902. Mary died 28 December 1922.
11(12)22415932   TRENT, Zollie
Zollie was born 17 March 1903.
11(12)22415933   TRENT, Pearlie Victoria
Pearlie was born 20 November 1906. Pearlie died 13 January 1933.
11(12)22415934   TRENT, Ossie
Ossie was born 29 July 1910.
11(12)22415935   TRENT, Edna
Edna was born 26 October 1916.
11(12)22415936   TRENT, Joseph Dale
Joseph was born 18 May 1923.
11(12)2241594 HALSEY, Beatrice
Beatrice was born 5 January 1883.
11(12)2241595 HALSEY, Elizabeth
Elizabeth was born 20 October 1886. Elizabeth died 2 April 1960.
11(12)2241596 HALSEY, Charles Calvin
Charles was born 2 May 1890. He married **HALSEY**, Elizabeth 20
April 1907. Charles died 1 April 1927 at 36 years of age.
11(12)22415961   HALSEY, Dane
Dane was born in Grayson Co., VA.

11(12)22415962   HALSEY, Richard Grimsley
Richard was born 4 September 1909. Richard died 8 October 1909.
11(12)22415963   HALSEY, Mary
Mary was born in Grayson Co., VA 10 September 1910.
11(12)22415964   HALSEY, Elizabeth
Elizabeth was born 15 August 1912. Elizabeth died 30 August 1912.
11(12)22415965   HALSEY, William Dock
William was born 4 October 1913. William died 18 July 1973.
11(12)22415966   HALSEY, James B.
James was born 30 October 1915.
11(12)22415967   HALSEY, Blaine
Blaine was born in Grayson Co., VA 6 December 1918.
11(12)22415968   HALSEY, Ruby
Ruby was born 31 March 1920.
11(12)22415969   HALSEY, Allen Sampson
Allen was born 16 December 1923. Allen died 24 September 1973.
11(12)2241596(10)   HALSEY, Beatrice
Beatrice was born 18 July 1926.
11(12)2241597 HALSEY, Robert Jackson
Robert was born 10 May 1892.
11(12)2241598 HALSEY, Myrtle Victoria
Myrtle was born 15 April 1894.
11(12)2241599 HALSEY, Samuel Allie
Samuel was born 12 May 1896. Samuel died 19 January 1962.
11(12)224159(10)   HALSEY, Herman
Herman was born circa 1898.
11(12)22416   HALSEY, Matilda
She married **COX**, Samuel. Matilda was born 22 April 1817. Matilda
died August 1913 at 96 years of age.
11(12)224161   COX, David
He married **PARSONS**, Mary.
11(12)2241611 COX, John
11(12)2241612 COX, Maude
11(12)2241613 COX, Joseph
11(12)224162   COX, Elbert
He married **COX**, Dillie.
11(12)2241621 COX, Little Rush
11(12)2241622 COX, David Romulus
11(12)224163   COX, Robert
11(12)224164   COX, Calvin
11(12)224165   COX, Allen
11(12)224166   COX, William R. 'Will'
He married **HALSEY**, Sarah Caroline (Hash). He married
RUTHERFORD, Nellie. He married **JONES**, Malinda. William was born 21
April 1837. William died 25 October 1922 at 85 years of age.
11(12)2241661 COX, Samuel
He married **COX**, Polly.

11(12)2241662 COX, Isom
11(12)2241663 COX, Joseph Franklin
He married **JONES**, Alice L.. Joseph was born 22 March 1867.
Joseph died 18 December 1954 at 87 years of age.
11(12)2241664 COX, Haywood
Haywood was born 18 July 1870. He married **PIERCE**, Clyde Chloa
7 September 1911. Haywood died 5 November 1919 at 49 years of age.
11(12)2241665 COX, Ida
Ida was born 5 March 1880. She married **WADDELL**, Jones Huston
in Grayson Co., VA, 25 December 1900. Ida died 17 July 1976.
11(12)224167   COX, Jashua
He married **JONES**, Namie. Jashua was born 29 November 1843.
Jashua died 26 May 1879 at 35 years of age.
11(12)224168   COX, Octavia
She married **ANDERSON**, Jess. Octavia was born circa 1846.
11(12)224169   COX, Jaruth
She married **JENKINS**, Hiram Munsey. Jaruth was born 6
September 1849. Jaruth died 6 March 1917 at 67 years of age.
11(12)2241691 JENKINS, Carl E.
11(12)2241692 JENKINS, George
George was born circa 1875. George died circa 1937.
11(12)2241693 JENKINS, Clyde Lowery
Clyde was born 16 April 1878. Clyde died 11 May 1950.
11(12)2241694 JENKINS, John Muncy
He married **CORNETT**, Lura. He married **CORNETT**, Flora. John
was born 3 October 1881. John died 4 December 1961 at 80 years of age.
11(12)22416941   JENKINS, Johnnie
Johnnie was born 29 November 1914.
11(12)22416942   JENKINS, Bill
Bill was born 14 March 1916.
11(12)22416943   JENKINS, Anna
Anna was born 2 March 1918.
11(12)22416944   JENKINS, Joseph
Joseph was born 10 April 1927.
11(12)2241695 JENKINS, Moe
Moe was born 12 July 1895.
11(12)22416(10)   COX, Sedelia 'Della'
Sedelia was born 31 March 1856. She married **MORTON**, Thomas
W. 6 January 1872. Sedelia died 10 October 1941 at 85 years of age.
11(12)22416(10)1   MORTON, William E.
William was born 27 September 1874.
11(12)22416(10)2   MORTON, F. Edd
F. was born 27 September 1874. F. died 2 April 1945.
11(12)22416(10)3   MORTON, Sam T.
Sam was born 25 December 1876. Sam died 24 November 1947.
11(12)22416(10)4   MORTON, L. B. 'Viola'
L. was born 12 July 1879. L. died 12 July 1953 at 74 years of age.

11(12)22416(10)5   MORTON, E. Jack
E. was born 19 July 1884.
11(12)22416(10)6   MORTON, Maude Elizabeth
Maude was born 20 October 1886.
11(12)22416(10)7   MORTON, Dell
Dell was born 28 March 1891.
11(12)22416(10)8   MORTON, Thomas Kell
Thomas was born 30 June 1893.
11(12)22416(10)9   MORTON, Joseph W.
Joseph was born 9 August 1895. Joseph died 18 December 1950.
11(12)22416(10)(10)   MORTON, Zenna R.
Zenna was born 16 February 1900.
11(12)22416(11)   COX, George Washington
George was born in Mouth of Wilson, Grayson Co., VA 1 June 1856.
He married **DELP**, Polly Ann 12 April 1889. George died 3 June 1929.
11(12)22416(11)1   COX, Robert Jashua
Robert was born 20 January 1890.
11(12)22416(11)2   COX, Gleaves
Gleaves was born 22 October 1891. Gleaves died 22 August 1973
in Apache Junction, AZ, at 81 years of age.
11(12)22416(11)3   COX, Claude S.
Claude was born 2 April 1893. Claude died 11 October 1927.
11(12)22416(11)4   COX, Arlene L.
Arlene was born 8 February 1895.
11(12)22416(11)5   COX, I. Vealine
I. was born 18 December 1896.
11(12)22416(11)6   COX, Drewey
Drewey was born 31 October 1898.
11(12)22416(11)7   COX, Dewey
Dewey was born 31 October 1898.
11(12)22416(11)8   COX, Nannie M.
Nannie was born 26 January 1902.
11(12)22416(11)9   COX, Montaque G.
Montaque was born 3 March 1904. Montaque died 6 November
1965 at 61 years of age.
11(12)22417   HALSEY, Loucinda
Loucinda was born 22 June 1822. She married **PARSONS**, William
B. Dr. in Ashe Co., NC, circa 1846. Loucinda died 3 July 1887.
11(12)224171   PARSONS, Lafayette Listen
Lafayette was born circa 1842. He married **HALSEY**, Polly Ann 25
April 1876.
11(12)2241711 PARSONS, Carrie E.
Carrie was born circa 1878. Carrie died circa 1958.
11(12)2241712 PARSONS, William C.
William was born circa 1880. William died 2 April 1963 in Milesville,
SD, at 82 years of age.
11(12)2241713 PARSONS, Charlie M.

Charlie was born 15 June 1884. He married **HASH**, Bettie 23 December 1906. Charlie died 1 May 1949 at 64 years of age.
11(12)22417131   PARSONS, Thomas
Thomas was born 10 October 1910.
11(12)22417132   PARSONS, Page
Page was born 12 March 1916. He married **HALSEY**, Carolyn DeEtte 9 September 1944.
11(12)224171321   PARSONS, Linda Joe
Linda was born 31 May 1946.
11(12)224171322   PARSONS, Gaynell
Gaynell was born 9 May 1950.
11(12)224171323   PARSONS, Mary Martha
Mary was born 27 December 1959.
11(12)22417133   PARSONS, Rex
Rex was born 12 October 1920. He married **HALSEY**, Oakie in MD, March 1942.
11(12)224171331   PARSONS, Barbara Jean
Barbara was born 30 March 1945.
11(12)224171332   PARSONS, Robert Wade
Robert was born 18 August 1947.
11(12)224171333   PARSONS, Don Ray
Don was born 1 April 1951.
11(12)224171334   PARSONS, Patricia Lee
Patricia was born 17 February 1954.
11(12)22417134   PARSONS, Edna
Edna was born February 1923.
11(12)22417135   PARSONS, Dallas Glenn
Dallas was born 21 November 1926. He married **HALSEY**, Edith Bryant 27 August 1949.
11(12)224171351   PARSONS, David Glenn
David was born 15 March 1956.
11(12)224171352   PARSONS, Vickie Lynn
Vickie was born 19 October 1957.
11(12)224171353   PARSONS, Camela
Camela died. Camela was born 14 November 1964.
11(12)224171354   PARSONS, Paul Wesley
Paul was born 20 October 1969.
11(12)22417136   PARSONS, Claude
Claude was born 6 September 1929.
11(12)2241714 PARSONS, Carl
Carl was born 16 January 1892. Carl died 16 August 1973.
11(12)2241715 PARSONS, Beulah Mae
Beulah was born 25 May 1895. She married **OSBORNE**, Andy 17 April 1917.
11(12)22417151   OSBORNE, Pauline Marie
Pauline was born August 1921.
11(12)22417152   OSBORNE, Samuel Wilson

Samuel was born 2 August 1923. Samuel died 9 February 1945.
11(12)2241716 PARSONS, Mattie Mae
Mattie was born 29 December 1900.
11(12)224172   PARSONS, Mastin
Mastin was born circa 1844.
11(12)224173   PARSONS, Caldone
She married **STOMPER**, Elbert. Caldone was born 14 January
1847. Caldone died 4 September 1941 at 94 years of age.
11(12)224174   PARSONS, J. Rush C.
J. was born circa 1848.
11(12)22418   HALSEY, Morris
His body was interred in Cease Halsey, Cemetery. Morris was born
In Grayson Co., VA circa 1825. He married **HASH**, Sophina (Finie) in Ashe
Co., N.C., circa 1847. Morris Halsey was a private in Company I, 51st
Virginia Infantry, enlisting from Fox Creek in Grayson County, VA on 28 June
1861. He received a medical discharge on 13 June 1862 because of
disabilities caused by the effects of typhoid fever caught in October 1861. He
was 37 years old at the time of discharge. Morris had a dark complexion with
dark hair and gray eyes. He was five feet eleven inches tall.
11(12)224181   HALSEY, Rena
She married **HALSEY**, James (Big Jim).
11(12)224182   HALSEY, Jim 'Calloway'
11(12)224183   HALSEY, Annie
She married **ANDERSON**, Floyd 26 February 1871.
11(12)2241831 ANDERSON, Hoyt
11(12)2241832 ANDERSON, Tilden
11(12)2241833 ANDERSON, Rena
11(12)2241834 ANDERSON, Mintie
Mintie was born. She married **HALSEY**, Lewis Bruce in Grayson
Co., VA, 27 October 1917.
11(12)2241835 ANDERSON, James Monroe 'Boat'
James was born circa 1874.
11(12)2241836 ANDERSON, Pete
Pete was born 22 December 1882. Pete died 21 September 1974 in
Fairwood, at 91 years of age.
11(12)2241837 ANDERSON, Famzy
Famzy was born 10 December 1884. Famzy died 14 February 1931.
11(12)224184   HALSEY, Grimsley
Grimsley was born circa 1857. He married **DOWELL**, Mary 4
September 1879. Grimsley died 30 January 1892 at 34 years of age.
11(12)2241841 HALSEY, Felix Cebert
Felix was born 20 June 1879. He married **WOOD**, Eva Ann 21 May
1906. Felix died circa 1974.
11(12)22418411   HALSEY, Wyndle
He married **LONG**, Geneva. Wyndle was born 20 March 1909.
11(12)224184111   HALSEY, Donald
11(12)224184112   HALSEY, Shirley

11(12)224184113   **HALSEY, Richard**
11(12)224184114   **HALSEY, Janice**
11(12)22418412   **HALSEY, Frances Virginia**
Frances was born 22 February 1912.
11(12)22418413   **HALSEY, George**
George was born 3 June 1915. He married **TESTERMAN**, Ester in Grayson Co., VA, 22 August 1934.
11(12)224184131   **HALSEY, James**
11(12)224184132   **HALSEY, Randolph**
11(12)224184133   **HALSEY, Barbara**
11(12)224184134   **HALSEY, Roger**
11(12)224184135   **HALSEY, Linda**
11(12)224184136   **HALSEY, Lana**
11(12)22418414   **HALSEY, Ralph Virgil**
Ralph was born 29 August 1918.
11(12)22418415   **HALSEY, Albert**
He married **COMER**, Virginia. Albert was born 14 April 1922.
11(12)224184151   **HALSEY, Brenda**
11(12)224184152   **HALSEY, Joseph**
11(12)224184153   **HALSEY, Danny**
11(12)224184154   **HALSEY, Valerie**
11(12)224184155   **HALSEY, Vickie**
11(12)22418416   **HALSEY, Felix Cebert, Jr.**
Felix was born 23 July 1926. Felix died 23 May 1971.
11(12)2241842 HALSEY, Fannie
Fannie was born 14 May 1884. She married **PARSONS**, Joseph T. in Grayson Co., VA, 22 December 1913. Fannie died 24 June 1958.
11(12)22418421   **PARSONS, Hurtle**
11(12)22418422   **PARSONS, Oscar**
Oscar was born in Kanawha, VA circa 1909. Oscar died 26 August 1975 at 66 years of age.
11(12)22418423   **PARSONS, Donnie**
Donnie was born circa 1912.
11(12)22418424   **PARSONS, Blaine**
Blaine was born circa 1917. Blaine died circa 1917.
11(12)22418425   **PARSONS, Garland**
Garland was born circa 1919. Garland died circa 1919.
11(12)22418426   **PARSONS, Garnet**
Garnet was born circa 1919. Garnet died circa 1940.
11(12)2241843 HALSEY, Carrie Loucinda
Carrie was born 3 September 1887. She married **PARSONS**, John H. in Grayson Co., VA, 5 May 1903. Carrie died 11 January 1978 in Fairwood, VA, at 90 years of age.
11(12)22418431   **PARSONS, Stella Emma**
Stella was born 8 February 1905.
11(12)22418432   **PARSONS, Wanette Blanche**
Wanette was born 11 June 1907.

11(12)22418433   PARSONS, Cebert E.
Cebert was born 29 December 1909.
11(12)22418434   PARSONS, Roscoe L.
Roscoe was born 20 April 1912. Roscoe died 12 April 1958.
11(12)22418435   PARSONS, Eugene F.
Eugene was born 25 May 1914. Eugene died 30 July 1944.
11(12)22418436   PARSONS, Rosie Ina
Rosie was born 30 September 1916.
11(12)22418437   PARSONS, Donna Ruth
Donna was born 27 May 1919.
11(12)22418438   PARSONS, Golda
Golda was born 17 November 1921.
11(12)22418439   PARSONS, Charlotte June
Charlotte was born 31 March 1924.
11(12)2241844 HALSEY, Elizabeth
Elizabeth was born 14 March 1889. She married **HALSEY**, Charles
Calvin 20 April 1907.
11(12)2241845 HALSEY, Dema Ellen
She married **PARSONS**, Joseph T.. Dema was born 12 August
1892. Dema died 24 February 1913 at 20 years of age.
11(12)2241846 HALSEY, Anna Belle
Anna was born circa 1894.
11(12)224185   HALSEY, Joseph Melvin
His body was interred in Cease Halsey, Cemetery. He married
RUTHERFORD, Nancy Caroline. Joseph was born 10 November 1860.
Joseph died 3 January 1949 at 88 years of age.
11(12)2241851 HALSEY, Mintie E.
Mintie was born 5 August 1886. She married **RICHARDSON**,
Munsey in Grayson Co., VA, 6 July 1906. Mintie died 1 November 1971.
11(12)22418511   RICHARDSON, Dewey Lee
Dewey was born 9 July 1907.
11(12)22418512   RICHARDSON, Kindeth Raymond
Kindeth was born 30 January 1909.
11(12)22418513   RICHARDSON, Edith Virginia
Edith was born 21 March 1911.
11(12)22418514   RICHARDSON, Mabel Marie
Mabel was born 19 August 1913.
11(12)22418515   RICHARDSON, Georgia Viola
Georgia was born 6 September 1915.
11(12)22418516   RICHARDSON, Harry Albert
Harry was born 8 September 1917.
11(12)22418517   RICHARDSON, Bertha Louise
Bertha was born 16 September 1919.
11(12)22418518   RICHARDSON, Brida Irene
Brida was born 29 January 1922.
11(12)22418519   RICHARDSON, Hicks Ellis
Hicks was born 29 March 1924.

11(12)2241851(10)   RICHARDSON, Rudolph Tilson
Rudolph was born 6 July 1926.
11(12)2241851(11)   RICHARDSON, Ardle Lester
Ardle was born 26 June 1929.
11(12)2241851(12)   RICHARDSON, Clara Hortense
Clara was born 29 January 1932.
11(12)2241852 HALSEY, Edgar Jackson
Edgar was born 25 December 1887. He married JONES, Minnie in Grayson Co., VA, 6 July 1911. He married ANDERSON, Rachel Isabelle circa 1914. Edgar died 22 August 1957 at 69 years of age.
11(12)22418521   HALSEY,
He was born 5 July 1912. He died 5 July 1912.
11(12)22418522   HALSEY,
He was born 5 July 1912. He died 30 July 1912.
11(12)22418523   HALSEY, Jones Anderson
Jones was born 27 October 1915.
11(12)22418524   HALSEY, Annie Rose
Annie was born 24 May 1917.
11(12)22418525   HALSEY, Beulah
Beulah was born 22 February 1920.
11(12)22418526   HALSEY, Hazel
Hazel was born 23 November 1921.
11(12)22418527   HALSEY, Blanche
Blanche was born 28 September 1923.
11(12)22418528   HALSEY, Geneva
Geneva was born 21 October 1925.
11(12)22418529   HALSEY, Ellis
Ellis was born 8 November 1927.
11(12)2241852(10)   HALSEY, Albert Clay
Albert was born 22 January 1930.
11(12)2241852(11)   HALSEY, Bobby
Bobby was born 3 March 1932.
11(12)2241852(12)   HALSEY, Lester Lee
Lester was born 13 January 1935.
11(12)2241852(13)   HALSEY, Wade Arnold
Wade was born 16 September 1939.
11(12)2241853 HALSEY, Annie
Annie was born 12 August 1889. Annie died 7 April 1935.
11(12)2241854 HALSEY, Belle Flora
Belle was born 12 August 1889. She married ANDERSON, Stanley E. in Grayson Co., VA, 17 March 1913.
11(12)22418541   ANDERSON, Raymond
Raymond was born 14 February 1914.
11(12)22418542   ANDERSON, Burgess Hicks
Burgess was born 2 May 1916.
11(12)22418543   ANDERSON, Dwight H.
Dwight was born 29 August 1917.

11(12)22418544   ANDERSON, Zettie Mae
Zettie was born 14 May 1919.

11(12)22418545   ANDERSON, Virginia
Virginia was born 14 June 1924.

11(12)22418546   ANDERSON, Donna Lee
Donna was born 26 March 1926.

11(12)22418547   ANDERSON, Staley F.
Staley was born 26 May 1927.

11(12)22418548   ANDERSON, Nina Belle
Nina was born 11 July 1929. Nina died 11 July 1929.

11(12)2241855 HALSEY, Tom Creed
Tom was born 14 April 1892. He married **SUITTS**, Nannie in
Grayson Co., VA, 18 April 1930.

11(12)22418551   HALSEY, Rex
Rex was born 24 February 1931. He married **WRIGHT**, Grace 22
July 1955.

11(12)224185511   HALSEY, Ronald Rex
Ronald was born 6 October 1964.

11(12)22418552   HALSEY, Eva
Eva was born 8 October 1932. She married **CAMPBELL**, Andrew
Jack in Grayson Co., VA, 11 May 1955.

11(12)224185521   CAMPBELL, Dennis Carson
Dennis was born 1 January 1957.

11(12)224185522   CAMPBELL, Robert Barry
Robert was born 13 May 1961.

11(12)22418553   HALSEY, Carnet
Carnet was born 19 September 1934. He married **OSBORNE**,
Carolene in Grayson Co., VA, 10 June 1955.

11(12)224185531   HALSEY, Michael David
Michael was born 2 January 1957.

11(12)224185532   HALSEY, Sherry Diane
Sherry was born 2 January 1957.

11(12)224185533   HALSEY, James Edward
James was born 9 April 1963.

11(12)22418554   HALSEY, Louise
Louise was born 9 June 1936. She married **ADAMS**, Billy Dean 26
September 1957.

11(12)224185541   ADAMS, Jerry Ray
Jerry was born 15 August 1961.

11(12)224185542   ADAMS, Larry Douglas
Larry was born 26 May 1969.

11(12)22418555   HALSEY, Tommy Clay
Tommy was born 14 September 1940.

11(12)22418556   HALSEY, Douglas Green
Douglas was born 15 August 1943. He married **HASH**, Jean in
Grayson Co., VA, 6 August 1963.

11(12)224185561   HALSEY, Cynthia Down

Cynthia was born 25 June 1965.
11(12)2241856 HALSEY, Paul E.
Paul was born 28 May 1897. He married **ANDERSON**, Mary in Grayson Co., VA, 18 February 1922.
11(12)22418561   HALSEY, William Rodney
William was born 11 February 1923.
11(12)22418562   HALSEY, Carley Rex
Carley was born 17 October 1924.
11(12)22418563   HALSEY, Carrie Pauline
Carrie was born 9 March 1927.
11(12)22418564   HALSEY, Dailey Cicero
Dailey was born 24 May 1929.
11(12)22418565   HALSEY, Essie Mae
Essie was born 12 July 1931.
11(12)22418566   HALSEY, Donna Lois
Donna was born 19 August 1937.
11(12)22418567   HALSEY, Richard Lee
Richard was born 7 July 1946.
11(12)2241857 HALSEY, Winnie V.
Winnie was born 28 September 1900.
11(12)224186   HALSEY, Thomas J.
Thomas was born circa 1863. He married **MURRAY**, Elizabeth E. 'Lizzie' 4 June 1904. Thomas died circa 1954 in Gold Hill.
11(12)2241861 HALSEY, Gladys
11(12)2241862 HALSEY, Annie Lee
Annie was born 11 January 1891. Annie died 5 March 1933.
11(12)2241863 HALSEY, Polly Jane
Polly was born 2 April 1895.
11(12)2241864 HALSEY, Rita
Rita was born 2 May 1898.
11(12)2241865 HALSEY, Mack
Mack was born 10 April 1902. Mack died 13 March 1967 in Whitehead, NC, at 64 years of age.
11(12)2241866 HALSEY, Roosevelt
Roosevelt was born circa 1905. He married **DOWELL**, Annie 'Polly' in Grayson Co., VA, 19 July 1933.
11(12)22418661   HALSEY, Charles Thomas
11(12)22418662   HALSEY, Louella
11(12)22418663   HALSEY, Jessie Ruth
Jessie was born 21 August 1934.
11(12)2241867 HALSEY, Beulah
Beulah was born 9 October 1906. She married **DOWELL**, James in Grayson Co., VA, 6 September 1922.
11(12)22418671   DOWELL, Mabel Virginia
Mabel was born 17 September 1922.
11(12)22418672   DOWELL, Polly
Polly was born 13 May 1925.

11(12)22418673   DOWELL, Susie
Susie was born 29 September 1932.
11(12)2241868 HALSEY, Hallie
Hallie was born 22 March 1908. She married **ANDERS**, Posey 24 August 1924.
11(12)22418681   ANDERS, Kermit
Kermit was born 11 May 1926.
11(12)22418682   ANDERS, Hurley
Hurley was born in Glenn Allen, WV 9 December 1928.
11(12)22418683   ANDERS, Muncy
Muncy was born 23 July 1929.
11(12)22418684   ANDERS, Odus
Odus was born 4 October 1932.
11(12)22418685   ANDERS, Louise
Louise was born 16 March 1937.
11(12)22418686   ANDERS, Ima Jean
Ima was born 6 May 1943.
11(12)22418687   ANDERS, De Ette
De was born 12 March 1945.
11(12)22418688   ANDERS, Dorothy Mae
Dorothy was born 7 May 1949.
11(12)2241869 HALSEY, Donna
Donna was born circa 1910. She married **PERRY**, Robert 30 March 1931.
11(12)22418691   PERRY, Dailey
11(12)22418692   PERRY, Arnold
11(12)22418693   PERRY, RoElla
11(12)22418694   PERRY, John Thomas
11(12)22418695   PERRY, Buck Ransom
11(12)224186(10)   HALSEY, Amos
Amos was born 2 June 1913. He married **DOWELL**, Drucie Ada in Grayson Co., VA, 6 May 1937.
11(12)224186(10)1   HALSEY, James Glenn
James was born 4 April 1938.
11(12)224186(10)2   HALSEY, Hobart
Hobart was born 3 January 1941.
11(12)224186(10)3   HALSEY, Mack Arthur
Mack was born 14 February 1944.
11(12)224186(10)4   HALSEY, Randy
Randy was born 20 August 1946.
11(12)224186(11)   HALSEY, Shirley
Shirley was born circa 1916.
11(12)224186(12)   HALSEY, Bethel
Bethel was born 6 July 1917. She married **DOWELL**, Josh circa 1950.
11(12)224186(12)1   DOWELL, June Ellen
June was born 1 June 1954.

11(12)224186(13)   HALSEY, Neecie
Neecie was born 28 March 1919. She married **PUGH**, Walker 10 September 1944.
11(12)224186(13)1   PUGH, Nancy
Nancy was born 12 June 1945.
11(12)224186(13)2   PUGH, Scotty
Scotty was born 7 April 1950.
11(12)224186(13)3   PUGH, Samuel
Samuel was born 14 October 1953.
11(12)224186(14)   HALSEY, Roscoe
Roscoe was born 7 May 1922.
11(12)224186(15)   HALSEY, Lasca
Lasca was born 5 January 1925. She married **CARICO**, Joe Charles in Sparta, NC, July 1956.
11(12)224186(15)1   CARICO, Brenda
Brenda was born 8 July 1957.
11(12)224186(15)2   CARICO, Joe Charles, Jr.
Joe was born 14 August 1961.
11(12)224187   HALSEY, William
William was born 6 January 1866. He married an unknown person in Grayson Co. VA, 15 January 1887. He married **HALSEY**, Loudora 15 January 1887. He married **HASH**, Alice (Cox) 31 August 1889. He married **TRIPLETT**, Mrs. Clemmie (McMeans) 9 February 1909. He married **MCMEANS**, Clemmie 9 February 1910. William died 18 January 1934.
11(12)2241871   HALSEY, Wiley
He married **HASH**, Emmie Caroline. Wiley was born 15 February 1885. Wiley died 10 March 1952 at 67 years of age.
11(12)22418711   HALSEY, Blanche
Blanche was born 20 May 1919. She married **HASH**, Grover 29 May 1944. Blanche died 6 October 1979 at 60 years of age.
11(12)224187111   HASH, Bonnie Sue
Bonnie was born 3 July 1945.
11(12)2241872 HALSEY, Effie
Effie was born 3 August 1887. She married **BURCHETTE**, Felix 24 January 1913. Effie died 7 March 1955 at 67 years of age.
11(12)22418721   BURCHETTE, Claude
Claude was born 1 March 1916.
11(12)22418722   BURCHETTE, Edna
Edna was born 3 June 1918.
11(12)2241873 HALSEY, Ahart
Ahart was born 29 December 1887. He married **ANDERSON**, Lura Beatrice 17 March 1905. Ahart died 22 December 1955 at 67 years of age.
11(12)22418731   HALSEY, Hardin G.
Hardin was born. His body was interred in Tomstone Cem., Sugar Grove, VA. Hardin died 18 May 1990.
11(12)22418732   HALSEY, Virgie
Virgie was born 25 June 1906. Virgie died 22 April 1992.

11(12)22418733   HALSEY, James Rhoa
James was born 5 April 1909. He married **HALSEY**, Lessie Lee in Grayson Co., VA, 24 December 1946.
11(12)22418734   HALSEY, Bertha
Bertha was born 10 December 1911. Bertha died 13 September 1967 at 55 years of age.
11(12)22418735   HALSEY, Frances H.
Frances was born 25 April 1915. Frances died 5 October 1967.
11(12)22418736   HALSEY, Lonnie S.
Lonnie was born 27 December 1917.
11(12)22418737   HALSEY, Raymond Vaughn
Raymond was born 7 May 1924. Raymond died 7 September 1961.
11(12)22418738   HALSEY, Greenberry
Greenberry was born circa 1926.
11(12)2241874 HALSEY, Carlie
Carlie was born 7 March 1895. Carlie died 4 December 1959.
11(12)2241875 HALSEY, Cauzada
Cauzada was born circa 1898. Cauzada died circa 1927.
11(12)2241876 HALSEY, Rena
She married **PRATT**, Parley. Rena was born 25 October 1898.
11(12)22418761   PRATT, Ralph
11(12)22418762   PRATT, Wilma D.
Wilma was born 3 May 1934.
11(12)2241877 HALSEY, Rissie Caroline
Rissie was born 14 October 1900. She married **BROWN**, Talmage 7 September 1918.
11(12)22418771   BROWN, Eunice
Eunice was born 28 July 1920.
11(12)22418772   BROWN, Vivian
Vivian was born 10 May 1923. Vivian died 27 September 1979.
11(12)22418773   BROWN, Ray
Ray was born 2 August 1928.
11(12)22418774   BROWN, Jimmy Carol
Jimmy was born 16 September 1934.
11(12)2241878 HALSEY, Laura B.
She married **JONES**, Sollie. Laura was born 11 August 1902.
11(12)22418781   JONES, Dorothy
11(12)22418782   JONES, Lorene
11(12)22418783   JONES, Ivan
11(12)22418784   JONES, Richard Lewis
11(12)22418785   JONES, Joe Ann
11(12)2241879 HALSEY, Harmon Lonnie
Harmon was born 3 July 1904. He married **BROWN**, Mattie 10 April 1927.
11(12)22418791   HALSEY, Jaunita
11(12)22418792   HALSEY, Letha Faye 'Susie'
Letha was born 24 April 1934.

11(12)22418793   HALSEY, Joyce Carol
Joyce was born 11 November 1943.
11(12)224187(10)   HALSEY, Maynard Virgil
Maynard was born 25 December 1907. He married **BROWN**, Zenna in Sparta, NC, 26 December 1930.
11(12)224187(10)1   HALSEY, Ella Jean
11(12)224188   HALSEY, Polly Ann
Polly was born 7 February 1868. She married **DOWELL**, Simon M. in Sparta, NC, 30 May 1886. Polly died 1 November 1951.
11(12)2241881 DOWELL, Charlie Sylvester
Charlie was born 7 July 1888. Charlie died 2 November 1972.
11(12)2241882 DOWELL, Leona
Leona was born 28 January 1892.
11(12)2241883 DOWELL, Darcas
Darcas was born 8 March 1894.
11(12)2241884 DOWELL, James
James was born 28 July 1896. He married **HALSEY**, Beulah in Grayson Co., VA, 6 September 1922. James died circa 1962.
11(12)2241885 DOWELL, Jincy
Jincy was born 29 December 1900. Jincy died 9 May 1952.
11(12)2241886 DOWELL, Lula
Lula was born 17 October 1906.
11(12)2241887 DOWELL, Joshua
Joshua was born 7 August 1907.
11(12)224189   HALSEY, Stephen L.
Stephen was born 9 September 1872. He married **OSBORNE**, Ruth in Grayson Co., VA, 23 February 1906. Stephen died 27 June 1952.
11(12)2241891 HALSEY, Reece
Reece was born 26 July 1908. Reece died 31 December 1951.
11(12)2241892 HALSEY, Zelma
Zelma was born 2 February 1912. She married **BROWN**, Howard 19 October 1935.
11(12)22418921   BROWN, James Marion
James was born 15 January 1940.
11(12)22418922   BROWN, William Rufus
William was born 10 November 1941.
11(12)2241893 HALSEY, Geneva
Geneva was born 7 August 1914. She married **ROBERTS**, Harry 21 November 1935.
11(12)22418931   ROBERTS, Walter L.
Walter was born 22 October 1936.
11(12)22418932   ROBERTS, Geraldine
Geraldine was born 9 May 1939.
11(12)22418933   ROBERTS, Michael
Michael was born 15 April 1942.
11(12)22418934   ROBERTS, Barfora
Barfora was born 27 September 1944.

11(12)22418935   ROBERTS, Bonnie
Bonnie was born 14 May 1946.
11(12)22418936   ROBERTS, Keith
Keith was born 6 January 1951.
11(12)22418937   ROBERTS, Karen
Karen was born 6 January 1951.
11(12)2241894 HALSEY, Flossie Mae
Flossie was born 1 May 1917.
11(12)2241895 HALSEY, Charles Victor
Charles was born 16 August 1919. He married **WRIGHT**, Wilma 20 January 1945.
11(12)22418951   HALSEY, Randall
Randall was born 12 November 1945.
11(12)22418952   HALSEY, Roger
Roger was born 25 January 1947.
11(12)22418953   HALSEY, Samuel
Samuel was born 31 May 1950.
11(12)22418954   HALSEY, John Stephen
John was born 8 August 1954.
11(12)2241896 HALSEY, Earl
Earl was born 28 September 1921.
11(12)2241897 HALSEY, Virginia Ruth
Virginia was born 15 March 1925.
11(12)22418(10)   HALSEY, Benjamin Dallas
Benjamin was born 26 May 1875. He married **PHIPPS**, Mazie Jane in Grayson Co., VA, 16 February 1895. Benjamin died 6 February 1957.
11(12)22418(10)1   HALSEY, Victoria
Victoria was born. She married **BARTON**, Johnny.
11(12)22418(10)11   BARTON, Johnny, Jr.
11(12)22418(10)12   BARTON, Lavina
11(12)22418(10)13   BARTON, Bennie
11(12)22418(10)14   BARTON, Wilburn
11(12)22418(10)15   BARTON, Lillie Mae
11(12)22418(10)16   BARTON, Mattie Faye
11(12)22418(10)17   BARTON, Daisy
11(12)22418(10)2   HALSEY, Ben Kilby
He married **BUMGARDNER**, Ethel 14 September 1932. He married **MOONEY**, Retha 24 June 1937.
11(12)22418(10)21   HALSEY, Berline
11(12)22418(10)22   HALSEY, Arnold
11(12)22418(10)23   HALSEY, Audrey Ailene
Audrey was born 13 January 1951.
11(12)22418(10)3   HALSEY, Adah
11(12)22418(10)4   HALSEY, Lessie Jane
Lessie died 13 March 1929.
11(12)22418(10)5   HALSEY, Hattie Mae
She married **SMITH**, Howard Evander. Hattie was born circa 1898.

Hattie died 27 March 1945 at 46 years of age.
11(12)22418(10)51 SMITH,
He was born circa 1915.
11(12)22418(10)52 SMITH, Ben Lee
Ben was born 26 April 1917.
11(12)22418(10)53 SMITH, Howard Evander, Jr.
Howard was born 20 September 1919.
11(12)22418(10)54 SMITH, James Luther
James was born 4 October 1921. James died 12 March 1947.
11(12)22418(10)55 SMITH, Mazie Anna
Mazie was born 9 February 1924.
11(12)22418(10)56 SMITH, Mattie Faye
Mattie was born 18 February 1926.
11(12)22418(10)57 SMITH, Bitha lleta
Bitha was born 31 January 1928.
11(12)22418(10)58 SMITH, William Walter
William was born 9 April 1930.
11(12)22418(10)59 SMITH, Margaret Mae
Margaret was born 25 March 1932. Margaret died 17 October 1935.
11(12)22418(10)5(10) SMITH, Dale Tanner
Dale was born 15 January 1934.
11(12)22418(10)5(11) SMITH, Charles LeVern
Charles was born 11 April 1936.
11(12)22418(10)5(12) SMITH, Robert Ford
Robert was born 4 February 1938.
11(12)22418(10)5(13) SMITH, Joe Neal
Joe was born 12 July 1940.
11(12)22418(10)5(14) SMITH, Tommy Rogers
Tommy was born 18 April 1944.
11(12)22418(10)6 HALSEY, Mettie Beatrice
Mettie was born 2 June 1902.
11(12)22418(10)7 HALSEY, Joseph
Joseph was born 28 March 1904. He married **BILLINGS**, Lucy 27
February 1925.
11(12)22418(10)71 HALSEY, Carolyn DeEtte
Carolyn was born 30 December 1925. She married **PARSONS**,
Page 9 September 1944.
11(12)22418(10)72 HALSEY, Myrtle Kate
Myrtle was born 1 March 1928. Myrtle died 14 May 1930.
11(12)22418(10)73 HALSEY, Edith Bryant
Edith was born 26 June 1930. She married **PARSONS**, Dallas
Glenn 27 August 1949.
11(12)22418(10)74 HALSEY, Loretta Ruth
Loretta was born 16 July 1934. She married **HENSEL**, Robert
Charles 2 July 1955.
11(12)22418(10)741 HENSEL, Robert Charles, Jr.
Robert was born 6 March 1956.

11(12)22418(10)742   HENSEL, Rodney Todd
Rodney was born 30 November 1958.
11(12)22418(10)75   HALSEY, Mazie Lavon
Mazie was born 29 January 1937.
11(12)22418(10)76   HALSEY, Ellen Bernice
Ellen was born 9 March 1941. She married **RAY**, Howard 9 October 1959.
11(12)22418(10)761   RAY, Teressa
Teressa was born 24 August 1960.
11(12)22418(10)762   RAY, Cammy
Cammy was born 10 March 1964.
11(12)22418(10)8   HALSEY, Margie Lee
Margie was born 16 August 1908. She married **BILLINGS**, Lonzo 3 February 1925.
11(12)22418(10)81   BILLINGS, Hattie Alene
Hattie died 13 January 1933.
11(12)22418(10)82   BILLINGS, Nonna Jean
Nonna died 28 December 1937.
11(12)22418(10)83   BILLINGS, Lacy
Lacy was born 21 December 1925. Lacy died 11 June 1946.
11(12)22418(10)84   BILLINGS, Carrie
Carrie was born 7 September 1927.
11(12)22418(10)85   BILLINGS, William
William was born 7 December 1929.
11(12)22418(10)86   BILLINGS, Retha Mae
Retha was born 7 April 1934.
11(12)22418(10)87   BILLINGS, Fannie Evelyn
Fannie was born 7 May 1938.
11(12)22418(10)88   BILLINGS, Jimmy Dale
Jimmy was born 20 April 1945.
11(12)22418(10)89   BILLINGS, Larry Dean
Larry was born 23 March 1951.
11(12)22418(10)8(10)   BILLINGS, Jerry Michael
Jerry was born 9 April 1953.
11(12)22418(10)9   HALSEY, Howard
Howard was born 5 January 1913. He married **SPARKS**, Mollie in Grayson Co., VA, 1 November 1938.
11(12)22418(10)91   HALSEY, Glenn
Glenn was born 29 February 1940.
11(12)22418(10)92   HALSEY, Troy
Troy was born 30 August 1941.
11(12)22418(10)93   HALSEY, Mazie
Mazie was born 12 July 1943.
11(12)22418(10)94   HALSEY, Lois
Lois was born 19 July 1949.
11(12)22418(10)(10)   HALSEY, Floyd Talmage
Floyd was born 2 August 1917.

11(12)22418(10)(11)   HALSEY, Fannie
Fannie was born 2 June 1919. She married **DOWELL**, Carl 28 October 1940.
11(12)22418(10)(11)1   DOWELL, Dinsel
Dinsel was born 4 September 1940.
11(12)22418(10)(11)2   DOWELL, Carl, Jr.
Carl, was born 18 July 1942.
11(12)22418(10)(11)3   DOWELL, Nancy
Nancy was born 6 October 1944.
11(12)22418(10)(11)4   DOWELL, Ralph
Ralph was born 11 March 1947.
11(12)22418(10)(11)5   DOWELL, Ernest
Ernest was born 1 May 1948.
11(12)22418(10)(11)6   DOWELL, Thomas
Thomas was born 5 August 1959.
11(12)22419   HALSEY, Polly
Polly was born 21 February 1832. She married **HASH**, Lazarus M. circa 1848. Polly died 8 February 1907 at 74 years of age.
11(12)224191   HASH, Lutitia 'Fishie'
Lutitia was born in Piney Creek, NC. Her body was interred in Lazarus Hash Cem. She married **BURCHETT**, William 8 January 1880.
11(12)2241911 BURCHETT, Emory
11(12)2241912 BURCHETT, Bert
11(12)2241913 BURCHETT, Josie
11(12)2241914 BURCHETT, Zollie
11(12)2241915 BURCHETT, Meack
11(12)2241916 BURCHETT, Joseph
11(12)2241917 BURCHETT, Kyle
11(12)2241918 BURCHETT, Mastin Columbus
Mastin was born 24 October 1883. Mastin died 21 July 1968.
11(12)224192 HASH, Walter G.
11(12)224193 HASH, John
11(12)224194 HASH, Mastin
11(12)224195 HASH, James L. B.
He married **GREGORY**, Amanda 7 December 1879.
11(12)224196 HASH, Josephine
She married **RUTHERFORD**, Andy M.
11(12)2241961 RUTHERFORD, Maggie
Maggie was born 7 July 1870. Maggie died 1 January 1963.
11(12)224197 HASH, Etta
She married **ESTEP**, Cap.
11(12)224198 HASH, Nancy Emoline
She married **MCMEANS**, J. Rufus. Nancy was born 1 November 1849. Nancy died 19 August 1934 at 84 years of age.
11(12)2241981 MCMEANS, Drucey Caroline
Drucey died 16 June 1968.
11(12)2241982 MCMEANS, William M.

William was born 10 May 1866. William died 9 May 1945.
11(12)2241983 MCMEANS, Clemmie
Clemmie was born circa 1871. Clemmie died circa 1943.
11(12)2241984 MCMEANS, James Harlow
James was born 2 August 1872. James died 4 March 1954.
11(12)2241985 MCMEANS, John A.
John was born 6 November 1878. John died 1 April 1916.
11(12)2241986 MCMEANS, Loudemia
Loudemia was born 29 April 1887. Loudemia died 15 September 1973 at 86 years of age.
11(12)2241987 MCMEANS, Etta
Etta was born 23 April 1890. Etta died 13 February 1965.
11(12)2241988 MCMEANS, Roy Lazarus
Roy was born 19 April 1893. Roy died 14 December 1963.
11(12)2241989 MCMEANS, H. Iley
H. was born 16 December 1895. H. died 11 January 1927.
11(12)224199   HASH, Cansada
She married **HALSEY**, Ira Franklin. Cansada was born 12 March 1851. Cansada died 7 November 1937 at 86 years of age.
11(12)22419(10)   HASH, Alice (Cox)
Her body was interred in Cecil Halsey Cem. Alice was born circa 1860. She married **COX**, Isom 25 February 1881. She married **HALSEY**, William 31 August 1889. Alice died circa 1909.
11(12)22419(11)   HASH, Joseph Marshall
He married **BLAND**, Elizabeth Jane. Joseph was born 27 December 1862. Joseph died 6 November 1955 at 92 years of age.
11(12)22419(11)1   HASH, Pearlie Mae
Pearlie was born 10 July 1886. Pearlie died 13 June 1888.
11(12)22419(11)2   HASH, Emmie Caroline
Emmie was born circa 1887. Emmie died 8 March 1937.
11(12)22419(11)3   HASH, Ellen
Ellen was born circa 1889. Ellen died circa 1911.
11(12)22419(11)4   HASH, Bettie
Bettie was born circa 1891.
11(12)22419(11)5   HASH, Grover Cleveland
Grover was born 7 April 1894. Grover died 4 May 1964.
11(12)22419(11)6   HASH, Mintie Clyde
Mintie was born 1 January 1895.
11(12)22419(11)7   HASH, Guy Swanson
Guy was born circa 1896. Guy died 25 December 1905.
11(12)22419(11)8   HASH, Carrie Viola
Carrie was born circa 1899. Carrie died circa 1916.
11(12)22419(12)   HASH, William Emory
His body was interred in Piney Creek Cem, NC. William was born in Piney Creek, NC 10 March 1870. He married **MUNDY**, Namie Virginia 15 September 1895. William died 15 June 1958 at 88 years of age.
11(12)22419(12)1   HASH, Etta Mae

Etta was born 27 July 1896.

11(12)22419(12)2   HASH, William Paul

William was born 10 March 1898.

11(12)22419(12)3   HASH, Ola Pearl

Ola was born 19 December 1900.

11(12)22419(12)4   HASH, Oma Cleo

Oma was born 9 April 1903.

11(12)22419(12)5   HASH, Donna Raye

Donna was born 20 May 1905.

11(12)22419(12)6   HASH, Ivan Eugene

Ivan was born 13 November 1907.

11(12)22419(12)7   HASH, Nina Lee

Nina was born 8 May 1910.

11(12)22419(12)8   HASH, Neal W.

Neal was born 8 May 1910.

11(12)22419(12)9   HASH, Leonard Wayne

Leonard was born 14 March 1913.

11(12)22419(12)(10)   HASH, Ruby Virginia

Ruby was born 8 February 1915.

11(12)2241(10)   HALSEY, Henry

He married **STANFORD-MILES**, Nancy Jane. Henry was born circa 1839.

G. H. Mathews, into Company I, 51st Virginia Infantry, enlisted Henry Halsey, at Fox Creek, VA, on Friday, 28 June 1861 for a period of 12 months, along with every other able bodied man from Grayson County. Henry was with his cousins and neighbors from southwestern Virginia from the Counties of Grayson, Wythe, Bland, Patrick, Wise, Washington, Nelson and Amherst, who made up the 51st Virginia, which was organized two months after the first battle at Bull Run. Most had little, if any, military training. Their forte was farming.

The 51st Virginia Infantry fought the unforgotten war as the unit was separated from the Army of northern Virginia and received very little attention. Henry and his fellow soldiers fought on many battlefields with the same tenacity and determination for the same principles. They adapted to several types of warfare such, as in the Kanawha Valley it was "bush-fighting". At Fort Donelson it was "trench" warfare which required great stamina. The rapid marches and offensive type maneuvers required physical conditioning and courage. Disease and severe weather and lack of supplies killed more men from the 51st Virginia than did battle. Henry joined I Co. at Fox Creek. After several days of military training and electing John P. Wolfe from Washington County as Captain, Colonel Wharton, accepted the unit as part of the 51st Virginia along with six other companies, making a final total of eleven companies.

He was 29 years old when he departed from the Mouth of Wilson for Fox Creek. Henry was with several cousins. They were Ezekiel, Greenberry, James C., Mastin, Morris, Thomas and Will C. Halsey. Henry and the 51st Virginia Infantry Regiment left Wytheville by the Virginia and Tennessee

Railroad to Camp Joe Johnston at Bonsack's Depot for extensive training. By August 1861, the 51st was in the Kanawha Valley (now WV), which was the location of the largest salt producer for the South and also supplied food from the fertile farms. The unit was under General John B. Floyd. Many of his fellow soldiers had not received weapons. Some had brought old muskets that allowed the use of minnie balls and buck shot both advantages for mountain fighting. The first muster was held in October for the period from June 28 to October 31, 1861. Henry was listed as present for duty. At Russellville, the Confederate capital of Kentucky, Henry received his first pay. Also, in spite of the rain and snow the camp at Russellville was comfortable with huts with fireplaces and chimneys. After Fort Henry fell on February 6th, the Confederates started a buildup at Fort Donelson on the Cumberland River, near what is now the "Land Between the Lakes" (Lake Barkley on the Cumberland and Kentucky Lake on the Tennessee). Fort Donelson guarded the route to eastern Tennessee and the Confederate supplies at Nashville. Henry as part of the 51st moved by steamboat from Clarksville to Fort Donelson for the purpose of strengthening defenses. Henry was among the captured and was probably taken to Fort Douglas near Chicago. He was released about three months later in late May or early June. He made his way home to Mouth of Wilson, arriving there sometime before September 1862. Henry rejoined the 51st Virginia Infantry sometime before Captain M. B. Tate, Quartermaster paid him, on August 1, 1862. He also was present for duty at the muster held on November 1, 1862 for the period from July 31st to October 31st.

While Henry was being held prisoner in late March 1862, the regiment withdrew from Tennessee to near Abingdon, VA, camping near Glade Spring. This break allowed time for the wounded to recuperate at Emory and Henry College. The men received their first leave since the beginning as the leaders were trying desperately to recruit men. In early May the 51st was reorganized at Wytheville with new elections of officers. The third muster was dated December 31, 1862 for the period of November and December. Henry was listed as present for duty. William F. Moore, Assistant Quartermaster last paid him, on November 1, 1862. The forth muster was dated February 28, 1863, for January and February 1863. Henry was listed as present for duty and being last paid by Captain Moore on December 31, 1862. The fifth muster, dated April 30, 1863, was for March and April 1863. It listed Henry as being last paid on February 28, 1863 by W. F. Moore, and that he was present for duty. Henry made the sixth muster on July 2, 1863 for the months of May and June 1863. He was listed as present for duty. His last pay was on April 30, 1863 by Captain Moore. The seventh muster was dated November 4, 1863 and was for the period from June 30 to October 31, 1863. Henry was listed as present for duty and being last paid by Captain Moore. Henry was listed on a "Receipt for clothing for the third year, 1864", issued on September 17, 1864. He again appeared on a "Receipt for clothing" for the 4th year, dated March 10, 1864. Henry is listed on a "Receipt for clothing for the second quarter" dated June 27, 1864. Henry is listed on three separate "Receipt for clothing", 1864, dated November 9th and 17th, and

December 25, 1864.

11(12)2241(10)1	HALSEY, Worth
11(12)2241(10)2	HALSEY, Lee
11(12)2241(10)3	HALSEY, Anna Lee
11(12)2241(10)4	HALSEY, Mattie
11(12)2241(10)5	HALSEY, Polly
11(12)2241(10)6	HALSEY, Elizabeth 'Betty'

She married **MILES**, William Jesse. Elizabeth was born circa 1862.
She married **ROSS**, Robert 25 April 1880.

11(12)2241(10)61   MILES, Joe

11(12)2241(11) HALSEY, William Cecil 'Cease'

His body was interred in Cease Halsey, Cemetery, Grayson Co. VA.
He married **HASH**, Rebecca. William was born in Grayson Co, VA circa
1840. William died 4 March 1932 at 91 years of age. It is said that Cecil
Halsey gave Daniel Daugherty a farm to go to the Civil War in his place. He
evidently did. Daugherty was a laborer staying with Nancy Dixon and family
according to the 1850 U.S. Census of Ashe County, N.C. (Page 95).
(Reference: "The Halsey Genealogy" by Rufus Clinton Halsey, 1980)

11(12)2241(11)1   HALSEY, T. Blair

His body was interred in Cease Halsey, Cemetery, Mo. of Wilson Cr,
VA. T. was born 27 October 1858. T. died 30 July 1906 at 47 years of age.

11(12)2241(11)2   HALSEY, Polly Jane

Polly was born 28 August 1863. She married **BRYANT**, Lewis
Napoleon in Grayson Co., VA, 3 December 1882. Polly died 12 December
1949 at 86 years of age.

11(12)2241(11)21   BRYANT, Joseph Jackson

Joseph was born 19 November 1883. Joseph died 11 December
1883 at less than one year of age.

11(12)2241(11)22   BRYANT, Gincy Cordell

Gincy was born circa 1885. Gincy died 2 June 1971.

11(12)2241(11)23   BRYANT, William Bays

William was born 16 February 1888. William died 8 September 1968

11(12)2241(11)24   BRYANT, Stephen Alex 'Eck'

Stephen was born 28 March 1890.

11(12)2241(11)25   BRYANT, Edgar Saxon

Edgar was born 14 February 1898.

11(12)2241(11)26   BRYANT, James Blair

James was born 20 May 1901. He married **HALSEY**, Drucie 22 May
1929. James died 31 December 1970 at 69 years of age.

11(12)2241(11)261   BRYANT, Louis Jackson

Louis was born 9 October 1935.

11(12)2241(11)262   BRYANT, Carole Sue

Carole was born 28 December 1938.

11(12)2241(11)3   HALSEY, James Jackson

His body was interred in Fox Creek, Cemetery, VA. James was born
16 January 1866. He married **HALSEY**, Ada Ann in Grayson Co., VA, 2
January 1890. James died 31 October 1956 at 90 years of age.

11(12)2241(11)4   HALSEY, Gincy
Gincy was born 5 May 1868. She married **THOMAS**, Joseph Jerome 'Joe' September 1889. Gincy died 29 July 1949 at 81 years of age.
11(12)2241(11)41   THOMAS, Edgar Carlisle
Edgar was born 20 January 1890. Edgar died 4 July 1928.
11(12)2241(11)42   THOMAS, Edison McCauly
Edison was born 20 February 1893.
11(12)2241(11)43   THOMAS, Saxon
Saxon was born 23 July 1895. Saxon died 28 July 1896.
11(12)2241(11)44   THOMAS, Paul Jerome
Paul was born 6 July 1897. Paul died 28 October 1952.
11(12)2241(11)5   HALSEY, Nancy H.
Nancy was born 10 May 1872. She married **HALSEY**, James Gordon in Grayson Co., VA, 21 December 1892. Nancy died 30 May 1906.
11(12)2241(11)51   HALSEY, Jincy Mae
She married **JONES**, Evans. She married **BLACK**, Steve.
11(12)2241(11)511   JONES, Edith Mae
She married **LUTE**, Earl.
11(12)2241(11)5111   LUTE, Steve
11(12)2241(11)5112   JUTE, Harry
11(12)2241(11)512   BLACK, Anna Marie
11(12)2241(11)52   HALSEY, Anna Pearl
Anna was born 20 September 1895.
11(12)2241(11)53   HALSEY, Clyde M.
Clyde was born 15 December 1902. She married **ANDERSON**, Russell 1 July 1948. Clyde died 14 March 1970 at 67 years of age.
11(12)2241(11)531   HALSEY, Lewis
11(12)2241(11)54   HALSEY, William Roosevelt
William was born 4 June 1905. He married **PENDRY**, Virginia in Grayson Co., VA, 11 April 1931.
11(12)2241(11)541   HALSEY, William Ford
William was born 23 May 1932.
11(12)2241(11)542   HALSEY, Musetta Pearl
Musetta was born 22 April 1934.
11(12)2241(11)543   HALSEY, Shirley Mae
Shirley was born 27 November 1936.
11(12)2241(11)544   HALSEY, Ronald Rex
Ronald was born 21 June 1940.
11(12)2241(11)545   HALSEY, Mack B.
Mack was born 24 September 1944.
11(12)2241(11)6   HALSEY, William Terry
William was born 20 October 1881. He married **HALSEY**, Verdie Elizabeth 21 October 1899. William died 18 July 1920 at 38 years of age.
11(12)2241(11)61   HALSEY, Beulah V.
She married **GRIFFITH**, Robert J. in Grayson Co., VA, 5 February 1919.
11(12)2241(11)611   GRIFFITH, Robert Winfield

11(12)2241(11)612   GRIFFITH, Emma Clay
11(12)2241(11)613   GRIFFITH, Winnie Loretta
11(12)2241(11)614   GRIFFITH, Samuel Terry
Samuel was born 7 September 1925.
11(12)2241(11)615   GRIFFITH, Mary Ruth
Mary was born 14 March 1928.
11(12)2241(11)616   GRIFFITH, Garnet Howard
Garnet was born 17 June 1931.
11(12)2241(11)62   HALSEY, John May
John was born 8 April 1902. He married **HALSEY**, Virginia Mildred 17 December 1949. John died 21 July 1966 at 64 years of age.
11(12)2241(11)621   HALSEY, J. C.
J. was born in Ashe Co., NC.
11(12)2241(11)622   HALSEY, Linda
Linda was born 9 December 1957.
11(12)2241(11)623   HALSEY, James
James was born 9 August 1961.
11(12)2241(11)63   HALSEY, Winnie
She married **WILLARD**, A. L.. Winnie was born 23 June 1904.
11(12)2241(11)631   WILLARD, Roger Allen
Roger was born 11 December 1927.
11(12)2241(11)632   WILLARD, Lonnie Lee
Lonnie was born 7 February 1943.
11(12)2241(11)633   WILLARD, Jerry Wade
Jerry was born 20 October 1948. Jerry died 16 December 1951.
11(12)2241(11)64   HALSEY, Allen Jackson
Allen was born 30 November 1906. He married **ANDERSON**, Lola 16 February 1924. He married **BROWN**, Virgie (Neugent) in Sparta, NC, 29 March 1961.
11(12)2241(11)641   HALSEY, William Bradley
11(12)2241(11)642   HALSEY, Edison
11(12)2241(11)643   HALSEY, Ira Cecil
11(12)2241(11)644   HALSEY, Sandra Sue
11(12)2241(11)645   HALSEY, Zollie Beatrice
Zollie was born circa 1921. She married **BELL**, Claude Lester in Grayson Co., VA, 19 December 1942.
11(12)2241(11)6451   BELL, Lucille
Lucille was born 25 November 1943.
11(12)2241(11)6452   BELL, Ruth
Ruth was born 25 September 1945.
11(12)2241(11)6453   BELL, Claude Lester, Jr.
Claude was born April 1947.
11(12)2241(11)6454   BELL, Bonnie
Bonnie was born 20 November 1949.
11(12)2241(11)6455   BELL, Cecil
Cecil was born 18 June 1951.
11(12)2241(11)6456   BELL, Raymond

Raymond was born 1 June 1954.
11(12)2241(11)646   HALSEY, Oakie
Oakie was born 10 June 1924. She married **PARSONS**, Rex in MD, March 1942.
11(12)2241(11)647   HALSEY, Allen Blake (Tom)
Allen was born 14 June 1929. He married **PUGH**, Clettie Clo. 24 December 1953.
11(12)2241(11)6471   HALSEY, Susan Gale
Susan was born 26 July 1954.
11(12)2241(11)6472   HALSEY, Lorrie Ann
Lorrie was born 4 June 1960.
11(12)2241(11)6473   HALSEY, Steve Allen
Steve was born 10 February 1962.
11(12)2241(11)648   HALSEY, Charles Neaues (Sam)
Charles was born 20 August 1936. He married **HASH**, Jessie Jean in Sparta, NC, 9 August 1957.
11(12)2241(11)6481   HALSEY, Michael Charles
Michael was born 16 January 1958.
11(12)2241(11)6482   HALSEY, Anna Lee
Anna was born 25 June 1961.
11(12)2241(11)6483   HALSEY, Terry Dale
Terry was born 29 April 1963.
11(12)2241(11)649   HALSEY, Nell Ruth
She married **THOMAS**, Teddie. Nell was born 31 December 1938.
11(12)2241(11)6491   THOMAS, Jerry
11(12)2241(11)6492   THOMAS, Mickie
11(12)2241(11)6493   THOMAS, Danny
11(12)2241(11)6494   THOMAS, Sandy
11(12)2241(11)64(10)   HALSEY, David Jackson
David was born 15 February 1962.
11(12)2241(11)65   HALSEY, Edwin
Edwin was born 11 April 1909. He married **HARTZOG**, Viola 27 October 1935.
11(12)2241(11)651   HALSEY, Edward Terry
Edward was born 1 October 1936.
11(12)2241(11)652   HALSEY, Franklin
Franklin was born 18 December 1938.
11(12)2241(11)653   HALSEY, Rutha Ann
Rutha was born 10 June 1946.
11(12)2241(11)654   HALSEY, Elizabeth
Elizabeth was born 24 March 1952.
11(12)2241(11)655   HALSEY, Donald
Donald was born 2 September 1953.
11(12)2241(11)66   HALSEY, Stella
Stella was born 3 December 1911. She married **LOWE**, Grady Patterson 26 December 1931.
11(12)2241(11)661   LOWE, Evelyn

Evelyn was born 26 November 1935.
11(12)2241(11)662   LOWE, Elvin Patterson
Elvin was born 26 August 1942.
11(12)2241(11)663   LOWE, Elizabeth
Elizabeth was born 16 February 1949.
11(12)2241(11)67   HALSEY, William
William was born 1 September 1914. He married **MCMEANS**, Pauline 4 October 1937.
11(12)2241(11)671   HALSEY, Lena Ruth
Lena was born 25 September 1939.
11(12)2241(11)672   HALSEY, Stella Jean
Stella was born 15 September 1941.
11(12)2241(11)673   HALSEY, Carol
Carol was born 20 August 1943.
11(12)2241(11)674   HALSEY, Joane
Joane was born 4 March 1947.
11(12)2241(11)675   HALSEY, Terry
Terry was born 21 April 1948.
11(12)2241(11)676   HALSEY, Peggy
Peggy was born 31 December 1950.
11(12)2241(11)677   HALSEY, Johnnie
Johnnie was born 8 September 1953.
11(12)2241(11)678   HALSEY, Dennis
Dennis was born 30 November 1957.
11(12)2241(11)68   HALSEY, Geneva P.
Geneva was born 27 February 1917. Geneva died 6 March 1932.
11(12)2242   HALSEY, Mary
Mary was born. She married **ROBINSON**, Andrew. She married **VANNOY**, Nathaniel 29 December 1819.
11(12)2243   HALSEY, Sarah or Sally
She married **PERDY**, Pleasants. Sarah was born in Grayson Co, VA. She married **DAVIS**, Peter 11 May 1825.
11(12)2244   HALSEY, Olive
She married **CREEP**, (Crep or Cress) David 8 July 1834.
11(12)2245   HALSEY, Clibsley
Clibsley died 20 March 1857.
11(12)2246   HALSEY, Amos
He married **HOWELL**, Elizabeth.
11(12)22461   HALSEY, Mary
11(12)22462   HALSEY, Margaret
11(12)22463   HALSEY, Eveline
11(12)22464   HALSEY, Virginia
11(12)22465   HALSEY, William
William was born 11 August 1817. He married **CREP**, Mary Ann in Grayson County, VA, 11 November 1834. William died 11 August 1869.
11(12)224651   HALSEY, Calvin P.
He married **PICKLE**, Hannah in Grayson Co., VA, 2 February 1868.

11(12)2246511   HALSEY, J. C.
        J. was born circa 1874.
11(12)224652   HALSEY, Ananias
        Ananias was born in Smythe Co., VA circa 1836.
11(12)22466   HALSEY, James Harry
        He married **BROWN**, Mahala C.. James was born in N.C. circa
1819.
11(12)224661   HALSEY, Noah Jeptha
11(12)224662   HALSEY, Jesse James
11(12)224663   HALSEY, Lloyd L.
11(12)224664   HALSEY, J. W.
11(12)224665   HALSEY, Elizabeth C.
        Elizabeth was born circa 1859.
11(12)224666   HALSEY, Zachariah
        Zachariah was born circa 1862.
11(12)224667   HALSEY, Mary Lou
        Mary was born circa 1864.
11(12)224668   HALSEY, Lelitha Evaline
        Lelitha was born circa 1866.
11(12)224669   HALSEY, Rachel
        Rachel was born circa 1868.
11(12)22467   HALSEY, George Washington
        He married Elizabeth. George was born in N.C. circa 1821. Data for
George's family taken from U.S. Census of 1870, for Wolfe County,
Kentucky. He also purchased a farm in Wolfe County on 11 February 1861
from J. H. Amyx.
11(12)224671   HALSEY, Caroline
        Caroline was born in Kanawha, VA circa 1849.
11(12)224672   HALSEY, Mary B.
        Mary was born in Kentucky circa 1860.
11(12)22468   HALSEY, David
        He married **WHITEHEAD**, Anna. David was born 14 May 1831.
David died 29 September 1895 at 64 years of age.
11(12)224681   HALSEY, James B.
        James was born circa 1855.
11(12)224682   HALSEY, Joseph Marion
        Joseph was born 14 February 1856. Joseph died 12 January 1974.
11(12)224683   HALSEY, William P.
        William was born circa 1864.
11(12)224684   HALSEY, Margaret E.
        Margaret was born circa 1866.
11(12)224685   HALSEY, George
        George was born circa 1868.
11(12)22469   HALSEY, Sylvester
        He married **COOK**, Abigail. He married **MURPHY**, Ellen. Sylvester
was born 9 September 1833. Sylvester died 20 October 1902.
11(12)224691   HALSEY, Lou Ellen

11(12)224692   HALSEY, Caroline
    She married **HUTTON**, Taylor.
11(12)2246921 HUTTON, Price
11(12)2246922 HUTTON, Cecelia
11(12)2246923 HUTTON, Bohannon
11(12)224693   HALSEY, Emma
11(12)224694   HALSEY, William
    William was born circa 1860.
11(12)224695   HALSEY, Joseph
    He married **DRAKE**, Emma. Joseph was born circa 1863. Joseph
died circa 1936.
11(12)2246951 HALSEY, Sarah Ellen
11(12)2246952 HALSEY, Charles Courtney
11(12)2246953 HALSEY, Marion Curtis
    Marion was born 13 July 1885. Marion died 24 September 1926.
11(12)2246954 HALSEY, Kelly Marton
    He married **SWEENY**, Lennis. Kelly was born 2 January 1889. Kelly
died 20 January 1964 at 75 years of age.
11(12)22469541   HALSEY, Elsie
    He married **BACH**, Kate.
11(12)224695411   HALSEY, Elsie, Jr.
11(12)224695412   HALSEY, Glenn
11(12)224695413   HALSEY, Quinton
11(12)22469542   HALSEY, Earl
11(12)22469543   HALSEY, Hershel
11(12)2246955 HALSEY, Howard Richmond
    Howard was born 3 March 1892.
11(12)2246956 HALSEY, Lula Mae
    Lula was born circa 1897. Lula died circa 1944.
11(12)2246957 HALSEY, Jerry Dorsey
    Jerry was born 21 April 1901. Jerry died 19 August 1977.
11(12)2246958 HALSEY, Pearl Edna
    Pearl was born 23 April 1904. Pearl died 12 July 1925.
11(12)224696   HALSEY, George Washington
    He married **BYRD**, Matilda Ann. George was born 15 January 1867.
11(12)2246961 HALSEY, George Washington, Jr.
11(12)2246962 HALSEY, Matilda Ann
11(12)2246963 HALSEY, Cinda
11(12)224697   HALSEY, Elizabeth
    Elizabeth was born 14 April 1868. Elizabeth died 27 February 1911.
11(12)224698   HALSEY, Robert
    Robert was born 1 January 1878. Robert died 3 January 1911.
11(12)224699   HALSEY, Laura
    She married W.H.H.. Laura was born 16 October 1881. Laura died
5 February 1904 at 22 years of age.
11(12)2246991 Everett
11(12)2246992 Bud

11(12)2246993 Lizzie
11(12)2246(10) HALSEY, Olly
Olly was born 8 July 1834.
11(12)2247   HALSEY, Sarah
Sarah was born in Grayson Co, VA 29 April 1783. She married
HOWELL, William in Grayson County, VA, 7 March 1800.
11(12)22471   HOWELL, Lydia
She married COLE, James 1 March 1826.
11(12)22472   HOWELL, Amos
He married EDWARDS, Rhoda. Amos was born in Grayson County,
VA circa 1799. Amos died circa 1867.
11(12)224721   HOWELL, Martha
She married GRAYBEAL, John. Martha was born circa 1820.
Martha died circa 1863.
11(12)2247211 GRAYBEAL, Mary Ann
Mary was born in Ashe County, NC 5 July 1838. She married
HARDIN, William P. circa 1860. She married JONES, John W. circa 1868.
She married MCCARROLL, Evan circa 1877. Mary died 9 April 1886.
11(12)22472111   HARDIN, Minerva Evoline
Minerva was born in Ashe County, NC December 1861. She
married WELLS, Alexander Haywood 'Jeff' 30 March 1881. Minerva died
October 1921 at 59 years of age.
11(12)224721111   WELLS, Jincie Virginia
Jincie was born in Big Wilson Creek, Grayson Co., VA 8 April 1882.
She married MINK, Joseph E. 1 March 1906. Jincie died 17 March 1968.
11(12)224721112   WELLS, Robert Bruce
Robert was born 10 March 1885. He married SPENCER, Etta 9
April 1905. Robert died 8 November 1919 at 34 years of age.
11(12)224721113   WELLS, Rush Cole
Rush was born 27 November 1887. He married MCMILLAN, Lou 15
March 1905. Rush died 22 March 1948 at 60 years of age.
11(12)224721114   WELLS, Maude McKee
Maude was born 16 March 1889. She married PUGH, William H. 4
July 1908.
11(12)224721115   WELLS, George Conn
George was born 2 April 1891. George died 17 March 1960.
11(12)224721116   WELLS, James Alexander
He married MINK, Grace. James was born 20 April 1893. James
died 15 June 1964 at 71 years of age.
11(12)224721117   WELLS, Jeston M.
She married PLUMMER, Steven M.. Jeston was born 6 April 1895.
11(12)224721118   WELLS, Mary
She married PARSONS, Jesse J.. Mary was born 3 July 1897.
Mary died 12 February 1971 at 73 years of age.
11(12)224721119   WELLS, Clyde
Clyde was born 6 March 1899. Clyde died 7 November 1902.
11(12)22472111(10)   WELLS, Joseph Franklin

Joseph was born 19 February 1901. He married **COX**, Cynthia Anna in Bristol, TN, 14 April 1922. Joseph died 2 May 1943 at 42 years of age.

11(12)22472111(10)1   WELLS, Minnie Evoline

Minnie was born in Volney, Grayson Co., VA 29 March 1923. She married **HALL**, Henry F. 23 July 1942.

11(12)22472111(10)2   WELLS, Jeff Cox

Jeff was born in Volney, Grayson Co., VA 2 September 1924. He married **HEDGEBETH**, Sarah Leigh 29 July 1950.

11(12)22472111(10)3   WELLS, Joseph Franklin, Jr.

Joseph was born in Volney, Grayson Co., VA 12 December 1933.

11(12)22472111(10)4   WELLS, Carol Sue

She married **MCGRADY**, Joseph B.. Carol was born 29 August 1935.

11(12)22472111(10)5   WELLS, Robert Bryan

Robert was born in Volney, Grayson Co., VA 27 July 1938. He married **KYKER**, Ruby L. 30 December 1960.

11(12)22472111(11)   WELLS, Ruth Evoline

She married **DANIEL**, H. Beecher. Ruth was born 14 January 1904.

11(12)22472112   HARDIN, Martha Ann

Martha was born 13 May 1863. She married **YOUNG**, Frank 9 January 1879. Martha died 30 September 1950 at 87 years of age.

11(12)22472113   JONES, Caroline Alice

She married **YOUNG**, Mack. Caroline was born circa 1869. Caroline died circa 1930.

11(12)22472114   JONES, Sarah Catherine

She married **PERKINS**, Gordon. Sarah was born 7 June 1872.

11(12)22472115   MCCARROLL, Frank

He married **PRICE**, Emma. Frank was born circa 1877. Frank died circa 1933.

11(12)2247212 GRAYBEAL, Rhoda

She married **GREEN**, Richard. Rhoda was born circa 1839.

11(12)2247213 GRAYBEAL, Peter

Peter was born circa 1840. He married **HARDIN**, Catherine circa 1867. Peter died circa 1904.

11(12)2247214 GRAYBEAL, Sarah Jane

She married **GREER**, John Calvin. Sarah was born 20 September 1843. Sarah died 18 June 1902 at 58 years of age.

11(12)2247215 GRAYBEAL, David

He married **ASHLEY**, Bethenia. David was born 11 September 1846.

11(12)2247216 GRAYBEAL, Jacob

He married **WILCOXEN**, Alice. Jacob was born circa 1848. Jacob died circa 1934.

11(12)224722   HOWELL, Margaret 'Peggy'

Margaret was born circa 1823. Margaret died 15 September 1888.

11(12)224723   HOWELL, William

He married **HALSEY**, Celia. William was born 16 May 1826.

William died 8 October 1905 at 79 years of age.
11(12)2247231 HOWELL, Wiley
     Wiley was born 28 May 1848. He married **YOUNG**, Malinda Elvirety 5 May 1867. Wiley died 14 August 1926 at 78 years of age.
11(12)22472311 HOWELL, David Cyrus
     David was born 21 June 1870. He married an unknown person before 1901. He married **NORRIS**, Eliza Ellen 26 February 1901. David died 9 April 1941 at 70 years of age.
11(12)224723111 HOWELL, Wiley Washington
     Wiley was born in Ashe County, NC 5 April 1902. He married **TAYLOR**, Bessie Lou in West Jefferson, NC, 26 August 1926. Wiley died 30 July 1961 in Mooresville, NC, at 59 years of age.
11(12)2247231111 HOWELL, Marvin Taylor
     Marvin was born in Mooresville, NC 8 December 1937. He married **LOWE**, Betty Anne in Mooresville, NC, 26 January 1957.
11(12)22472311111 HOWELL, Alex Wayne
     Alex was born in Charlotte, NC 25 May 1970.
11(12)224724 HOWELL, Olive
     She married **STANSBURY**, Nathan. Olive was born circa 1830.
11(12)224725 HOWELL, Mary Polly
     She married **HARTZOG**, James. Mary was born 1 June 1832.
11(12)224726 HOWELL, David
     David was born circa 1836.
11(12)224727 HOWELL, Lindsey 'Lucy'
     Lindsey was born 8 February 1842. She married **GRAYBEAL**, Calvin Monroe 31 August 1865. Lindsey died 14 August 1926.
11(12)224728 HOWELL, Sultane
     Sultane was born circa 1845. Sultane died before 1850.
11(12)22473 HOWELL, David
     David was born in Grayson County, VA 6 September 1803. He married **DUGGER**, Mary 14 March 1830. David died 1 April 1889.
11(12)224731 HOWELL, Malinda
     Malinda was born 12 January 1831.
11(12)224732 HOWELL, Amos
     Amos was born 9 April 1832.
11(12)224733 HOWELL, John Senter
     John was born 12 August 1833. He married **COOK**, Delphia 3 May 1854.
11(12)224734 HOWELL, Matilda
     Matilda was born 26 February 1835.
11(12)224735 HOWELL, Martha
     Martha was born 30 March 1837.
11(12)224736 HOWELL, Rhoda
     Rhoda was born 2 June 1839. She married **HARDIN**, Frank 20 March 1866. Rhoda died 26 January 1911 at 71 years of age.
11(12)224737 HOWELL, William
     William was born 2 January 1843.

11(12)224738   HOWELL, James
James was born 27 September 1845.
11(12)22474   HOWELL, Peggy
She married **LORANCE**, George. Peggy was born circa 1807.
11(12)2248   HALSEY, Margaret
She married **HASH**, Joseph. Margaret was born in Grayson Co, VA 24 October 1785.
11(12)22481   HASH, Phoebe
She married **MATHENY**, .
11(12)224811   MATHENY, Polly
11(12)22482   HASH, Evalina
11(12)22483   HASH, Rachel
She married **HAGA**, Jacob.
11(12)224831   HAGA, (Infant)
11(12)224832   HAGA, (Infant)
11(12)224833   HAGA, Edie
11(12)224834   HAGA, Clementine
11(12)224835   HAGA, Margaret
11(12)224836   HAGA, Harriett
11(12)224837   HAGA, Mary 'Mollie'
11(12)22484   HASH, Margaret
11(12)22485   HASH, Polly
11(12)22486   HASH, Joseph, Jr. 'Rimer Joe'
He married **COLE**, Polly.
11(12)224861   HASH, Isom
11(12)224862   HASH, Phoebe
11(12)224863   HASH, America
11(12)224864   HASH, Zilda
11(12)224865   HASH, Cynthia
Cynthia was born 31 March 1846. Cynthia died circa 1906.
11(12)224866   HASH, Floyd
Floyd was born 2 May 1847. Floyd died 15 March 1929.
11(12)224867   HASH, Watson
Watson was born 15 February 1864. Watson died 17 June 1939.
11(12)224868   HASH, Boyden
Boyden was born 23 August 1866. Boyden died 8 February 1890.
11(12)22487   HASH, William 'Blind Fox Billy'
He married **HASH**, Polly (Glass). William was born 25 January 1809. He married **BORHAM**, Jane 18 October 1833. William died 11 May 1895 at 86 years of age.
11(12)224871   HASH, Levi
Levi was born 25 January 1833.
11(12)224872   HASH, Eli G.
Eli was born 15 September 1835.
11(12)224873   HASH, Elsie
Elsie was born 7 January 1838.
11(12)224874   HASH, Calvin

Calvin was born 28 March 1840.
11(12)224875   HASH, Elizabeth
Elizabeth was born 5 January 1842.
11(12)224876   HASH, William
William was born 7 January 1844.
11(12)224877   HASH, Abel
Abel was born 7 July 1846.
11(12)224878   HASH, Zebedee
Zebedee was born 7 December 1848.
11(12)224879   HASH, Wiley
Wiley was born 7 December 1848.
11(12)22487(10)   HASH, Mary Jane
Mary was born 26 May 1850.
11(12)22487(11)   HASH, Sarah Caroline
Sarah was born 1 May 1851.
11(12)22487(12)   HASH, Loudema
Loudema was born 8 May 1853.
11(12)22487(13)   HASH, Alice
Alice was born 8 April 1863.
11(12)22487(14)   HASH, Emaline
Emaline was born 23 March 1865.
11(12)22487(15)   HASH, Martha Jane
Martha was born 23 March 1865.
11(12)22487(16)   HASH, William Mathas
William was born 14 April 1868. William died 14 May 1895.
11(12)22487(17)   HASH, Lee F.
Lee was born 29 January 1873. Lee died 13 September 1959.
11(12)22488   HASH, Zebedee
He married **HACKLER**, Frankie. Zebedee was born circa 1810. He married **WARD**, Evaline 5 December 1841.
11(12)224881   HASH, Zachariah
11(12)224882   HASH, Tobitha
11(12)224883   HASH, Zilla
11(12)224884   HASH, William Troy
11(12)224885   HASH, Weldon
11(12)224886   HASH, Fieldon
11(12)224887   HASH, Letcher Z.
11(12)224888   HASH, Ludema
11(12)224889   HASH, Polly Ann
11(12)22488(10)   HASH, Augusta
11(12)22488(11)   HASH, Louise
11(12)22488(12)   HASH, Jennie
11(12)22488(13)   HASH, Joseph N.
Joseph was born circa 1858.
11(12)22489   HASH, Rebecca
She married **WARD**, Nathan. Rebecca was born circa 1824.
11(12)224891   WARD, Margaret 'Peggy Ann'

11(12)224892   WARD, Lucinda
11(12)2248(10) HASH, Abraham
He married **WARD**, Sallie. Abraham was born circa 1830. He
married **MCGRADY**, Rebecca 13 March 1864. He married **CULLOP**,
Elizabeth 1 July 1879. He married **COX**, Jane (Jennings) 11 February 1894.
Abraham died circa 1902.

11(12)2248(10)1	**HASH, Louise**
11(12)2248(10)2	**HASH, Cora**
11(12)2248(10)3	**HASH, Sarah**
11(12)2248(10)4	**HASH, Emory Columbus**
11(12)2248(10)5	**HASH, Senmour C.**
11(12)2248(10)6	**HASH, Albert G.**
11(12)2248(10)7	**HASH, Peyton G.**
11(12)2248(10)8	**HASH, Dennis**

Dennis was born 18 January 1859. Dennis died 13 July 1941.

11(12)2248(10)9   HASH, Walter A.
Walter was born 21 March 1878. Walter died circa 1962.

11(12)2249   HALSEY, Rachel Persilla
She married **PACELY**, Isaac. Rachel was born in Grayson Co, VA
26 April 1787.

11(12)224(10)   HALSEY, Sylvester
Sylvester was born in Grayson Co, VA circa 1788. He married
YOUNG, Mary 24 July 1828. Sylvester died 12 July 1856 at 68 years of age.

11(12)224(10)1 HALSEY, Major
11(12)224(10)2 HALSEY, Celia
She married **HOWELL**, Felix.

11(12)224(10)21	**HOWELL, Felix**
11(12)224(10)22	**HOWELL, Willy**
11(12)224(10)23	**HOWELL, Lee**

11(12)224(10)3 HALSEY, William
William was born circa 1831. He married **HASH**, Loudema in Ashe
Co., N.C., 6 May 1858. William died 1 April 1901 at 69 years of age.

11(12)224(10)31   HALSEY, Polly Ann
She married **WALKER**, Houston. Polly was born 2 November 1859.
Polly died 14 March 1929 at 69 years of age.

11(12)224(10)311	**WALKER, Florence**
11(12)224(10)312	**WALKER, Josephine**
11(12)224(10)313	**WALKER, Kate**
11(12)224(10)314	**WALKER, Lee**
11(12)224(10)315	**WALKER, Attie**
11(12)224(10)316	**WALKER, Reece**
11(12)224(10)32	**HALSEY, Celia Jane**

She married **WEISS**, Hershell Beauregard, Dr.. Celia was born 10
December 1861. She married **DELP**, John Marshall 13 March 1904. Celia
died 12 May 1935 at 73 years of age.

11(12)224(10)321   WEISS, William Authur
He married **VAUGHT**, Gincy. William was born 13 October 1882.

11(12)224(10)3211   **WEISS, Annie**
11(12)224(10)3212   **WEISS, Bronson H.**
11(12)224(10)3213   **WEISS, French**
11(12)224(10)3214   **WEISS, Mattie**
11(12)224(10)3215   **WEISS, Robert**
11(12)224(10)322   **WEISS, Lura Alice**
She married **ROGERS**, Hugh F.. Lura was born 10 June 1884. Lura died 31 December 1970 at 86 years of age.
11(12)224(10)3221   **ROGERS, Annie Lorraine**
11(12)224(10)323   **WEISS, Annie Loraine**
She married **PHIPPS**, Floyd. Annie was born 5 April 1886. Annie died 7 April 1914 at 28 years of age.
11(12)224(10)3231   **PHIPPS, Pauline**
11(12)224(10)324   **WEISS, Thomas Conley**
He married **WEAVER**, Annie. Thomas was born 30 April 1888. Thomas died May 1936 at 48 years of age.
11(12)224(10)3241   **WEISS, Ethel**
11(12)224(10)325   **WEISS, Glenn, Dr.**
Glenn, was born 27 August 1892. He married **DUNCAN**, Agnes 28 February 1918. Glenn, died 8 November 1922 at 30 years of age.
11(12)224(10)3251   **WEISS, Dean**
Dean was born 23 December 1918.
11(12)224(10)3252   **WEISS, Vinton**
Vinton was born 28 December 1919. Vinton died 21 October 1921.
11(12)224(10)326   **WEISS, Mattie Josephine**
Mattie was born 22 August 1896.
11(12)224(10)327   **DELP, Ruby Dale**
Ruby was born 15 January 1906. She married **HALSEY**, Polk 24 June 1923.
11(12)224(10)3271   **HALSEY, Opal Evangeline**
Opal was born circa 1924. She married **VICKERS**, James C. in Grayson Co., VA, 27 August 1948.
11(12)224(10)32711   **VICKERS, James Glenn**
James was born circa 1949.
11(12)224(10)32712   **VICKERS, Robert Laird**
Robert was born circa 1952.
11(12)224(10)3272   **HALSEY, Valetta**
Valetta was born circa 1926. She married **SALOMA**, Herman circa 1950.
11(12)224(10)32721   **SALOMA, Pamela Kathryn**
Pamela was born circa 1953.
11(12)224(10)32722   **SALOMA, Mark Emmanuel**
Mark was born circa 1955.
11(12)224(10)32723   **SALOMA, Roy Anthony**
Roy was born circa 1957.
11(12)224(10)32724   **SALOMA, Lori Valetta**
Lori was born circa 1959.

11(12)224(10)3273   HALSEY, Ollie
    Ollie was born circa 1928. She married **EBERTS**, Kenneth circa 1952.
11(12)224(10)32731   EBERTS, Rose Ann
    Rose was born circa 1952.
11(12)224(10)32732   EBERTS, Becky Dale
    Becky was born circa 1954.
11(12)224(10)32733   EBERTS, Zeno Kay
    Zeno was born circa 1956.
11(12)224(10)32734   EBERTS, Debby Lena
    Debby was born circa 1958.
11(12)224(10)3274   HALSEY, Mattie Jean
    Mattie was born circa 1931. She married **O'CONNER**, James L., II 26 September 1950.
11(12)224(10)32741   O'CONNER, Sharon Ann
    Sharon was born 1 July 1951.
11(12)224(10)32742   O'CONNER, James L., III
    James was born 2 November 1952.
11(12)224(10)32743   O'CONNER, Kathleen Marie
    Kathleen was born 27 May 1955.
11(12)224(10)32744   O'CONNER, Mary Jane
    Mary was born 28 December 1959.
11(12)224(10)3275   HALSEY, Lorraine
    Lorraine was born circa 1933.
11(12)224(10)3276   HALSEY, Glenna
    Glenna was born circa 1936.
11(12)224(10)3277   HALSEY, Mary Ann
    Mary was born circa 1938.
11(12)224(10)3278   HALSEY, Barbara Dale
    Barbara was born circa 1941.
11(12)224(10)3279   HALSEY, Pauline
    Pauline was born circa 1944.
11(12)224(10)327(10)   HALSEY, Charlie
    Charlie was born circa 1947.
11(12)224(10)33   HALSEY, Thomas Jackson 'Bud'
    Thomas was born 17 September 1866. He married **MCMILLAN**, Mattie 9 December 1891. He married **HALL**, Savannah in Ashe Co., NC, 10 July 1895.
11(12)224(10)331   HALSEY, Byrant
11(12)224(10)332   HALSEY, Ruth
11(12)224(10)333   HALSEY, Venilla
11(12)224(10)334   HALSEY, Mildred
11(12)224(10)335   HALSEY, Lucy.
11(12)224(10)336   HALSEY, Jesse
11(12)224(10)34   HALSEY, Sylvester
    Sylvester was born 30 November 1868. He married **HALSEY**, Ennice 18 January 1905. Sylvester died circa 1937.

11(12)224(10)341   HALSEY, Wade
Wade was born 5 November 1902. Wade died September 1991.
11(12)224(10)342   HALSEY, Paul
Paul was born 26 November 1904. Paul died May 1990.
11(12)224(10)343   HALSEY, Greek
Greek was born 17 November 1906. He married **WHITTINGTON**, Ella 17 May 1927.
11(12)224(10)3431   HALSEY, Blanche
Blanche was born 11 December 1928.
11(12)224(10)3432   HALSEY, William Greek
William was born 16 May 1934. William died 25 July 1948.
11(12)224(10)3433   HALSEY, Clarence
Clarence was born 13 August 1936.
11(12)224(10)3434   HALSEY, Donald Ray
Donald was born 27 July 1939.
11(12)224(10)344   HALSEY, Conley Weiss
He married **SCHRITCHFIELD**, Virginia. Conley was born 2 September 1910. He married **LUCAS**, Margaret 10 March 1931.
11(12)224(10)3441   HALSEY, Conrad Eugene
Conrad was born June 1933.
11(12)224(10)3442   HALSEY, Nancy
Nancy was born 25 December 1936.
11(12)224(10)3443   HALSEY, Robert Curtis
Robert was born May 1938.
11(12)224(10)3444   HALSEY, Gilbert
Gilbert was born June 1940.
11(12)224(10)3445   HALSEY, David
David was born December 1942.
11(12)224(10)345   HALSEY, Hurshel Hix
Hurshel was born 17 November 1912. He married **ANDERSON**, Dany Othello 28 March 1934.
11(12)224(10)3451   HALSEY, Hurshel Hix, Jr.
Hurshel was born 21 February 1935. He married **CRAIG**, Erma Louise Draper 15 March 1964.
11(12)224(10)3452   HALSEY, Betty Gaye
Betty was born 1 June 1936. She married **NELSON**, James Bobby 8 April 1955.
11(12)224(10)3453   HALSEY, Johnny Vester
Johnny was born 30 September 1946. He married **SHELTON**, Sandra Jane 24 November 1966.
11(12)224(10)34531   HALSEY, Tanya Caroline
Tanya was born 21 August 1971.
11(12)224(10)34532   HALSEY, John Christopher
John was born 28 October 1981.
11(12)224(10)346   HALSEY, Hobert Sylvester
Hobert was born in Grayson County, VA 14 December 1917. He married **REYNOLDS**, Rebecca Jean 27 June 1942. Hobert died 27 May

1974 in Elkton, MD, at 56 years of age.

11(12)224(10)3461   HALSEY, Hobert Sylvester, Jr.

Hobert was born in Elkton, MD 11 April 1945. He married **DOWDELL**, Mary Jane in Elkton, MD, 9 January 1965. He married **PHILLIPS**, Carol Marie in Elkton, MD, 2 February 1980.

11(12)224(10)34611   HALSEY, Beverly Lynn

Beverly was born in Cecil County, MD 3 August 1965.

11(12)224(10)34612   HALSEY, William Earl

William was born in Cecil County, MD 7 November 1966.

11(12)224(10)3462   HALSEY, Joseph Wayne

Joseph was born in No. East, MD 29 September 1946. He married **PENDLETON**, Sharon E. in Elkton, MD, 22 December 1973. Joseph Wayne Halsey joined the U.S. Marines on January 3, 1966, and went to Viet Nam in July 1966. He was wounded on May 29, 1967, and discharged in 1969 with more than 90% disability.

11(12)224(10)347   HALSEY, Kate

Kate was born 22 January 1922.

11(12)224(10)348   HALSEY, Ruth

Ruth was born 16 May 1925. She married **CASSAVERA**, Sam 4 February 1944.

11(12)224(10)3481   CASSAVERA, Sam, Jr.

Sam, was born 9 September 1945.

11(12)224(10)3482   CASSAVERA, Sue Carol

Sue was born 22 December 1950.

11(12)224(10)3483   CASSAVERA, Anthony

Anthony was born 7 July 1957.

11(12)224(10)35   HALSEY, James K. Polk

James was born 8 January 1871. James died 10 September 1892.

11(12)224(10)36   HALSEY, William Reece

William was born 14 May 1873.

11(12)224(10)37   HALSEY, Benjamin Franklin

Benjamin was born 18 April 1875. He married **PUGH**, Bina R. in Grayson Co., VA, 6 July 1895. Benjamin died 9 May 1924.

11(12)224(10)371   HALSEY, Glenn

Glenn was born circa 1897. Glenn died circa 1897.

11(12)224(10)372   HALSEY, W. Ray

W. was born 14 November 1898. He married **MCMEANS**, Venie 21 April 1919.

11(12)224(10)3721   HALSEY, James Franklin 'Jay'

He married **PENNINGTON**, Lillie Mae. James was born 20 March 1920. He married **HASH**, Ruby in Sparta, NC, 23 April 1941.

11(12)224(10)37211   HALSEY, Bina Carleta

Bina was born 10 April 1943.

11(12)224(10)37212   HALSEY, Juda

Juda was born 1 March 1951.

11(12)224(10)37213   HALSEY, Glenna Jaylene

Glenna was born 28 June 1953.

11(12)224(10)37214   HALSEY, Debbie Gay
Debbie was born 21 September 1957.
11(12)224(10)3722   HALSEY, Robert
He married **KEY**, Della. Robert was born 28 March 1923.
11(12)224(10)37221   HALSEY, Barbara Alice
Barbara was born 23 July 1943.
11(12)224(10)37222   HALSEY, Linda Faye
Linda was born 30 June 1945. Linda died 1 July 1945.
11(12)224(10)37223   HALSEY, Carol Sue
Carol was born 4 October 1946.
11(12)224(10)3723   HALSEY, Lizzie Lee
Lizzie was born 13 March 1926. She married **DOGAN**, Ethan
Eugene, Sr. 15 July 1946.
11(12)224(10)37231   DOGAN, Patricia Ann
Patricia was born 13 March 1947.
11(12)224(10)37232   DOGAN, Ethan Eugene, Jr.
Ethan was born 28 November 1950.
11(12)224(10)3724   HALSEY, Artie
Artie was born 1 January 1929. He married **HALL**, Claudia 23
December 1948.
11(12)224(10)37241   HALSEY, Sandra
Sandra was born 25 September 1949.
11(12)224(10)37242   HALSEY, David
David was born 3 June 1951.
11(12)224(10)37243   HALSEY, Dale
Dale was born 23 May 1958.
11(12)224(10)3725   HALSEY, Rose Zella
Rose was born 25 May 1932.
11(12)224(10)3726   HALSEY, Heury
Heury was born 22 June 1935. He married **TAYLOR**, Peggy 27
June 1959.
11(12)224(10)37261   HALSEY, Juda
Juda was born 7 April 1960.
11(12)224(10)37262   HALSEY, Pamela
Pamela was born 17 February 1966.
11(12)224(10)3727   HALSEY, Bert
He married **DAVIS**, Janice. Bert was born 16 October 1939.
11(12)224(10)37271   HALSEY, Neal
11(12)224(10)37272   HALSEY, Michael
11(12)224(10)37273   HALSEY, Debri
11(12)224(10)373   HALSEY, Eugenia
Eugenia was born 17 August 1902. She married **PENNINGTON**, R.
Hurley 3 January 1922.
11(12)224(10)3731   PENNINGTON, Maxine
Maxine was born 31 December 1922.
11(12)224(10)3732   PENNINGTON, Margaret
Margaret was born 22 June 1925.

11(12)224(10)3733   PENNINGTON, Gayle
Gayle was born 31 March 1928.
11(12)224(10)374   HALSEY, Nannie Lou
Nannie was born 19 December 1904. She married **HARDING**,
Glenn W. 21 April 1921.
11(12)224(10)3741   HARDING, Vivian Margaret
Vivian was born 5 October 1921.
11(12)224(10)3742   HARDING, Barbara Frances
Barbara was born 23 August 1924.
11(12)224(10)3743   HARDING, Robert Wallick
Robert was born 16 February 1927.
11(12)224(10)3744   HARDING, Glenn Halsey
Glenn was born 19 July 1929.
11(12)224(10)3745   HARDING, Iva Lou
Iva was born 1 March 1945.
11(12)224(10)375   HALSEY, Elva Odell
Elva was born 13 June 1907.
11(12)224(10)376   HALSEY, Ben Rogers
Ben was born 19 January 1910. He married **REEDY**, Edith 28 July
1928.
11(12)224(10)3761   HALSEY, Elizabeth Ann
Elizabeth was born 25 September 1929.
11(12)224(10)3762   HALSEY, Lois Frances
Lois was born 11 November 1931.
11(12)224(10)3763   HALSEY, Billy Rogers
Billy was born 18 May 1935.
11(12)224(10)38   HALSEY, Leander
Leander was born 6 February 1878. Leander died 6 April 1878.
11(12)224(10)39   HALSEY, John McNeal
John was born 15 June 1879. He married **KIRK**, Attie 12 October
1900. He married **BLEVINS**, Emma Lenora 7 April 1906. John died 7
December 1942 at 63 years of age.
11(12)224(10)391   HALSEY,
He was born 16 April 1901. He died 16 April 1901.
11(12)224(10)392   HALSEY, J. Carl
J. was born 18 May 1907. J. died 21 August 1956.
11(12)224(10)393   HALSEY, Glenn R.
Glenn was born 18 November 1908. He married **JONES**, Celia
Ennice 2 January 1933.
11(12)224(10)3931   HALSEY, Robert Dean
Robert was born 6 December 1933.
11(12)224(10)3932   HALSEY, Rex Lee
Rex was born 19 June 1935.
11(12)224(10)3933   HALSEY, Glenna Sue
Glenna was born 17 September 1939.
11(12)224(10)3934   HALSEY, Polly Ann
Polly was born 25 November 1942.

11(12)224(10)3935   HALSEY, Charles Neal
Charles was born 5 April 1945.
11(12)224(10)394   HALSEY, Attie Lenora
Attie was born 20 April 1911.
11(12)224(10)395   HALSEY, Zenna Mae
She married **FRANKLIN**, J. Warren. Zenna was born 19 February
1917.
11(12)224(10)3951   FRANKLIN, Joe Warren
11(12)224(10)3952   FRANKLIN, Laura Dale
11(12)224(10)396   HALSEY, Dale York
Dale was born 16 December 1918.
11(12)224(10)397   HALSEY, Beale K.
Beale was born 23 November 1920. He married **ELLER**, Hazel 24
September 1943.
11(12)224(10)3971   HALSEY, Sammy Roy
Sammy was born 30 September 1944.
11(12)224(10)3972   HALSEY, Doris Ann
Doris was born 8 December 1945.
11(12)224(10)3973   HALSEY, Jerry Lee
Jerry was born 8 December 1948.
11(12)224(10)3974   HALSEY, Joyce Kay
Joyce was born 12 August 1951.
11(12)224(10)3975   HALSEY, David Eller
David was born 20 March 1957.
11(12)224(10)3976   HALSEY, Karen Aretta
Karen was born 4 August 1960.
11(12)224(10)398   HALSEY, Gladys Lavaun
Gladys was born 2 May 1926. She married **CALLISON**, Gilmer
Woods 18 August 1951.
11(12)224(10)3981   CALLISON, Alice Woods
Alice was born in Roanoke, VA 16 August 1955.
11(12)224(10)3982   CALLISON, Sue Ann
Sue was born in Roanoke, VA 18 November 1957.
11(12)224(10)399   HALSEY, Thelma Irene
Thelma was born 13 February 1929. Thelma died 29 July 1936.
11(12)224(10)39(10)   HALSEY, Shirly Ann
Shirly was born 23 September 1931. She married **HASH**, Max
Harold 22 April 1950.
11(12)224(10)39(10)1   HASH, Nancy Ellen
Nancy was born 9 December 1955.
11(12)224(10)39(10)2   HASH, Thelma Jane
Thelma was born 30 March 1957.
11(12)224(10)39(10)3   HASH, Kenneth Max
Kenneth was born 5 December 1958.
11(12)224(10)39(10)4   HASH, Gary Rex
Gary was born 24 December 1960.
11(12)224(10)3(10)   HALSEY, Cornelia

Cornelia was born 15 June 1879. Cornelia died 15 June 1879.
11(12)224(10)3(11)   HALSEY, Herschell Fielding
Herschell was born 13 December 1881. He married **DEBOARD**,
Mary Elizabeth 9 May 1908. Herschell died 13 January 1945.
11(12)224(10)3(11)1   HALSEY, Leigh Buckner
Leigh was born 16 October 1908. Leigh died 23 June 1922.
11(12)224(10)3(11)2   HALSEY, Mary Virginia
Mary was born 18 April 1910.
11(12)224(10)3(11)3   HALSEY, Voctor Conley
Voctor was born 14 August 1911.
11(12)224(10)3(11)4   HALSEY, Dorothy Irene
Dorothy was born 3 January 1914. Dorothy died 8 March 1914.
11(12)224(10)3(11)5   HALSEY, Edward Max
Edward was born 12 January 1915. Edward died 12 February 1915.
11(12)224(10)3(11)6   HALSEY, Edith Rose
Edith was born 23 March 1917.
11(12)224(10)3(11)7   HALSEY, Herschell Fielding, Jr.
Herschell was born 10 April 1919. Herschell died January 1981 in
Indep, Grayson Co., VA, at 61 years of age.
11(12)224(10)3(11)8   HALSEY, William Franklin
William was born 31 March 1923. William died 26 April 1975.
11(12)224(10)3(11)9   HALSEY, Lucien DeBoard
Lucien was born 22 December 1925. He married **HALL**, Patricia
Joan 19 August 1950. He married **FERGUSON**, Shirley (Dawson) in Laural,
MD, 9 May 1964. Lucien died 1 May 1972 at 46 years of age.
11(12)224(10)3(11)91   HALSEY, Karen Lucienne
Karen was born 6 June 1951.
11(12)224(10)3(11)92   HALSEY, Mary Patricia
Mary was born 3 June 1952.
11(12)224(10)3(11)93   HALSEY, Richard Edward
Richard was born 12 April 1954.
11(12)224(10)3(11)94   HALSEY, Mona Rae
Mona died. Mona was born 5 August 1956.
11(12)224(10)3(12)   HALSEY, Florence Belle
Florence was born 9 March 1884. She married **DIXON**, John
Franklin 10 July 1902. Florence died 11 January 1955 at 70 years of age.
11(12)224(10)3(12)1   DIXON, Wilma
Wilma was born 22 August 1903. Wilma died 14 September 1933.
11(12)224(10)3(12)2   DIXON, William Gilbert
William was born 15 December 1905. William died 15 December
1905 at less than one year of age.
11(12)224(10)3(12)3   DIXON, Thomas Conley
Thomas was born 18 March 1907. Thomas died 18 March 1907.
11(12)224(10)3(12)4   DIXON, William Neal
William was born 15 May 1908. William died 15 May 1908.
11(12)224(10)3(12)5   DIXON, Lena Lou
Lena was born 28 November 1910.

11(12)224(10)3(12)6   DIXON, Anna Odell
Anna was born 21 November 1913.
11(12)224(10)3(12)7   DIXON, Maggie Lee
Maggie was born 16 July 1916. Maggie died 16 July 1916.
11(12)224(10)3(12)8   DIXON, Agnes Alice
Agnes was born 16 July 1916. Agnes died 16 July 1916.
11(12)224(10)3(12)9   DIXON, Lola Valentine
Lola was born 14 February 1918. Lola died September 1972.
11(12)224(10)3(12)(10) DIXON, Claude Swanson
Claude was born 21 January 1922. Claude died circa 1924.
11(12)224(10)3(12)(11) DIXON, Jaunita Marie
Jaunita was born circa 1923. Jaunita died circa 1923.
11(12)224(10)3(12)(12) DIXON, Mary Virginia
Mary was born 28 May 1924.
11(12)224(10)3(12)(13) DIXON, Forrest 'Bud'
Forrest was born 10 July 1925.
11(12)224(10)4 HALSEY, Ezekial
Ezekial was born circa 1837. He married **HALSEY**, Fidella Ann
'Dilla' 19 September 1856. Ezekial died circa 1869.
11(12)224(10)5 HALSEY, Thomas
He married **COX**, Margaret 'Peggy'. Thomas was born in Grayson
County, VA circa 1842. Thomas died 22 April 1865 in Point Lookout, MD, at
22 years of age.
     Enlisted in Company I, 51st Virginia Infantry, on 28 June 1861 from
Fox Creek in Grayson County. He received a medical discharge on 18 July
1862 for "predisposition to phythisis pulmonalis" at age twenty. Thomas had
a dark complexion with black eyes and black hair. He was five feet four
inches tall. He listed his occupation as a soldier. Later muster rolls show
Thomas enlisting again from Grayson County on 30 April 1863. He died a
prisoner of war at Point Lookout, MD on 22 April 1865 of dropsey.
11(12)224(10)51   HALSEY, Polly Ann
Polly was born 14 March 1856. She married **PARSONS**, Lafayette
Listen 25 April 1876. Polly died 16 February 1924 at 67 years of age.
11(12)224(10)52   HALSEY, John Wiley
John was born circa 1860.
11(12)224(10)53   HALSEY, Greenberry, Dr.
Greenberry, was born 12 March 1863. He married **BRYANT**, Bettie
Cordelia 16 July 1890. Greenberry, died 3 April 1908 at 45 years of age.
11(12)224(10)531   HALSEY, Hattie Mae
Hattie was born in Fox, VA 24 March 1891. She married **HICKS**,
Carlisle Preston in Grayson Co., VA, 9 August 1911. She married **PAISLEY**,
Edwin Lee 11 November 1964.
11(12)224(10)5311   HICKS, Rosamond Cordello
Rosamond was born 7 September 1912. She married
COULTHARD, Marvin C. 10 February 1940.
11(12)224(10)53111   COULTHARD, Curtis Carmel
Curtis was born 6 July 1941.

11(12)224(10)53112   COULTHARD, June Marie
    June was born 4 March 1943.
11(12)224(10)53113   COULTHARD, Marvin David
    Marvin was born 22 November 1949.
11(12)224(10)5312   HICKS, Paul Preston
    Paul was born 13 September 1914.
11(12)224(10)5313   HICKS, Leon Carlisle
    Leon was born 29 September 1916. He married **SMITH**, Dorothy L.
26 December 1939.
11(12)224(10)53131   HICKS, Earl Preston
    Earl was born 26 May 1941.
11(12)224(10)53132   HICKS, Norvell Dennis
    Norvell was born 4 February 1943.
11(12)224(10)53133   HICKS, Leon Carlisle, Jr.
    Leon was born 7 April 1946.
11(12)224(10)53134   HICKS, Clifford Henry
    Clifford was born 3 November 1953.
11(12)224(10)5314   HICKS, Zell Rebecca
    Zell was born 1 December 1918. Zell died 16 February 1930.
11(12)224(10)5315   HICKS, Rodehaver Halsey
    Rodehaver was born 16 February 1921.
11(12)224(10)5316   HICKS, Henry Greene
    Henry was born 14 June 1923. Henry died 4 April 1945.
11(12)224(10)5317   HICKS, June Octavia
    June was born 6 July 1928. She married **COUNTS**, Dennis Reed 15
July 1950.
11(12)224(10)53171   COUNTS, Susan Elizabeth
    Susan was born 3 September 1951.
11(12)224(10)53172   COUNTS, Betty Rebecca
    Betty was born 13 January 1955.
11(12)224(10)53173   COUNTS, Dennis Reed, Jr.
    Dennis was born 17 December 1956.
11(12)224(10)532   HALSEY, William Kyle
    William was born in Fox, VA 7 November 1892. William died 1
October 1939 at 46 years of age.
11(12)224(10)533   HALSEY, Ruth Bryant
    Ruth was born in Fox, VA 1 April 1895. She married **COX**, Fields
Mack 4 November 1914.
11(12)224(10)5331   COX, Mary Bryant
    Mary was born 5 March 1916. She married **ROSE**, Paul W. 9 May
1937. Mary died 7 December 1971 at 55 years of age.
11(12)224(10)53311   ROSE, Betsey Lynn
    Betsey was born 2 October 1941.
11(12)224(10)53312   ROSE, Mary Carol
    Mary was born 10 April 1943.
11(12)224(10)53313   ROSE, |Rose| Dorothy
    |Rose| was born 16 February 1946.

11(12)224(10)53314   ROSE, Paula Ruth
Paula was born 18 July 1952.
11(12)224(10)53315   ROSE, Nancy Jean
Nancy was born 23 April 1956.
11(12)224(10)5332   COX, Nell Rose
Nell was born 22 April 1918.
11(12)224(10)5333   COX, Fields Mack, Jr.
Fields was born 4 February 1921.
11(12)224(10)5334   COX, Bettie Emaline
Bettie was born 10 September 1923.
11(12)224(10)5335   COX, Thomas Melville
Thomas was born 15 October 1930.
11(12)224(10)534   HALSEY, Walker Hale
He married **LAWSON**, Marie. Walker was born in Fox, VA 5 March
1897.
11(12)224(10)5341   HALSEY, Charles Lewis
He married **COVAN**, Dolly Mae.
11(12)224(10)53411   HALSEY, Linda Marie
11(12)224(10)53412   HALSEY, Charles Lewis, Jr.
11(12)224(10)53413   HALSEY, Catherine Lynn
11(12)224(10)5342   HALSEY, Helen Marie
11(12)224(10)5343   HALSEY, Margaret Hope
She married **HAINES**, Donn Vaughn.
11(12)224(10)53431   HAINES, Jess Vaughn
11(12)224(10)53432   HAINES, Jacqueline Marie
11(12)224(10)53433   HAINES, Jerrold Harley
11(12)224(10)535   HALSEY, French Wise
He married **ALBRIGHT**, Claire A.. French was born in Fox, VA 25
February 1899. French died 8 February 1947 at 47 years of age.
11(12)224(10)5351   HALSEY, Virginia Ruth
She married **KOBSIEH**, Donald J.
11(12)224(10)53511   KOBSIEH, Barbara Joan
11(12)224(10)53512   KOBSIEH, Kathryn Louise
11(12)224(10)53513   KOBSIEH, John Harold
11(12)224(10)5352   HALSEY, Billie Hale
He married **BOBULOSKY**, Patricia.
11(12)224(10)53521   HALSEY, Deborah Kay
11(12)224(10)53522   HALSEY, Denise Claire
11(12)224(10)53523   HALSEY, Doreen Rose
11(12)224(10)53524   HALSEY, Robert
11(12)224(10)5353   HALSEY, Robert Harold
11(12)224(10)5354   HALSEY, Jack Wise
He married **SKIDMORE**, Patricia.
11(12)224(10)53541   HALSEY, Elizabeth Ann
11(12)224(10)53542   HALSEY, Jean
11(12)224(10)53543   HALSEY, William Robert
11(12)224(10)53544   HALSEY, Sally Ann

11(12)224(10)536   HALSEY, Lasca Emeline
Lasca was born in Bridle Creek, VA 18 February 1901.
11(12)224(10)537   HALSEY, Thomas Gwynn
Thomas was born in Bridle Creek, VA 4 July 1903.
11(12)224(10)54   HALSEY, Celia Jane
Celia was born 9 April 1865. She married **ROSE**, Ben R. 27 April 1884. Celia died 18 May 1941 at 76 years of age.
11(12)224(10)541   ROSE, Muncie
11(12)224(10)542   ROSE, Birtie
Birtie was born 16 August 1885.
11(12)224(10)543   ROSE, Richard Lee
Richard was born 6 May 1888. Richard died 1 April 1957.
11(12)224(10)544   ROSE, Thomas M.
Thomas was born 18 July 1891. Thomas died 8 November 1918.
11(12)224(10)545   ROSE, Jennie
Jennie was born 29 March 1894. Jennie died 7 January 1956.
11(12)224(10)546   ROSE, Caroline F. 'Callie'
Caroline was born 20 May 1897. Caroline died 7 April 1934.
11(12)224(10)547   ROSE, Walker C.
Walker was born 6 January 1900.
11(12)224(10)548   ROSE, Kyle Cox
His body was interred in Bridle Creek Cem, VA. Kyle was born 10 September 1902. Kyle died circa 1976.
11(12)224(10)6 HALSEY, Greenberry
His body was interred in Oak Hill Cem, VA. He married **HASH**, Drucilla Ann. Greenberry was born 10 December 1842. Greenberry died 10 December 1919 at 77 years of age. Corporal, Company I, 51st Virginia Infranty, Field and Staff (28 June 1861) Grayson County. He went from Private to Second Corporal between 31 October 1861 and 31 October 1862. He began to appear on the Field and Staff muster roll during this time. He was promoted from Second Corporal to First Corporal between 31 October 1862 and 31 December 1862.
11(12)224(10)61   HALSEY, Robena E
She married **ANDERSON**, John C. L. 11 September 1889.
11(12)224(10)611   ANDERSON, Barum
11(12)224(10)612   ANDERSON, Greene
11(12)224(10)613   ANDERSON, Grace
11(12)224(10)614   ANDERSON, Beulah
11(12)224(10)615   ANDERSON, Robert
11(12)224(10)616   ANDERSON, Robena
11(12)224(10)617   ANDERSON, Tommy
11(12)224(10)62   HALSEY, John Ander
John was born 13 September 1871. He married **HASH**, Maggie Robena in Ashe Co., NC, 25 December 1891. John died 30 August 1942.
11(12)224(10)621   HALSEY, Margaret
She married **LAXTON**, Hayden. She married **VAUGHT**, Blaine.
11(12)224(10)622   HALSEY, Christie

Christie was born 25 December 1892. She married **HASH**, Charlie Gleason 25 February 1913.

11(12)224(10)6221   HASH, Ruth Montana
Ruth was born 5 January 1914.

11(12)224(10)6222   HASH, Virginia
Virginia was born 17 March 1915.

11(12)224(10)6223   HASH, Logene
Logene was born 31 August 1916.

11(12)224(10)6224   HASH, Charlotte
Charlotte was born 28 July 1918.

11(12)224(10)6225   HASH, Kelly
Kelly was born 25 May 1920.

11(12)224(10)6226   HASH, June
June was born 18 July 1922.

11(12)224(10)6227   HASH, Susie
Susie was born 26 August 1924.

11(12)224(10)6228   HASH, Kathleen
Kathleen was born 4 May 1928.

11(12)224(10)6229   HASH, John Alex
John was born 9 May 1930.

11(12)224(10)622(10)   HASH, Joseph Dale
Joseph was born 24 June 1932.

11(12)224(10)623   HALSEY, Hardin
Hardin was born 9 March 1895. Hardin died 18 December 1896.

11(12)224(10)624   HALSEY, Creola
Creola was born 23 February 1897. Creola died 25 January 1898.

11(12)224(10)625   HALSEY, Polk
Polk was born 29 May 1899. He married **DELP**, Ruby Dale 24 June 1923. Polk died 16 November 1970 at 71 years of age.

11(12)224(10)626   HALSEY, Senna Viola
Senna was born 3 April 1901. She married **MARTIN**, Sloan 12 June 1923.

11(12)224(10)6261   MARTIN, Euelyn Frances
Euelyn was born 10 May 1924.

11(12)224(10)6262   MARTIN, Dean Lance
Dean was born 9 May 1927.

11(12)224(10)627   HALSEY, Bays M.
His body was interred in Fox Creek, VA. Bays was born 4 May 1906. Bays died 16 February 1992 at 85 years of age.

11(12)224(10)628   HALSEY, Walter R.
Walter was born circa 1907.

11(12)224(10)629   HALSEY, Ovid Emerson
Ovid was born 11 December 1908. He married **DOWELL**, Mattie Faye in Grayson Co., VA, 24 December 1955. Ovid died 22 August 1968.

11(12)224(10)6291   HALSEY, Emerson
Emerson was born 3 June 1957.

11(12)224(10)6292   HALSEY, Dorothy

Dorothy was born 15 December 1958.
11(12)224(10)6293   HALSEY, David Lee
David was born 7 April 1967.
11(12)224(10)62(10)   HALSEY, John Greene
His body was interred in Fox Creek, VA. John was born 19 March 1913. He married **SPENCER**, Ione in Grayson Co., VA, 22 April 1938. John died 2 December 1988 at 75 years of age.
11(12)224(10)62(10)1   HALSEY, Staley Codean
Staley was born 7 February 1939.
11(12)224(10)62(11)   HALSEY, Reba
Reba was born circa 1916. She married **HASH**, Gelene 20 January 1939.
11(12)224(10)62(11)1   HASH, Ronald Emerson
11(12)224(10)62(11)2   HASH, Larry
11(12)224(10)62(11)3   HASH, Robert Lewis
11(12)224(10)63   HALSEY, Leander
Leander was born 13 September 1871. Leander died 5 November 1877 at 6 years of age.
11(12)224(10)64   HALSEY, Lura Ellen
Lura was born 1 February 1874. She married **PARSONS**, Hardin Ellis in Sparta, NC, 28 June 1891. Lura died 6 October 1963.
11(12)224(10)641   PARSONS, Greek
Greek was born 9 May 1892. Greek died 2 February 1965.
11(12)224(10)642   PARSONS, David Crockett
David was born 15 June 1894. David died 9 September 1959.
11(12)224(10)643   PARSONS, Isaac Greene
Isaac was born 12 February 1897. Isaac died 25 January 1957.
11(12)224(10)644   PARSONS, Allie
Allie was born 4 March 1900. Allie died 11 February 1962.
11(12)224(10)645   PARSONS, Mary Stansbury
Mary was born 17 July 1902.
11(12)224(10)646   PARSONS, John Britton
John was born 26 May 1905. John died 17 January 1961.
11(12)224(10)647   PARSONS, Myrtle Kate
Myrtle was born 25 October 1907.
11(12)224(10)648   PARSONS, Mattie Mae
Mattie was born 14 February 1910. Mattie died 20 June 1965.
11(12)224(10)649   PARSONS, Betty Ruth
Betty was born 4 October 1912.
11(12)224(10)64(10)   PARSONS, Hardin Ellis, Jr.
Hardin was born 26 November 1916. Hardin died 18 April 1937.
11(12)224(10)65   HALSEY, Walter Crockett
Walter was born 11 July 1876. He married **HASH**, Myrtle 11 December 1897. Walter died 26 December 1970 at 94 years of age.
11(12)224(10)651   HALSEY, Colonel Lee
Colonel was born 3 October 1899. Colonel died 27 August 1965.
11(12)224(10)652   HALSEY, William Webb

William was born 7 September 1901. He married **YOUNG**, Hattie 24 June 1923.

11(12)224(10)6521   HALSEY, Katherine
Katherine was born 21 July 1924.

11(12)224(10)6522   HALSEY, William Webb
William was born 16 October 1929.

11(12)224(10)653   HALSEY, Lola Audrey
Lola was born 21 October 1903. Lola died November 1987 in Roanoke, VA, at 84 years of age.

11(12)224(10)654   HALSEY, Robert Breece
Robert was born 7 March 1906.

11(12)224(10)655   HALSEY, Ella Mae
Ella was born 29 May 1909. Ella died 10 April 1921.

11(12)224(10)656   HALSEY, Fred
Fred was born 19 August 1911. He married **WAGG**, Annie Mae 25 May 1931. Fred died 30 December 1972 at 61 years of age.

11(12)224(10)6561   HALSEY, Dean
Dean was born 1 March 1932.

11(12)224(10)6562   HALSEY, Elizabeth Louise
Elizabeth was born 16 February 1934. She married **BYRD**, Talmage 11 September 1953. Elizabeth died 4 October 1967 at 33 years of age.

11(12)224(10)65621   BYRD, Joseph
11(12)224(10)65622   BYRD, Jimmy
11(12)224(10)65623   BYRD, William
11(12)224(10)6563   HALSEY, Stanley Hale
Stanley was born 2 March 1936.

11(12)224(10)6564   HALSEY, John Crockett
John was born 21 February 1939.

11(12)224(10)6565   HALSEY, Robert Gleason
Robert was born 15 October 1942.

11(12)224(10)6566   HALSEY, Edwin Louis
Edwin was born 13 February 1945.

11(12)224(10)6567   HALSEY, Earl J.
Earl was born 22 April 1952.

11(12)224(10)6568   HALSEY, Zola Mae
Zola was born 25 February 1955.

11(12)224(10)657   HALSEY, Crockett Carr
Crockett was born 10 September 1913.

11(12)224(10)658   HALSEY, Zollie Irene
Zollie was born 3 January 1919.

11(12)224(10)659   HALSEY, Glenn Byron
Glenn was born 20 April 1921. Glenn died 6 August 1944.

11(12)224(10)65(10)   HALSEY,
He was born circa 1922.

11(12)224(10)66   HALSEY, Dora F.
Dora was born 21 March 1879. She married **PARSONS**, David Johnson in Sparta, NC, 24 December 1894. Dora died 22 September 1964.

11(12)224(10)661   PARSONS, Zollie Burnace
Zollie was born 12 December 1895.

11(12)224(10)662   PARSONS, Isaac Halsey
Isaac was born 12 June 1898. Isaac died 11 March 1902.

11(12)224(10)663   PARSONS, Drucilla Evaline
Drucilla was born 19 September 1900.

11(12)224(10)664   PARSONS, French Joseph
French was born 4 August 1903.

11(12)224(10)665   PARSONS, Victoria Irene
Victoria was born 7 July 1906.

11(12)224(10)666   PARSONS, Della Clyde
Della was born 6 November 1908.

11(12)224(10)667   PARSONS, Robert Hardin
Robert was born 26 June 1911.

11(12)224(10)668   PARSONS, Frances Dora
Frances was born 5 June 1913.

11(12)224(10)669   PARSONS, David Crockett
David was born 14 September 1915.

11(12)224(10)66(10)   PARSONS, Carrie Mae
Carrie was born 4 March 1918.

11(12)224(10)66(11)   PARSONS, Hazel Ruth
Hazel was born 26 April 1921. Hazel died 10 February 1943.

11(12)224(10)67   HALSEY, Cornelia Fuqua
Cornelia was born 29 July 1881. She married **HASH**, Walter Abram
13 October 1900. Cornelia died 1 February 1963 at 81 years of age.

11(12)224(10)671   HASH, Wayne Hatcher
Wayne was born 29 October 1901.

11(12)224(10)672   HASH, Hazel Gladys
Hazel was born 11 March 1905. She married **WOODS**, John Wythe
3 September 1928.

11(12)224(10)6721   WOODS, John Wythe, Jr.
John was born 21 September 1929.

11(12)224(10)6722   WOODS, Walter Ralph
Walter was born 2 December 1931.

11(12)224(10)6723   WOODS, Harold Gray
Harold was born 14 August 1934.

11(12)224(10)6724   WOODS, Sallie Elizabeth
Sallie was born 27 December 1945.

11(12)224(10)673   HASH, Ruth Josephine
Ruth was born 20 April 1908.

11(12)224(10)674   HASH, Albert Garland
Albert was born 9 May 1913.

11(12)224(10)675   HASH, Walter Abram, Jr.
Walter was born 11 April 1921.

11(12)224(10)676   HASH, Elizabeth Ann
Elizabeth was born 18 July 1923. She married **MILES**, John 7
November 1941. Elizabeth died 6 June 1971 at 47 years of age.

11(12)224(10)6761   MILES, Patricia Ann
Patricia was born 2 December 1945. She married **BURRIS**, John
Gordon July 1973.
11(12)224(10)6762   MILES, John Richard
John was born 28 May 1955.
11(12)224(10)68   HALSEY, Myrtle M
Myrtle was born 21 July 1884. Myrtle died 21 July 1958.
11(12)224(10)69   HALSEY, Celia Clyde
Celia was born 14 October 1888. She married **HALSEY**, Vilas
Manning 31 December 1914. Celia died 23 December 1951.
11(12)224(10)691   HALSEY, Ralph Emerson
Ralph was born 26 February 1916.
11(12)224(10)692   HALSEY, Eva Rosamond
Eva was born 15 December 1917. Eva died 15 December 1917.
11(12)224(10)693   HALSEY, Thelma Pauline
Thelma was born 26 October 1918. She married **VAUGHT**, Hobson
T. 23 March 1941.
11(12)224(10)6931   VAUGHT, Harold Eugene
Harold was born 30 November 1946. Harold died 30 November
1946 at less than one year of age.
11(12)224(10)6932   VAUGHT, Shirley Ann
Shirley was born 14 October 1949.
11(12)224(10)6933   VAUGHT, Erdice Sue
Erdice was born 3 March 1953.
11(12)224(10)6934   VAUGHT, Hobson T., Jr.
Hobson was born 12 August 1955.
11(12)224(10)694   HALSEY, Anna Lois
Anna was born 14 August 1921. Anna died 14 August 1921.
11(12)224(10)695   HALSEY, Robert Manning
Robert was born 1 July 1922. Robert died 1 July 1922.
11(12)224(10)696   HALSEY, Talmage Kyle
Talmage was born 2 July 1923. Talmage died 2 July 1923.
11(12)224(10)697   HALSEY, William G.
William was born 16 August 1924. William died 16 August 1924.
11(12)224(10)698   HALSEY, Gwyn
Gwyn was born 5 July 1926.
11(12)224(10)699   HALSEY, Robena Sue
Robena was born 10 June 1930.
11(12)224(11)   HALSEY, William (Bucky) III
William was born in Grayson Co, VA circa 1789. He married **PEAK**,
Juda 27 April 1814. William died 28 August 1849 at 60 years of age.
11(12)224(11)1 HALSEY, Ira Josiah
He married **PARSONS**, Mary. Ira was born 22 April 1815. He
married **MCMILLAN**, Fannie 21 August 1834. Ira died 18 December 1861 in
old homestead, Piney Creek, N.C., at 46 years of age.
11(12)224(11)11   HALSEY, J. E. 'Dock'
He married **WILLIAMS**, Martha M. 25 December 1885.

11(12)224(11)111 HALSEY, George C.
11(12)224(11)12 HALSEY, Theisia
Theisia was born 13 March 1836.
11(12)224(11)13 HALSEY, Franklin Benjamin
Franklin was born 26 June 1838. He married **COX**, Polly Jane 13 April 1865. Franklin died 30 June 1899 at 61 years of age.
11(12)224(11)131 HALSEY, Virginia Florence
Virginia was born in Piney Creek, NC 20 July 1867. She married **HALSEY**, Benjamin Franklin 2 September 1881. Virginia died 19 August 1937 at 70 years of age.
11(12)224(11)132 HALSEY, Fannie
Fannie was born 24 January 1869. She married **OSBORNE**, John Calvin Breckenridge in Grayson Co., VA, 28 January 1885. Fannie died 26 June 1944 in Bridle Creek, VA, at 75 years of age.
11(12)224(11)1321 OSBORNE, Donna
Donna was born 3 June 1886. She married **CHOATE**, Glenn William 20 October 1909.
11(12)224(11)13211 CHOATE, William Paige
William was born in Rockwell, NC 4 August 1910.
11(12)224(11)13212 CHOATE, Pru
Pru was born 25 February 1912.
11(12)224(11)13213 CHOATE, Nell
Nell was born 5 October 1915.
11(12)224(11)1322 OSBORNE, Kyle
His body was interred in Arlington Cemete, VA. Kyle was born 11 December 1888. Kyle died 21 November 1956 at 67 years of age.
11(12)224(11)1323 OSBORNE, Claude
Claude was born 4 July 1892. Claude died 26 February 1955 in Roanoke, VA, at 62 years of age.
11(12)224(11)1324 OSBORNE, Mattie Belle
Mattie was born 5 July 1895. Mattie died 26 May 1966 in Bridle Cr., Cem., VA, at 70 years of age.
11(12)224(11)1325 OSBORNE, Edna
Edna was born 5 September 1902.
11(12)224(11)133 HALSEY, Martha Alice
Martha was born 12 January 1871. She married **WYATT**, William Glenn in Grayson Co., VA, 7 October 1898. Martha died 24 September 1953
11(12)224(11)1331 WYATT, Lola Lougene
Lola was born 11 November 1900. Lola died 7 February 1920 in Roanoke, VA, at 19 years of age.
11(12)224(11)1332 WYATT, Cora Virginia
Cora was born 14 August 1904.
11(12)224(11)1333 WYATT, Gladys Jaunita
Gladys was born in Independence, VA 12 August 1905.
11(12)224(11)134 HALSEY, Maggie Rafenia
She married **SALSO**, Chris. Maggie was born 3 February 1873. She married **WYATT**, Wiley Marshall in Sparta, NC, 14 April 1895.

11(12)224(11)1341   WYATT, Zenna
11(12)224(11)1342   WYATT, Ollie Reed
Ollie was born 11 March 1896.
11(12)224(11)1343   WYATT, Loy Otto
Loy was born 18 March 1898. Loy died December 1927.
11(12)224(11)135   HALSEY, Fielden McTier 'Mack'
Fielden was born 11 May 1874. He married **COX**, Zennobia in Sparta, NC, 13 April 1900. Fielden died 26 March 1954 at 79 years of age.
11(12)224(11)1351   HALSEY, Clarence Nebraska
Clarence was born 6 November 1902. He married **FINNEY**, Ileta in Grayson Co., VA, 25 October 1930. He married **REEVES**, 2 December 1968. Clarence died 9 February 1976 at 73 years of age.
11(12)224(11)13511   HALSEY, Edith Nell
Edith was born 21 June 1931.
11(12)224(11)13512   HALSEY, Hazel
Hazel was born 12 July 1944.
11(12)224(11)1352   HALSEY, Lucille Laska
Lucille was born 31 October 1905. She married **OSBORNE**, Fielden Z. 10 August 1929.
11(12)224(11)13521   OSBORNE, James Perry
James was born 15 August 1931.
11(12)224(11)13522   OSBORNE, Barbara Lucille
Barbara was born 21 June 1935.
11(12)224(11)13523   OSBORNE, Carolyn Virginia
Carolyn was born 10 March 1944.
11(12)224(11)1353   HALSEY, Frank Mack
Frank was born 28 August 1907. He married **WYNNE**, Margaret circa 1939.
11(12)224(11)13531   HALSEY, Frank Mack, Jr.
Frank was born 18 October 1939.
11(12)224(11)13532   HALSEY, Marjorie Mae
Marjorie was born 3 June 1941. She married **COFFEY**, Robert 28 August 1960.
11(12)224(11)135321   COFFEY, Elizabeth Wynne
Elizabeth was born in Kingsport, TN 14 July 1961.
11(12)224(11)135322   COFFEY, Robert Martin
Robert was born in Kingsport, TN 25 October 1963.
11(12)224(11)1354   HALSEY, Guy Wilson
Guy was born 10 June 1914. He married **CHITWOOD**, Jane 7 August 1958.
11(12)224(11)13541   HALSEY, Roger Guy
Roger was born 26 November 1959.
11(12)224(11)13542   HALSEY, William Franklin
William was born in Sparta, NC 27 August 1961.
11(12)224(11)13543   HALSEY, Mark Andrew
Mark was born in Sparta, NC 9 August 1964.
11(12)224(11)13544   HALSEY, Nancy Jane

Nancy was born in Sparta, NC 20 February 1966.
11(12)224(11)1355   HALSEY, Edith Grace
Edith was born 6 May 1916. Edith died 13 August 1920.
11(12)224(11)14   HALSEY, Juda
She married **DIXON**, James Marshall. Juda was born 16 December
1840. Juda died 3 June 1919 at 78 years of age.
11(12)224(11)141   DIXON, Emmett
11(12)224(11)142   DIXON, Andy
11(12)224(11)143   DIXON, Laura
11(12)224(11)144   DIXON, Emma J.
Emma was born in Nathan's Creek, NC (?) 4 July 1861. She married
HALSEY, Charles Lee in Sparta, NC, 2 January 1880. Emma died 22 March
1941 at 79 years of age.
11(12)224(11)145   DIXON, Preston C.
Preston was born 17 July 1864. He married **GOODMAN**, Lola M. 11
October 1883. Preston died 16 May 1941 at 76 years of age.
11(12)224(11)1451   DIXON, Sally
11(12)224(11)1452   DIXON, Caren
11(12)224(11)1453   DIXON, Arthur
11(12)224(11)1454   DIXON, Frank
11(12)224(11)1455   DIXON, Jennie
11(12)224(11)1456   DIXON, Mattie
11(12)224(11)1457   DIXON, Smith
11(12)224(11)1458   DIXON, Annie
11(12)224(11)1459   DIXON, Nellie
11(12)224(11)145(10)   DIXON, Myrtle
11(12)224(11)145(11)   DIXON, Lizzie
11(12)224(11)145(12)   DIXON, Juda M.
Juda was born 21 June 1887. Juda died 9 July 1945.
11(12)224(11)145(13)   DIXON, Marshall
Marshall was born 2 November 1908. Marshall died 5 April 1963.
11(12)224(11)146   DIXON, Wiley Gordon
Wiley was born 20 July 1867. He married **REEVES**, Cessie J. 21
November 1893. Wiley died 11 September 1945 at 78 years of age.
11(12)224(11)1461   DIXON, Nannie
11(12)224(11)1462   DIXON, Conley Chester
11(12)224(11)1463   DIXON, Thomas Walter
11(12)224(11)1464   DIXON, Mazie
11(12)224(11)1465   DIXON, Blanche
11(12)224(11)1466   DIXON, Drucy Mae
Drucy was born 5 October 1895. Drucy died 21 December 1904.
11(12)224(11)1467   DIXON, William A.
William was born 15 January 1900. William died 30 January 1900.
11(12)224(11)147   DIXON, Mollie
She married **COLVARD**, Jesse Reeves. Mollie was born circa 1880.
Mollie died circa 1922.
11(12)224(11)1471   COLVARD, Estle

11(12)224(11)1472   COLVARD, Howard
11(12)224(11)1473   COLVARD, Charlie
11(12)224(11)1474   COLVARD, Russell
11(12)224(11)1475   COLVARD, Neal Dixon
        Neal was born 23 January 1922.
11(12)224(11)148   DIXON, Ollie Bettie
        Ollie was born 11 March 1883. Ollie died 10 July 1885.
11(12)224(11)15   HALSEY, Andrew McMillan
        Andrew was born in Piney Creek, NC 26 July 1843. He married
WYATT, Susan Frances circa 1869. He married WEAVER, Lura 2 April
1901. Andrew died 12 June 1916 in Sinton, TX, at 72 years of age. His
body was interred June 1916 in Kingfisher Cem., Kingfisher, OK.
11(12)224(11)151   HALSEY, Fannie Elizabeth
        Fannie died in Wichita, KS. She married BELL, Harry Herbert.
Fannie was born 15 January 1868.
11(12)224(11)152   HALSEY, Minnie Adella 'Addie'
        Minnie was born in Jackson Co., MO 16 September 1869. She
married SMITH, Ira T. 24 December 1889. Minnie died circa 1948 in
Darrouzett, TX.
11(12)224(11)1521   SMITH, Maggie P.
        Maggie was born in KS October 1890.
11(12)224(11)1522   SMITH, Virgie M.
        Virgie was born in KS November 1892.
11(12)224(11)1523   SMITH, Ninnie E.
        Ninnie was born in OK October 1898.
11(12)224(11)153   HALSEY, Annie Laurie
        Annie was born in Grandview, Jackson Co., MO 14 January 1873.
She married JONES, Benjamin Allen in Kingfisher, OK, December 1891.
Annie died 1 January 1947 in El Monte, Los Angeles Co., CA.
11(12)224(11)154   HALSEY, John (Marshall?) Miller
        He married Alice. John was born in Grandview, MO 10 October
1873. He married GAUNT (DROKE?), Cora Bell circa 1893. John died 17
August 1955 in Grandview, MO, at 81 years of age. John Marshall Halsey
owned the first flour mill and cotton gin in Kansas. He later moved to south
Texas, San Patricia County, near Sinton, where he farmed several hundred
acres of land.
11(12)224(11)1541   HALSEY, Autrey
11(12)224(11)1542   HALSEY, Hope Louise
        Hope was born in Bridgeport, OK 22 July 1898. Hope died 29
October 1987 in San Antonio, TX, at 89 years of age.
11(12)224(11)1543   HALSEY, Opal Ruth
        Opal was born in Bridgeport, OK 12 February 1900. Opal died 2
May 1986 in San Antonio, TX, at 86 years of age.
11(12)224(11)1544   HALSEY, Andrew Martin 'Jack'
        Andrew was born in El Reno, OK 27 May 1907. He married
STAUFFER, Hazel Esther in Sequin, TX, 14 February 1927. Andrew died 6
February 1988 in San Antonio, TX, at 80 years of age.

11(12)224(11)15441   HALSEY, Tommie G. R.
Tommie was born in San Antonio, TX 24 July 1929.
11(12)224(11)15442   HALSEY, Colonel John Terrance
Colonel was born in San Antonio, TX 28 July 1931.
11(12)224(11)15443   HALSEY, Andrew Martin
Andrew was born in San Antonio, TX 25 August 1934.
11(12)224(11)1545   HALSEY, Ervin
Ervin was born in Bridgeport, OK 10 October 1914. Ervin died
February 1947 at 32 years of age.
11(12)224(11)155   HALSEY, Burgess Josiah
He married **CLARKSON**, Mary Susan 'Mayme'. Burgess was born
in Kansas City, MO 30 April 1875. He married **GAUNT**, Ella in
Independence, Jackson Co., MO, 20 December 1905. Burgess died 23
December 1962 in Los Angeles, CA, at 87 years of age.
11(12)224(11)156   HALSEY, Carolina Elizabeth 'Nina'
She married **YOUNT**, Jess. Carolina was born 12 September 1877.
Carolina died 25 July 1940 in Los Angeles, CA, at 62 years of age.
11(12)224(11)157   HALSEY, Joseph Horn
Joseph was born in Viola, Sedgwick Co., KS 21 November 1881. He
married **WILLEY**, Ida Myrtle in Clinton, Custer Co., OK, 11 April 1905.
Joseph died 14 December 1957 in Los Angeles, CA, at 76 years of age. His
body was interred 17 December 1957 in San Pedro, Los Angeles Co., CA.
11(12)224(11)1571   HALSEY, Andrew Raymond
Andrew was born in Butler, Custer Co., OK 2 August 1907. He
married **JACKSON**, Mabel Lorena 1945.
11(12)224(11)15711   HALSEY, Joseph Raymond 'Joe Ray'
He married Vicki. Joseph was born in Perryton, TX circa 1947.
11(12)224(11)157111   HALSEY, Casey
Casey was born 1976.
11(12)224(11)1572   HALSEY, Joseph LeRoy
Joseph was born in Booker, Ochiltree Co., TX 23 January 1923. He
married **SULLIVAN**, Mary Ella 'Faye' in Groom, Carson Co., TX, 14
November 1942. Joseph died 16 April 1969 in Los Angeles, CA, at 46 years
of age. His body was interred 19 April 1969 in Forest Lawn, Glendale, CA.
11(12)224(11)15721   HALSEY, Doris LaRae
Doris was born in Borger, Hutchinson Co., TX 19 January 1944. She
married **BROOKS**, James John in So. Lake Tahoe, CA, 30 March 1968.
11(12)224(11)157211   BROOKS, Joseph Kevin
Joseph was born in Glendale, CA 9 November 1962. Joseph died
11 June 1976 in Plano, TX, at 13 years of age. His body was interred 14
June 1976 in Plano, TX.
11(12)224(11)157212   BROOKS, Taragh Kathryn
She married an unknown person. She married **SCHOM**, Patrick
Paul. Taragh was born in Ojai, Ventura Co., CA 6 April 1971.
11(12)224(11)1572121   BROOKS, Kaitlyn LaRae
Kaitlyn was born in San Antonio, Baxar Co., TX 21 March 1995.
11(12)224(11)157213   BROOKS, Eireann Elizabeth

Eireann was born in Glendale, CA 6 August 1980.

11(12)224(11)157214   BROOKS, James Colin

James was born in Plano, TX 14 June 1983. James died 14 June 1983 in Plano, TX, at less than one year of age. His body was interred June 1983 in Forest Lawn, Glendale, CA.

11(12)224(11)15722   HALSEY, Sharon Lynn

Sharon was born circa 1945.

11(12)224(11)15723   HALSEY, Donna Jo

Donna was born circa 1950.

11(12)224(11)158   HALSEY, Beulah Viola Rose

She married **PEDIGO**, Clyde Thomas. Beulah was born in KS 18 July 1886. Beulah died 9 October 1921 in Bridgeport, Caddo Co., OK.

11(12)224(11)159   HALSEY, Andrew Frank

Andrew was born in Viola, Sedgwick Co., KS 4 January 1891. He married **CASE**, Verna Esther in Iola, KS, 3 March 1917. He married **STEELE**, Vada Martina Ryland in Wichita, KS, 10 December 1950. Andrew died 28 November 1964 in Wichita, KS, at 73 years of age.

11(12)224(11)16   HALSEY, Mary Jane

Mary was born 16 January 1848.

11(12)224(11)17   HALSEY, Fannie

Fannie was born 19 July 1849. She married **GAMBILL**, Jesse A. 6 June 1869. Fannie died 28 April 1910 at 60 years of age.

11(12)224(11)171   GAMBILL, Chasa Ellen 'Cora'

Chasa was born 17 May 1870. She married **HALSEY**, John Hamilton in Sparta, NC, 9 November 1889. Chasa died 3 January 1892.

11(12)224(11)172   GAMBILL, Lucy Jane

She married **WEAVER**, Felix Johnson. Lucy was born 30 April 1873.

11(12)224(11)1721   WEAVER, Fannie 'Faye'

11(12)224(11)1722   WEAVER, Robert Cicero

Robert was born 30 May 1908.

11(12)224(11)1723   WEAVER, Mabel Elizabeth

Mabel was born 18 July 1910.

11(12)224(11)173   GAMBILL, Tincy Ennis

Tincy was born 23 December 1874. Tincy died 28 September 1894.

11(12)224(11)174   GAMBILL, Cynthia Allie

Cynthia was born 7 October 1877. Cynthia died 12 August 1879.

11(12)224(11)175   GAMBILL, James Cicero, Dr.

James was born 3 January 1882. He married **LOWE**, Effie Stewart 2 February 1905. James died 10 January 1942 at 60 years of age.

11(12)224(11)1751   GAMBILL, Lenna Fannie

Lenna was born 3 November 1905.

11(12)224(11)1752   GAMBILL, Jessie Lee

Jessie was born 11 November 1907.

11(12)224(11)1753   GAMBILL, James Vance 'Zebb'

James was born 25 October 1909.

11(12)224(11)1754   GAMBILL, Mary Lucy

Mary was born 1 November 1911.

11(12)224(11)1755   GAMBILL, Ruth Elizabeth
Ruth was born 26 December 1916.
11(12)224(11)1756   GAMBILL, James Cicero, Jr.
James was born 14 May 1921.
11(12)224(11)1757   GAMBILL, Alda Lowe
Alda was born 1 September 1922.
11(12)224(11)1758   GAMBILL, Melba Lowe
Melba was born 1 September 1922.
11(12)224(11)1759   GAMBILL, Effie Lowe
Effie was born 3 July 1926.
11(12)224(11)176   GAMBILL,
He was born 17 July 1885. He died 17 July 1885.
11(12)224(11)18   HALSEY, Sarah Adeline
Sarah was born 18 July 1851. She married **PEAKE**, David C in Sparta, NC, 12 September 1870. Sarah died 6 March 1929.
11(12)224(11)181   PEAKE, Fannie
11(12)224(11)182   PEAKE, Vera Creed 'Nora'
11(12)224(11)183   PEAKE, Etta
Etta was born 7 December 1871. Etta died 18 December 1951.
11(12)224(11)184   PEAKE, Josiah S.
Josiah was born 11 April 1876. Josiah died 16 February 1943.
11(12)224(11)185   PEAKE, Charles
Charles was born circa 1880. Charles died circa 1935 in Rupert, WV.
11(12)224(11)186   PEAKE, John G.
John was born 29 April 1881. John died 5 June 1930.
11(12)224(11)187   PEAKE, Zora Cleatle
Zora was born 19 February 1887. Zora died 5 April 1966.
11(12)224(11)19   HALSEY, Newton C.
He married **PIERCE**, Alice. Newton was born 31 May 1855. Newton died 12 December 1948 at 93 years of age.
11(12)224(11)191   HALSEY, Charles Glenn
He married **HAMPTON**, Versie 13 April 1912.
11(12)224(11)1911   HALSEY, Eleanor Rose
Eleanor was born 27 September 1914.
11(12)224(11)1912   HALSEY, Charles Glenn, Jr.
Charles was born 14 July 1919.
11(12)224(11)192   HALSEY, Fannie Batrice
Fannie was born 27 December 1887. She married **YOUNG**, Luther 5 May 1912.
11(12)224(11)1921   YOUNG, Arthur Willard
Arthur was born 10 April 1913. Arthur died 16 July 1959.
11(12)224(11)1922   YOUNG, Edna
Edna was born 28 January 1915.
11(12)224(11)1923   YOUNG, Lloyd
He married **ROSS**, Virginia. Lloyd was born 11 March 1917.
11(12)224(11)19231   YOUNG, Franklin

11(12)224(11)19232   YOUNG, Frances Geneive
11(12)224(11)19233   YOUNG, Joseph
11(12)224(11)19234   YOUNG, Charles
11(12)224(11)1924   YOUNG, Donald
 Donald was born 5 August 1919. He married **MOSS**, Eula 20 January 1945.
11(12)224(11)19241   YOUNG, Donald Gene
11(12)224(11)19242   YOUNG, Gerald
11(12)224(11)19243   YOUNG, Regena
11(12)224(11)1925   YOUNG, Eva
 Eva was born 28 August 1923. She married **GREER**, Arthur 11 January 1941.
11(12)224(11)19251   GREER, Donald Richard
 Donald was born 9 April 1943.
11(12)224(11)19252   GREER, Michael Ray
 Michael was born 17 May 1953.
11(12)224(11)193   HALSEY, Estel Carley
 Estel was born 18 July 1889. Estel died 9 June 1898.
11(12)224(11)194   HALSEY, Mary Maletha
 Mary was born 31 January 1892. She married **YOUNG**, Harvey Otis 7 October 1919.
11(12)224(11)1941   YOUNG, Elmer Carl
 Elmer was born 26 July 1920.
11(12)224(11)1942   YOUNG, Mildred Ruth
 Mildred was born 30 December 1922.
11(12)224(11)1943   YOUNG, Burl Wayne
 Burl was born 22 July 1925.
11(12)224(11)1944   YOUNG, Gurald Harding
 Gurald was born 4 October 1927.
11(12)224(11)1945   YOUNG, Paul Otis
 Paul was born 1 March 1933.
11(12)224(11)195   HALSEY, Wayne Mack
 Wayne was born 6 September 1894. He married **PASLEY**, Dora Evelyn in Grayson Co., VA, 4 June 1919. Wayne died 6 March 1981.
11(12)224(11)1951   HALSEY, Bayne
11(12)224(11)1952   HALSEY, Alfred
11(12)224(11)1953   HALSEY, Doris
11(12)224(11)1954   HALSEY, Blanche
11(12)224(11)1955   HALSEY, Louise
11(12)224(11)1956   HALSEY, Edith
11(12)224(11)1957   HALSEY, Thelma
11(12)224(11)1958   HALSEY, Hilton
 Hilton was born 5 April 1920.
11(12)224(11)1959   HALSEY, Wayne Warren
 Wayne was born in Landenberg, PA 21 August 1933. He married **HEATON**, Eileen May in Newark, DE, 12 November 1966.
11(12)224(11)19591   HALSEY, David Warren

David was born in Wilmington, DE 11 August 1971.
11(12)224(11)19592   HALSEY, Brian Keith
Brian was born in Wilmington, DE 27 August 1973.
11(12)224(11)196   HALSEY, Claude Swanson
Claude was born 21 July 1897. He married **HALSEY**, Lora Maude in Grayson Co., VA, 6 June 1918.
11(12)224(11)1961   HALSEY, Reba Lorraine
Reba was born 6 January 1920.
11(12)224(11)1962   HALSEY, Howard
Howard was born 29 April 1926.
11(12)224(11)1963   HALSEY, Lewis Gale
Lewis was born 15 June 1929. He married **BOGGS**, Beverly 29 September 1951.
11(12)224(11)1964   HALSEY, Delbert
Delbert was born 1 March 1942.
11(12)224(11)197   HALSEY, Zenna Lou
She married **MCGUIRE**, Charles Henry. Zenna was born 11 June 1900.
11(12)224(11)1971   MCGUIRE, Charles Eugene
Charles was born 4 May 1922.
11(12)224(11)1972   MCGUIRE, Alice Wilson
Alice was born 18 March 1924.
11(12)224(11)1973   MCGUIRE, Kettella Jewell
Kettella was born 13 October 1926.
11(12)224(11)198   HALSEY, Pressie
Pressie was born 6 December 1906.
11(12)224(11)199   HALSEY, Susie
Susie was born 18 July 1908.
11(12)224(11)1(10)   HALSEY, Victoria Ellen
She married **OSBORNE**, Enoch Senter. Victoria was born 11 May 1857. Victoria died 7 July 1889 at 32 years of age.
 11(12)224(11)1(10)1   OSBORNE, Mollie
She married **HAYES**, Montgomery L.. Mollie was born 21 October 1888.
11(12)224(11)1(10)11   HAYES, Windsor
Windsor was born 31 October 1910.
11(12)224(11)1(10)12   HAYES, Archie Dean
Archie was born 26 January 1912.
11(12)224(11)1(10)13   HAYES, Earl Osbourne
Earl was born 24 October 1913.
11(12)224(11)1(10)14   HAYES, Harold Windell
Harold was born 23 July 1917. Harold died 17 December 1923.
11(12)224(11)1(10)15   HAYES,
She was born 23 September 1919. She died 23 September 1919.
11(12)224(11)1(10)16   HAYES, Foxie Marshall
Foxie was born 16 December 1919.
11(12)224(11)1(10)17   HAYES, Edwin Needham

Edwin was born 4 September 1924.

11(12)224(11)1(10)18   HAYES, Jojnsie Elizabeth

Jojnsie was born 29 October 1926.

11(12)224(11)1(11)   HALSEY, John Monroe

John was born 8 March 1861. He married **YOUNG**, Lettie Sedalia 4 December 1883. John died 28 November 1926 in Grant, VA.

11(12)224(11)1(11)1   HALSEY, Lula Victoria

Lula was born 12 October 1884. She married **HASH**, Volney Wythe in Grayson County, VA, 27 September 1905. Lula died 15 February 1971.

11(12)224(11)1(11)11   HASH, Hazel Beatrice

Hazel was born circa 1906.

11(12)224(11)1(11)12   HASH, Kathleen Watts

Kathleen was born circa 1908. Kathleen died circa 1918.

11(12)224(11)1(11)13   HASH, John Wythe

John was born circa 1909.

11(12)224(11)1(11)14   HASH, Volney Wade

Volney was born 1 December 1913.

11(12)224(11)1(11)15   HASH, Donald H.

Donald was born circa 1917.

11(12)224(11)1(11)2   HALSEY, Jincy Alma

Jincy was born 24 September 1887. She married **WAGG**, James W. 15 January 1914.

11(12)224(11)1(11)21   WAGG, Hale

Hale died 11 December 1934.

11(12)224(11)1(11)22   WAGG, Edward

11(12)224(11)1(11)3   HALSEY, Virginia Evelyn

Virginia was born 17 July 1890. She married **BLEVENS**, John Franklin 10 May 1907. Virginia died 2 May 1965 at 74 years of age.

11(12)224(11)1(11)31   BLEVENS, Richard Allen

Richard was born in Welch, WV.

11(12)224(11)1(11)32   BLEVENS, Mark Stephen

11(12)224(11)1(11)33   BLEVENS, Phillips

11(12)224(11)1(11)34   BLEVENS, Carol Regina

11(12)224(11)1(11)35   BLEVENS, Clarence Bryan

Clarence was born 23 July 1908. Clarence died 1 January 1939.

11(12)224(11)1(11)36   BLEVENS, John Dale

He married **DEWAIN**, Rose. John was born 19 March 1912. He married **COWLING**, Evelyn circa 1942. He married **GILSTRAP**, Hazel circa 1949.

11(12)224(11)1(11)37   BLEVENS, Virginia Kathleen

Virginia was born 18 September 1921. She married **REYNOLDS**, George Luther 16 September 1944.

11(12)224(11)1(11)371   REYNOLDS, Barbara Jane

Barbara was born in Bluefield, WV 11 October 1949.

11(12)224(11)1(11)372   REYNOLDS, Lance Carlton

Lance was born in Kissimmee, FL 31 May 1954.

11(12)224(11)1(11)38   BLEVENS, Wade Jennings

Wade was born 28 May 1926.

11(12)224(11)1(11)4   HALSEY, Cleo Maude
Cleo was born 9 February 1893. She married **GOODSON**, Elijah
Jefferson, Sr. 15 March 1919. Cleo died 3 December 1975.

11(12)224(11)1(11)41   GOODSON, Elijah Jefferson

11(12)224(11)1(11)42   GOODSON, Tracy Ann

11(12)224(11)1(11)43   GOODSON, Marvin Coleman
Marvin was born 28 May 1921.

11(12)224(11)1(11)5   HALSEY, Maye Bryan
Maye was born 23 January 1897.

11(12)224(11)1(11)6   HALSEY, Lola Faye
Lola was born 11 April 1901. She married **TILGHMAN**, Stanley 9
October 1920.

11(12)224(11)1(11)7   HALSEY, Hazel Adelaide
She married **WHITE**, Charles Columbus. She married **ADAMS**,
Harry. Hazel was born 12 September 1903.

11(12)224(11)1(11)71   WHITE, Regina Darleen
She married Don. She married **SMITH**, Bill. Regina was born
February 1925.

11(12)224(11)1(11)711   Stephen

11(12)224(11)1(11)712   Leslie

11(12)224(11)1(11)713   SMITH, Lisa

11(12)224(11)1(11)714   SMITH, Kim

11(12)224(11)1(11)72   WHITE, Eleanor Hope
She married **ANTONACCI**, Joe Louis. She married **BRYTE**, William.
Eleanor was born February 1926.

11(12)224(11)1(11)721   ANTONACCI, Michael Joseph

11(12)224(11)1(11)722   BRYTE, Beverly Sue

11(12)224(11)1(11)723   BRYTE, Stephen Douglas

11(12)224(11)1(11)8   HALSEY, John Kent
He married **JOHNSON**, Mildred. John was born 20 June 1907.
John died 21 February 1965 at 57 years of age.

11(12)224(11)1(11)81   HALSEY, Kenneth

11(12)224(11)1(11)82   HALSEY, Stanley

11(12)224(11)1(11)83   HALSEY, Kermit

11(12)224(11)1(11)84   HALSEY, Johnnie

11(12)224(11)1(11)85   HALSEY, Jaunita

11(12)224(11)1(11)86   HALSEY, Dolores

11(12)224(11)1(11)87   HALSEY, Marvin

11(12)224(11)1(11)88   HALSEY, Mary

11(12)224(11)1(11)89   HALSEY, Melvin

11(12)224(11)1(11)8(10)   HALSEY, Roland

11(12)224(11)1(11)8(11)   HALSEY, Edwin

11(12)224(11)2 HALSEY, Caswell
Caswell was born 17 April 1818. He married **MCMILLAN**, Mahala
26 May 1836. Caswell died 27 October 1905 at 87 years of age.

11(12)224(11)21   HALSEY, William

He married **EDWARDS**, Phoebe. William was born 20 November 1837. William died 12 June 1913 at 75 years of age.

11(12)224(11)211   HALSEY, America J.

America was born in Piney Creek, NC 18 February 1861. She married **HALSEY**, William 25 December 1882. America died 7 November 1916 at 55 years of age.

11(12)224(11)212   HALSEY, Ellen Lee

Her body was interred in Fox Cr. Cemetery, VA. She married **REEVES**, George. Ellen was born in Piney Creek, NC 30 September 1863. Ellen died 30 August 1947 at 83 years of age.

11(12)224(11)2121   REEVES, Vella

11(12)224(11)2122   REEVES, John Mack

John was born 8 September 1892. He married **BEDWELL**, Nina Blanche 6 May 1922. John died 7 July 1954 in Fox, VA, at 61 years of age.

11(12)224(11)21221   REEVES, Ralph B.

Ralph was born 3 February 1923.

11(12)224(11)21222   REEVES, George Mack

George was born 17 January 1925.

11(12)224(11)21223   REEVES, Fred Lee

Fred was born 4 October 1927.

11(12)224(11)21224   REEVES, Clara Ruth

Clara was born 22 January 1930.

11(12)224(11)2123   REEVES, Walter

Walter was born 25 January 1894. Walter died 21 October 1922 in Fox, VA, at 28 years of age.

11(12)224(11)2124   REEVES, Dewey

Dewey was born circa 1898. Dewey died circa 1959.

11(12)224(11)213   HALSEY, George Vance 'Dick'

George was born in Piney Creek, NC 27 January 1866. He married **HALSEY**, Ada Selina in Ashe Co., NC, 25 March 1885.

11(12)224(11)214   HALSEY, John Elmore

John was born in Piney Creek, NC 4 July 1868. He married **WINGATE**, Mae in Sparta, NC, 22 August 1897. John died 10 September 1937 at 69 years of age.

11(12)224(11)2141   HALSEY, Nina Fay

Nina was born 23 July 1898. She married **WARD**, Clarence S. 25 June 1919.

11(12)224(11)21411   WARD, Stewart Elmore

Stewart was born 29 May 1921.

11(12)224(11)21412   WARD, June Elizabeth

June was born 5 June 1926.

11(12)224(11)2142   HALSEY, Paul

Paul was born 2 February 1900.

11(12)224(11)2143   HALSEY, Blanche

Blanche was born 1 March 1902. She married **EDWARD**, Ellege Y. 7 November 1925.

11(12)224(11)21431   EDWARD, Roy Ellege

Roy was born 17 February 1927. Roy died 3 May 1931.
11(12)224(11)21432   EDWARD, Robert Carey
He married **DAVIS**, Virginia. Robert was born 7 April 1937.
11(12)224(11)2144   HALSEY, Kate
Kate was born 20 April 1904. She married **CLARK**, William Royston
4 April 1925.
11(12)224(11)21441   CLARK, William Royston, Jr.
William was born 16 September 1927. William died 17 September
1927 at less than one year of age.
11(12)224(11)21442   CLARK, Joan
Joan was born 2 November 1928.
11(12)224(11)21443   CLARK, Richard Edward
Richard was born 3 June 1932.
11(12)224(11)2145   HALSEY, Ruby
Ruby was born 3 June 1907. She married **CAULFORD**, Byron H. 9
September 1927.
11(12)224(11)21451   CAULFORD, Jean
Jean was born 8 June 1928.
11(12)224(11)21452   CAULFORD, Mary Joyce
Mary was born 15 September 1931.
11(12)224(11)21453   CAULFORD, Billie Marie
Billie was born 6 September 1933.
11(12)224(11)21454   CAULFORD, Martha Ann
Martha was born 10 February 1936. Martha died 20 May 1938.
11(12)224(11)21455   CAULFORD, Winona
Winona was born 4 February 1938.
11(12)224(11)2146   HALSEY, Pearl
Pearl was born in Tilden, Nebr. 8 April 1910.
11(12)224(11)215   HALSEY, Fields M.
Fields was born in Piney Creek, NC 3 September 1870. Fields died
3 April 1890 at 19 years of age.
11(12)224(11)216   HALSEY, Charles A.
Charles was born in Piney Creek, NC 5 April 1873. He married
FENDER, Cornelia V. in Sparta, NC, 11 November 1899. Charles died 5
June 1920 at 47 years of age.
11(12)224(11)2161   HALSEY, Carl
Carl was born 24 August 1900. Carl died 9 July 1901.
11(12)224(11)2162   HALSEY,
He was born 25 April 1902. He died 25 April 1902.
11(12)224(11)2163   HALSEY, Mariam Mecca
Mariam was born 30 April 1903.
11(12)224(11)2164   HALSEY, William Dwight
William was born 1 October 1905.
11(12)224(11)2165   HALSEY, Ruth
Ruth was born 26 June 1907.
11(12)224(11)2166   HALSEY, Eugene
Eugene was born 28 March 1910.

11(12)224(11)2167   HALSEY, Carrie G.
Carrie was born 5 March 1913.
11(12)224(11)2168   HALSEY, Eulah
Eulah was born 24 July 1917.
11(12)224(11)217   HALSEY, Willie Reed
Willie was born in Piney Creek, NC 7 October 1876. Willie died 24 June 1899 at 22 years of age.
11(12)224(11)218   HALSEY, Edgar Franklin
Edgar was born in Piney Creek, NC 20 April 1880. He married **STANFORD**, Nancy Jan 22 January 1904. Edgar died circa 1951.
11(12)224(11)2181   HALSEY, Zita Lee
Zita was born 5 June 1905. She married **PUCKETT**, Walter 26 October 1926.
11(12)224(11)21811   PUCKETT, Ralph Gaines
Ralph was born 28 July 1933.
11(12)224(11)21812   PUCKETT, Donald Lee
Donald was born 19 March 1942.
11(12)224(11)2182   HALSEY, William Dean
William was born 18 September 1907. He married **GAMBILL**, Mary Blanche 4 August 1944.
11(12)224(11)21821   HALSEY, Robert Gambill
Robert was born 11 January 1947.
11(12)224(11)21822   HALSEY, James Dean
James was born 26 June 1949.
11(12)224(11)2183   HALSEY, Bays Franklin
Bays was born 7 December 1909. He married **WILKINS**, Mary 13 September 1947.
11(12)224(11)21831   HALSEY, Iris Jane
Iris was born 18 January 1949.
11(12)224(11)21832   HALSEY, Rita Ann
Rita was born 27 February 1951.
11(12)224(11)2184   HALSEY, Robert Hale
Robert was born 2 August 1912.
11(12)224(11)2185   HALSEY, Ava Ruth
Ava was born 22 June 1914. She married **BUSIC**, Clint 17 April 1935.
11(12)224(11)21851   BUSIC, Nancy Dora
Nancy was born 2 May 1939.
11(12)224(11)21852   BUSIC, Kathy Lee
Kathy was born 28 January 1941.
11(12)224(11)21853   BUSIC, William Franklin
William was born 5 March 1946.
11(12)224(11)21854   BUSIC, Barbara Lynn
Barbara was born 22 February 1948.
11(12)224(11)2186   HALSEY, Ella Jean
Ella was born 6 May 1916. She married **PERRY**, Bruce 9 February 1935.

11(12)224(11)21861   PERRY, Jimmie Lewis
Jimmie was born 10 February 1936. Jimmie died 4 August 1964.
11(12)224(11)21862   PERRY, Linda Ann
Linda was born 13 May 1942.
11(12)224(11)2187   HALSEY, Joseph McDowell
Joseph was born 28 April 1918. He married **REEVES**, Rosamond
16 February 1945.
11(12)224(11)21871   HALSEY, Larry Edward
Larry was born 23 July 1946.
11(12)224(11)21872   HALSEY, Patsy Gale
Patsy was born 4 October 1948.
11(12)224(11)21873   HALSEY, Pamelia Ailene
Pamelia was born 27 October 1952.
11(12)224(11)22   HALSEY, John Reed
He married **DIXON**, Mary Polly 'Pop'. John was born 14 February
1840. John died 1 April 1871 at 31 years of age.
11(12)224(11)221   HALSEY, Robert Lee
Robert was born in Piney Creek, NC 31 May 1864. He married
SENTER, Ellen E. 3 October 1886. Robert died 14 April 1952.
11(12)224(11)2211   HALSEY, Mamie Mildred
She married **WILLEY**, Ben. Mamie was born 8 August 1887. Mamie
died 18 March 1909 at 21 years of age.
11(12)224(11)22111   WILLEY, Gordon
Gordon was born 3 July 1906. Gordon died 1 September 1928.
11(12)224(11)22112   WILLEY, Mildred Cochrane
Mildred was born 3 March 1909.
11(12)224(11)2212   HALSEY, Calvin Orla
Calvin was born 7 April 1889. He married **MICKLE**, Clara 12 August
1907.
11(12)224(11)22121   HALSEY, Letha Cross
Letha was born 5 April 1908. Letha died 13 February 1961.
11(12)224(11)22122   HALSEY, Lea
Lea was born 5 April 1908.
11(12)224(11)22123   HALSEY, Eugene
Eugene was born 23 October 1918.
11(12)224(11)2213   HALSEY, Andrew Clyde
Andrew was born 3 April 1891. He married **WILLIAMS**, Jessie
Caroline 23 November 1909.
11(12)224(11)22131   HALSEY, Irene Dilts
Irene was born 24 September 1911.
11(12)224(11)22132   HALSEY, Wayne
Wayne was born 26 November 1913.
11(12)224(11)22133   HALSEY, William Clyde
William was born 10 October 1922.
11(12)224(11)22134   HALSEY, Jack Lee
Jack was born 13 January 1929.
11(12)224(11)2214   HALSEY, Roy Addison

Roy was born 19 February 1894. He married **SMALLEY**, Hallie Opal 6 October 1915.

11(12)224(11)22141   HALSEY, Dorothy Harnden
Dorothy was born 20 October 1916.

11(12)224(11)22142   HALSEY, Raymond
Raymond was born 21 February 1920.

11(12)224(11)22143   HALSEY, Richard
Richard was born 26 January 1924.

11(12)224(11)22144   HALSEY, Carole Butcher
Carole was born 20 October 1926.

11(12)224(11)2215   HALSEY, Maude Alice
Maude was born 3 March 1897. She married **CROTHERS**, Clarence Earl 23 December 1912.

11(12)224(11)22151   CROTHERS, Melvin
Melvin was born 11 March 1915.

11(12)224(11)22152   CROTHERS, Delsie Lorene
Delsie was born 6 April 1917.

11(12)224(11)22153   CROTHERS, Marjorie Ruth
Marjorie was born 10 September 1920. Marjorie died 11 April 1929.

11(12)224(11)22154   CROTHERS, Donna Lee
Donna was born 6 November 1931.

11(12)224(11)2216   HALSEY, Rosa Virginia
She married **MARTIN**, Fred. She married **LA BELLE**, Ed. Rosa was born 3 July 1899.

11(12)224(11)22161   MARTIN, Virginia
Virginia was born 13 March 1916.

11(12)224(11)22162   MARTIN, Leonard
Leonard was born 17 November 1919. Leonard died 28 April 1964.

11(12)224(11)22163   MARTIN, Maxine
Maxine was born 6 July 1921.

11(12)224(11)2217   HALSEY, Nellie Clair
Nellie was born 19 July 1901. She married **HOLT**, Mayberry 8 August 1917.

11(12)224(11)22171   HOLT, Goldie Mae
Goldie was born 11 January 1918. Goldie died 1 February 1935.

11(12)224(11)22172   HOLT, Mary Ellen
Mary was born 24 March 1921.

11(12)224(11)22173   HOLT, Ruby
Ruby was born 20 November 1922. Ruby died 12 September 1963.

11(12)224(11)22174   HOLT, Imogene
Imogene was born 11 November 1924.

11(12)224(11)22175   HOLT, Bettie Lee
Bettie was born 26 August 1926.

11(12)224(11)22176   HOLT, Robert Dale
Robert was born 11 February 1929.

11(12)224(11)22177   HOLT, Paul Ray
Paul was born 2 May 1933.

11(12)224(11)2218   HALSEY, Ruth Edna
She married **HOLT**, George. Ruth was born 25 January 1904. Ruth died 26 September 1961 at 57 years of age.
11(12)224(11)22181   HOLT, James
James was born 23 March 1923.
11(12)224(11)22182   HOLT, Peggy De
Peggy was born 14 October 1924.
11(12)224(11)22183   HOLT, Max
Max was born 6 October 1930.
11(12)224(11)22184   HOLT, Shirley
Shirley was born 13 May 1936.
11(12)224(11)2219   HALSEY, Roberta Elaine
Roberta was born 5 March 1906. She married **ROSS**, Delbert 3 March 1921. She married **HIGGINS**, John 13 March 1943.
11(12)224(11)22191   ROSS, Jeanne
Jeanne was born 19 November 1922.
11(12)224(11)222   HALSEY, Virginia
Virginia was born in Piney Creek, NC 5 January 1865. She married **MCMILLAN**, Drura R. Huston in Sparta, NC, 23 September 1883. Virginia died 17 May 1950 in Flat Ridge, VA, at 85 years of age.
11(12)224(11)2221   MCMILLAN, Grover Cleveland
Grover was born 1 November 1884. He married **MOXLEY**, Cora Ennice 27 February 1908. Grover died 15 July 1972 at 87 years of age.
11(12)224(11)22211   MCMILLAN, R. Gwyn
R. was born 3 January 1909. R. died 30 November 1916.
11(12)224(11)22212   MCMILLAN, Archie Martin
Archie was born 4 September 1910. Archie died 20 February 1973.
11(12)224(11)22213   MCMILLAN, Hazel Virginia
Hazel was born 13 July 1912.
11(12)224(11)22214   MCMILLAN, Mary Darene
Mary was born 26 November 1914.
11(12)224(11)22215   MCMILLAN, Roy Dean
Roy was born 4 February 1917.
11(12)224(11)22216   MCMILLAN, Ivory Malissa
Ivory was born 3 February 1919.
11(12)224(11)22217   MCMILLAN, Mildred Cleaver
Mildred was born 5 December 1920.
11(12)224(11)22218   MCMILLAN, Infant
Infant was born 20 October 1922. Infant died 20 October 1922.
11(12)224(11)22219   MCMILLAN, Infant
Infant was born 20 October 1922. Infant died 20 October 1922.
11(12)224(11)2221(10) MCMILLAN, Gilbert Greek
Gilbert was born 28 November 1923.
11(12)224(11)2221(11) MCMILLAN, Kyle Houston
Kyle was born 2 December 1925. Kyle died 8 June 1933.
11(12)224(11)2221(12) MCMILLAN, Ruby Lenora
Ruby was born 1 April 1929.

11(12)224(11)2222   MCMILLAN, Rudolph Faw
Rudolph was born 27 October 1886. He married **MOXLEY**, Rebecca
Ann in Sparta, NC, 2 July 1911. Rudolph died 3 January 1963.
11(12)224(11)22221   MCMILLAN, Faye
11(12)224(11)22222   MCMILLAN, Arnie
Arnie was born 22 March 1911.
11(12)224(11)22223   MCMILLAN, Stella
Stella was born 20 September 1912.
11(12)224(11)22224   MCMILLAN, Infant
Infant was born 20 November 1914. Infant died 20 November 1914.
11(12)224(11)22225   MCMILLAN, Mary
Mary was born 22 November 1917.
11(12)224(11)22226   MCMILLAN, Arlie Ray
Arlie was born 16 July 1921.
11(12)224(11)2223   MCMILLAN, Ollie Matilda
Ollie was born 12 October 1888.
11(12)224(11)2224   MCMILLAN, Polly Mahala
Polly was born 12 October 1888. Polly died 27 December 1888.
11(12)224(11)23   HALSEY, Ira Marshall
Ira was born 17 October 1842. He married **WHITEHEAD**, Amanda
in Sparta, NC, 5 August 1866. Ira died 6 October 1890 at 47 years of age.
11(12)224(11)231   HALSEY, Mary Jane
Mary was born in Piney Creek, NC 8 July 1867. She married **COX**,
Morgan L. 2 November 1884. Mary died 18 May 1960 in Bridle Creek, VA
(?), at 92 years of age.
11(12)224(11)2311   COX, Polly Ann
Polly was born 29 May 1888. Polly died 27 May 1890.
11(12)224(11)2312   COX, Olga
Olga was born 9 June 1890.
11(12)224(11)2313   COX, Willie
Willie was born 12 February 1892.
11(12)224(11)2314   COX, Cora Lee
Cora was born 12 January 1894.
11(12)224(11)2315   COX, Dora
Dora was born 15 November 1895. Dora died 14 February 1921.
11(12)224(11)2316   COX, Munsey
Munsey was born 15 December 1895.
11(12)224(11)2317   COX, Pearl
Pearl was born 9 March 1899. Pearl died 8 September 1973.
11(12)224(11)2318   COX, Oscar
Oscar was born 6 July 1902.
11(12)224(11)2319   COX, Estel
Estel was born 25 October 1905.
11(12)224(11)231(10)   COX, (Infant)
(Infant) was born circa 1907.
11(12)224(11)232   HALSEY, Nancy E.
Nancy was born in Piney Creek, NC 14 October 1869. Nancy died

February 1870 at less than one year of age.
11(12)224(11)233   HALSEY, Laura
Laura was born in Piney Creek, NC 25 August 1872. She married
FENDER, W. A. 'Bud' 19 September 1894.
11(12)224(11)2331   FENDER, Fred
11(12)224(11)2332   FENDER, William
11(12)224(11)2333   FENDER, Reba
11(12)224(11)2334   FENDER, Bruce
Bruce was born in Sparta, NC 10 March 1895.
11(12)224(11)2335   FENDER, Paul
Paul was born 13 July 1898.
11(12)224(11)2336   FENDER, Ben
Ben was born 16 February 1903.
11(12)224(11)234   HALSEY, Alex Addison
Alex was born in Piney Creek, NC 27 September 1874. He married
FENDER, Sue in Sparta, NC, 17 January 1891. Alex died 14 March 1956.
11(12)224(11)2341   HALSEY, Gertrude Vee
Gertrude was born 14 January 1895.
11(12)224(11)2342   HALSEY, Clarence Bayard
Clarence was born 23 March 1897.
11(12)224(11)2343   HALSEY, Wheeler Platt
Wheeler was born 30 April 1899.
11(12)224(11)2344   HALSEY, Laura Nadine
Laura was born 28 December 1900.
11(12)224(11)2345   HALSEY, Armond
Armond was born 20 February 1904. Armond died 4 August 1964.
11(12)224(11)2346   HALSEY, Doris
Doris was born 4 August 1914.
11(12)224(11)235   HALSEY, Ida
Ida was born in Piney Creek, NC 28 July 1881. She married MABE,
Rufus Monroe 'Boss' in Grayson Co., VA, 28 August 1900. Ida died 21 May
1962 at 80 years of age.
11(12)224(11)2351   MABE, Loyd Paul
Loyd was born 8 February 1901. Loyd died December 1962.
11(12)224(11)2352   MABE, Lonnie Marshall
Lonnie was born 30 August 1902.
11(12)224(11)2353   MABE, Vella
Vella was born 22 July 1909.
11(12)224(11)24   HALSEY, Narcissa 'Sessa'
Narcissa was born 14 January 1845. She married GAMBILL,
William S. 7 March 1869. Narcissa died 3 June 1913 at 68 years of age.
11(12)224(11)241   GAMBILL, Etta Mae
Etta was born 31 May 1870. She married REEVES, Van Worthy in
Sparta, NC, 30 November 1890. Etta died 17 September 1953.
11(12)224(11)2411   REEVES, William Lester
William was born 7 November 1891. William died 23 April 1962.
11(12)224(11)2412   REEVES, George Carl

George was born 21 January 1893. George died 26 January 1960.
11(12)224(11)2413   REEVES, Carrie Clea
Carrie was born 9 March 1894. Carrie died 4 June 1974.
11(12)224(11)2414   REEVES, Ethel Maie
Ethel was born 10 January 1896. Ethel died 15 January 1966.
11(12)224(11)2415   REEVES, Lon Mc
Lon was born 9 April 1898.
11(12)224(11)2416   REEVES, Robert DeFaw
Robert was born 3 March 1900. Robert died 29 August 1902.
11(12)224(11)2417   REEVES, Paul Lee
Paul was born 23 April 1902. Paul died 28 April 1966.
11(12)224(11)2418   REEVES, Lelia Rebecca
Lelia was born 3 April 1904.
11(12)224(11)2419   REEVES, Octavia Goode
Octavia was born 21 July 1909.
11(12)224(11)242   GAMBILL, Mack F.
He married **CAUDILL**, Mallie L.. Mack was born 18 July 1872.
11(12)224(11)2421   GAMBILL, Bruce
11(12)224(11)2422   GAMBILL, Ruth
11(12)224(11)2423   GAMBILL, Leff
11(12)224(11)243   GAMBILL, Lonnie Lee
Lonnie was born 30 May 1875. He married **TAYLOR**, Lavonna
Cordella 3 July 1901. Lonnie died 4 January 1940 at 64 years of age.
11(12)224(11)2431   GAMBILL, Paul
11(12)224(11)2432   GAMBILL, Blan
11(12)224(11)2433   GAMBILL, Blanche
11(12)224(11)2434   GAMBILL, Treva
11(12)224(11)2435   GAMBILL, Clyde
Clyde was born 11 March 1899. Clyde died 28 September 1928.
11(12)224(11)2436   GAMBILL, Pearl
Pearl was born 19 February 1901.
11(12)224(11)2437   GAMBILL, Kyle
Kyle was born 15 April 1904.
11(12)224(11)244   GAMBILL, Mattie Eudora 'Dora'
Mattie was born 28 January 1879. She married **EDWARDS**, John
Robert 1 February 1899. Mattie died 16 June 1956 at 77 years of age.
11(12)224(11)2441   EDWARDS, Edna
Edna was born 19 June 1905.
11(12)224(11)2442   EDWARDS, John Mc
John was born 5 June 1907.
11(12)224(11)245   GAMBILL, Ollie Mae
Ollie was born 4 December 1880. She married **PORTER**, Floyd
Arthur 14 January 1903. Ollie died 18 March 1925 at 44 years of age.
11(12)224(11)2451   PORTER, Verna Pauline
Verna was born 8 January 1906.
11(12)224(11)2452   PORTER, Kate Lee
Kate was born 26 March 1907.

11(12)224(11)2453   PORTER, Ruby Jane
Ruby was born 7 May 1908. Ruby died 30 July 1972.
11(12)224(11)2454   PORTER, Samuel Lewis
Samuel was born 28 July 1909.
11(12)224(11)2455   PORTER, Wilma May
Wilma was born 27 September 1911.
11(12)224(11)2456   PORTER, Fields Mc
Fields was born 1 March 1913.
11(12)224(11)2457   PORTER, Floyd Blan
Floyd was born 27 September 1914.
11(12)224(11)2458   PORTER, William Earl
William was born 1 April 1916.
11(12)224(11)2459   PORTER, Nannie Catherine
Nannie was born 9 August 1918.
11(12)224(11)245(10)   PORTER, James Ted
James was born 3 December 1921.
11(12)224(11)245(11)   PORTER, Infant
Infant was born 30 January 1925. Infant died 30 January 1925.
11(12)224(11)25   HALSEY, Nancy Adeline
Nancy was born 10 June 1847. She married **WYATT**, John Reed in
Sparta, NC, 26 December 1869. Nancy died 17 September 1888.
11(12)224(11)251   WYATT, Wiley Marshall
Wiley was born. He married **HALSEY**, Maggie Rafenia in Sparta,
NC, 14 April 1895.
11(12)224(11)252   WYATT, Cora Lee
Cora was born 25 October 1870. She married **HASH**, Granville R. 5
October 1889. Cora died 18 September 1912 in Roanoke, VA.
11(12)224(11)253   WYATT, Ollie Mae
Ollie was born 2 March 1875. She married **SMITH**, John Hawthorne
5 October 1895. Ollie died 28 January 1961 at 85 years of age.
11(12)224(11)2531   SMITH, Eula Mae
Eula was born 9 January 1897.
11(12)224(11)2532   SMITH, Annie Beatrice
Annie was born 4 August 1898.
11(12)224(11)2533   SMITH, John Reid
John was born 21 March 1903.
11(12)224(11)254   WYATT, William Glenn
William was born 11 November 1878. He married **HALSEY**, Martha
Alice in Grayson Co., VA, 7 October 1898. William died 20 September 1936.
11(12)224(11)255   WYATT, Geneva
Geneva was born 3 October 1881. Geneva died 1 January 1900.
11(12)224(11)256   WYATT, Lemma
Lemma was born 18 July 1885. Lemma died 17 September 1885.
11(12)224(11)257   WYATT, Nannie A.
Nannie was born 17 September 1888. Nannie died 4 November
1900 at 12 years of age.
11(12)224(11)26   HALSEY, Martha Alice

Martha was born 31 July 1854. She married **GAMBILL**, Robert Thompson 3 August 1880. Martha died 21 February 1931.

11(12)224(11)261   GAMBILL, Samuel Oscar

He married **TAYLOR**, Salina Cornelia. Samuel was born 26 January 1881. Samuel died 14 August 1970 at 89 years of age.

11(12)224(11)2611   GAMBILL, Anna Letha
11(12)224(11)2612   GAMBILL, Cora Lee
11(12)224(11)2613   GAMBILL, Samuel Oscar, Jr.
11(12)224(11)2614   GAMBILL, Gena Sue
11(12)224(11)2615   GAMBILL, Eula Mae

Eula was born 10 March 1908. Eula died 31 October 1967.

11(12)224(11)2616   GAMBILL, Infant

Infant was born 7 November 1911. Infant died 1 December 1911.

11(12)224(11)262   GAMBILL, Claudia S.

Claudia was born 21 November 1883. She married **PORTER**, William Letcher 1 February 1905. Claudia died 24 October 1967 in Galax, VA, at 83 years of age.

11(12)224(11)2621   PORTER, Beulah Clyde

Beulah was born 19 December 1905. Beulah died 14 August 1940.

11(12)224(11)2622   PORTER, Robert Thompson

Robert was born 29 October 1908.

11(12)224(11)263   GAMBILL, Robert Cleve

Robert was born 6 November 1885. He married **MCMILLON**, Maude Mae 11 February 1912.

11(12)224(11)2631   GAMBILL, Arthur T.

Arthur was born 13 March 1913.

11(12)224(11)2632   GAMBILL, Paul Dailey

Paul was born 11 February 1915.

11(12)224(11)2633   GAMBILL, Mary Madeline

Mary was born 1 December 1916.

11(12)224(11)2634   GAMBILL, Dorothy Mae

Dorothy was born 22 June 1921.

11(12)224(11)2635   GAMBILL, Robert Garner

Robert was born 25 March 1933.

11(12)224(11)264   GAMBILL, Bertie A.

Bertie was born 7 February 1888.

11(12)224(11)265   GAMBILL, Nannie C.

Nannie was born 7 July 1892.

11(12)224(11)266   GAMBILL, Johnnie

Her body was interred in Elk Creek Cem.. Johnnie was born 8 April 1895. Johnnie died 13 June 1896 at 1 year of age.

11(12)224(11)267   GAMBILL, Donnie C.

Her body was interred in Elk Creek Cem.. Donnie was born 10 July 1897. Donnie died 13 March 1949 at 51 years of age.

11(12)224(11)27   HALSEY, Charles Lee

Charles was born 11 March 1857. He married **DIXON**, Emma J. in Sparta, NC, 2 January 1880. Charles died 20 October 1907.

11(12)224(11)271   HALSEY, Mertie Alice
Mertie was born 11 February 1882. Mertie died 26 February 1882.
11(12)224(11)272   HALSEY, Grover Reed
Grover was born 12 July 1884. Grover died 18 April 1886.
11(12)224(11)273   HALSEY, Pearl
Pearl was born 11 June 1886. Pearl died 25 September 1956.
11(12)224(11)274   HALSEY, Walter Franklin
Walter was born 18 January 1888. He married **BLACK**, Ada Virginia
in Sparta, NC, 13 March 1915. Walter died 8 June 1966 at 78 years of age.
11(12)224(11)2741   HALSEY, Robert Wayne
Robert was born 28 December 1917.
11(12)224(11)2742   HALSEY, Eulah Maude
Eulah was born 18 April 1919. She married **HUMPHREY**, George
William 7 December 1939.
11(12)224(11)27421   HUMPHREY, William Edward
William was born in Meadow Grove, Nebr 9 October 1940.
11(12)224(11)27422   HUMPHREY, Evelyn Irene
Evelyn was born in Royal, Nebr 30 October 1941.
11(12)224(11)27423   HUMPHREY, Joyce Ann
Joyce was born in So. Dakota 20 July 1943.
11(12)224(11)27424   HUMPHREY, Walter Lee
Walter was born in Meadow Grove, Nebr 2 October 1944.
11(12)224(11)27425   HUMPHREY, George Eugene
George was born 4 August 1946.
11(12)224(11)27426   HUMPHREY, Barbara Janelle
Barbara was born 27 March 1948.
11(12)224(11)27427   HUMPHREY, John Franklin
John was born 7 August 1949.
11(12)224(11)27428   HUMPHREY, Betty Lou
Betty was born in Norfolk, Nebr 11 August 1951.
11(12)224(11)27429   HUMPHREY, Larry Dean
Larry was born in Tilden, Nebr 6 August 1953.
11(12)224(11)2742(10) HUMPHREY, Kay elaine
Kay was born in Tilden, Nebr 19 June 1955.
11(12)224(11)2742(11) HUMPHREY, Donna Rae
Donna was born in Tilden, Nebr 13 January 1957.
11(12)224(11)2742(12) HUMPHREY, Roger Allen
Roger was born 29 August 1958.
11(12)224(11)2742(13) HUMPHREY, Norma Jean
Norma was born in Tilden, Nebr 24 May 1961.
11(12)224(11)2742(14) HUMPHREY, Linda Lee
Linda was born in Tilden, Nebr 13 February 1963.
11(12)224(11)2743   HALSEY, Fred Lee
Fred was born 8 April 1921. He married **MEANS**, Etta Louise 11
March 1946. Fred died 4 April 1969 at 47 years of age.
11(12)224(11)27431   HALSEY, Rebecca Lee
Rebecca was born in Tilden, Nebr. 8 March 1947.

11(12)224(11)27432   HALSEY, Bonita Sue
Bonita was born in Tilden, Nebr. 16 November 1948.
11(12)224(11)27433   HALSEY, Jane Ellen
Jane was born in Tilden, NE 8 June 1951.
11(12)224(11)27434   HALSEY, Peggy Joan
Peggy was born in Tilden, NE 15 May 1955.
11(12)224(11)27435   HALSEY, Christine Joy
Christine was born in Tilden, NE 22 September 1959.
11(12)224(11)2744   HALSEY, Zollie Virginia
Zollie was born 30 December 1923. She married **KOHL**, Alfred 25
September 1947.
11(12)224(11)27441   KOHL, Edwin C.
Edwin was born 8 January 1949.
11(12)224(11)27442   KOHL, Shirley J.
Shirley was born 17 December 1952.
11(12)224(11)27443   KOHL, James W.
James was born 9 June 1954.
11(12)224(11)27444   KOHL, Barbara M.
Barbara was born 4 February 1957.
11(12)224(11)27445   KOHL, Franklin A.
Franklin was born 31 October 1959.
11(12)224(11)27446   KOHL, Diane V.
Diane was born 10 October 1964.
11(12)224(11)2745   HALSEY, Annie Emolene
Annie was born 12 February 1925. She married **SPARR**, Wayne
Isage 14 April 1945.
11(12)224(11)27451   SPARR, Rodney Wayne
Rodney was born in Tilden, Nebr 11 September 1946.
11(12)224(11)27452   SPARR, Patricia Ann
Patricia was born in Norfolk, Nebr 30 August 1948.
11(12)224(11)27453   SPARR, Robert Warren
Robert was born in Tilden, Nebr 30 January 1950.
11(12)224(11)27454   SPARR, Donald Ray
Donald was born in Tilden, Nebr 5 June 1952.
11(12)224(11)2746   HALSEY, Zella Ruth
Zella was born 30 January 1928. Zella died 25 October 1929.
11(12)224(11)2747   HALSEY, Walter Jack
Walter was born 9 June 1933. He married **MEYER**, Kathleen Joyce
in Meadow Grove, NE, 14 March 1953.
11(12)224(11)27471   HALSEY, Kenneth Eugene
Kenneth was born in Neligh, NE 18 February 1954.
11(12)224(11)27472   HALSEY, Jacklyn Kayleen
Jacklyn was born in Tilden, NE 16 October 1958.
11(12)224(11)275   HALSEY, Estel William
Estel was born 16 April 1894. He married **MCMILLAN**, Jennie in
Grayson Co., VA, 30 December 1922. He married **HALSEY**, Betty Ruth
(Caldwell) in Sparta, NC, 14 July 1949. Estel died 28 January 1954.

11(12)224(11)2751   HALSEY, Helen Estelle
11(12)224(11)2752   HALSEY, Katie Marie
Katie was born 20 January 1933.
11(12)224(11)276   HALSEY, Verna C.
She married **WARDEN**, J. Garfield. Verna was born 21 September 1895.
11(12)224(11)2761   WARDEN, Wiley Preston (Buddy)
11(12)224(11)2762   WARDEN, Mabel
Mabel was born 29 October 1921.
11(12)224(11)2763   WARDEN, Madge Janet
Madge was born 7 September 1923.
11(12)224(11)277   HALSEY, Nonnie
Nonnie was born 22 December 1898. She married **MUSGROVE**, Lonnie M. 16 July 1921.
11(12)224(11)2771   MUSGROVE, Howard
Howard was born 8 March 1922.
11(12)224(11)2772   MUSGROVE, George Cameron
George was born 25 February 1924.
11(12)224(11)2773   MUSGROVE, Pauline Elsie
Pauline was born 7 July 1926.
11(12)224(11)2774   MUSGROVE, Hazel
Hazel was born 28 July 1928. Hazel died 10 January 1931.
11(12)224(11)2775   MUSGROVE, Edna Ruth
Edna was born 6 May 1932.
11(12)224(11)2776   MUSGROVE, Robert Glenn
Robert was born 4 August 1934.
11(12)224(11)2777   MUSGROVE, Mary Lee
Mary was born 16 January 1936.
11(12)224(11)2778   MUSGROVE, Estle Jerry Dean
Estle was born 7 March 1942.
11(12)224(11)278   HALSEY, Ollie B.
Ollie was born 20 June 1901. She married **WARDEN**, Rex Savannah 2 June 1923.
11(12)224(11)2781   WARDEN, Mildred Irene
Mildred was born 28 January 1924.
11(12)224(11)2782   WARDEN, Charles Franklin
Charles was born 28 January 1926.
11(12)224(11)2783   WARDEN, Rex Savannah, Jr.
Rex was born 19 August 1932.
11(12)224(11)2784   WARDEN, Vonnie Wave
Vonnie was born 9 February 1936.
11(12)224(11)2785   WARDEN, Angelia Faye
Angelia was born 31 July 1941.
11(12)224(11)279   HALSEY, Zollie
She married **ROBBINS**, William. She married **REEVES**, Rufus Bower in Sparta, NC. Zollie was born 20 June 1901.
11(12)224(11)2791   ROBBINS, Virginia

11(12)224(11)2792   REEVES, Rufus Bower, Jr.
Rufus was born circa 1942. Rufus died circa 1977.
11(12)224(11)27(10)   HALSEY, Robert
Robert was born 2 January 1906.
11(12)224(11)28   HALSEY, Mary Elizabeth 'Molly'
Mary was born 2 March 1864. She married **HALSEY**, Samuel
Freeland 25 December 1882. Mary died 31 October 1944.
11(12)224(11)3 HALSEY, Ira
Ira was born 30 June 1820. He married **DIXON**, Zilphia 19 May
1861. Ira died 10 June 1901 at 80 years of age.
11(12)224(11)31   HALSEY, William
William was born 9 March 1863. He married **HALSEY**, America J.
25 December 1882. He married **MILES**, Myrtle 29 December 1918. William
died 2 August 1924 at 61 years of age.
11(12)224(11)311   HALSEY, Dora Ellen
Dora was born 3 December 1885. Dora died 19 July 1887.
11(12)224(11)312   HALSEY, Mertie Alice
Mertie was born 24 November 1887. Mertie died 26 November 1887
11(12)224(11)313   HALSEY, Luther Fields
Luther was born 13 February 1890. He married **ROUP**, Mayme
Virginia in Sparta, NC, 15 July 1914. Luther died 18 July 1961.
11(12)224(11)314   HALSEY, Jesse Willard
Jesse was born 2 November 1919. Jesse died 26 March 1943.
11(12)224(11)32   HALSEY, Juda Ennice
Juda was born 5 May 1865. She married **HASH**, William Weldon 30
September 1883. Juda died 29 October 1962 at 97 years of age.
11(12)224(11)321   HASH, Mack Linea
Mack was born 22 August 1884. Mack died 17 April 1955.
11(12)224(11)322   HASH, Carl Lewis
Carl was born 22 November 1887. He married **WOODRUFF**, Sadie
W. 13 February 1920. Carl died 16 March 1976 at 88 years of age.
11(12)224(11)3221   HASH, William Alexander
William was born 13 February 1921.
11(12)224(11)3222   HASH, Lewis Jackson
He married **HARRIS**, Gladys. Lewis was born 9 September 1922.
11(12)224(11)3223   HASH, Hugh Chatham
Hugh was born 9 May 1934.
11(12)224(11)323   HASH, Lula
Lula was born 14 September 1889.
11(12)224(11)324   HASH, Jacks or Bruce
Jacks was born 29 January 1892.
11(12)224(11)325   HASH, Zella
Zella was born 26 January 1896. Zella died 29 August 1978.
11(12)224(11)326   HASH, (Infant)
(Infant) was born 21 June 1900. (Infant) died 21 June 1900.
11(12)224(11)327   HASH, (Infant)
(Infant) was born 1 October 1902. (Infant) died 1 October 1902.

11(12)224(11)33   HALSEY, James Harlow
James was born 7 November 1867. He married **WOODRUFF**, Flora 26 December 1894. He married **PIERCE**, Lelia Mae 13 February 1898. James died 23 January 1933 at 65 years of age.
11(12)224(11)331   HALSEY, (Infant)
(Infant) was born 12 April 1896. (Infant) died 12 April 1896.
11(12)224(11)332   HALSEY, Rufus Clinton
Rufus was born 16 February 1899. He married **LANDRETH**, Margaret Lacy in Jacksonville, FL, 1 June 1929. He married **PASLEY**, Iona Annette in Marion, VA, 18 April 1957.
11(12)224(11)3321   HALSEY, James Clinton
James was born in Winston Salem, NC 4 April 1941. He married **FIELDS**, Nancy Rosamond in Mouth Of Wilson, VA, 26 June 1965.
11(12)224(11)3322   HALSEY, Rosemary
Rosemary was born in Winston Salem, NC 27 October 1943. She married **FREEMAN**, Byron 29 March 1968.
11(12)224(11)33221   FREEMAN, Laura Landreth
Laura was born in Durham, NC 21 November 1969.
11(12)224(11)33222   FREEMAN, Elizabeth Halsey
Elizabeth was born in Chapel Hill, NC 14 May 1974.
11(12)224(11)333   HALSEY, Eugene Bower
Eugene was born 16 March 1901.
11(12)224(11)334   HALSEY, Hazel Ileen
Hazel was born 4 September 1902.
11(12)224(11)335   HALSEY, Lilian Marie
Lilian was born 4 July 1909. She married **WALKER**, Ralph in Ashville, NC, 3 June 1938.
11(12)224(11)3351   WALKER, James
James was born 24 January 1942.
11(12)224(11)3352   WALKER, Eugene
Eugene was born 16 January 1944.
11(12)224(11)336   HALSEY, Bettie Jaunita
Bettie was born 19 August 1911.
11(12)224(11)337   HALSEY, Wallace Beverly
Wallace was born 12 November 1922. He married **CAUDILL**, Elsie Mae 12 February 1944.
11(12)224(11)3371   HALSEY, Bettie Lou
Bettie was born 8 February 1948.
11(12)224(11)34   HALSEY, Matilda Jane 'I'
Matilda was born 9 February 1870. She married **EDWARDS**, Andrew Morris 11 January 1893. Matilda died 21 September 1966.
11(12)224(11)341   EDWARDS, (Infant)
(Infant) was born 8 February 1895. (Infant) died 8 February 1895.
11(12)224(11)342   EDWARDS, Edna Izetta
Edna was born 28 September 1898. She married **WEAVER**, Donald Watson in Roanoke, VA, 24 September 1919.
11(12)224(11)3421   WEAVER, Donald Watson, Jr.

Donald was born in Galax, VA 16 January 1921.

11(12)224(11)3422   WEAVER, Edward Maurice
Edward was born 21 December 1923. Edward died 1 June 1945.

11(12)224(11)3423   WEAVER, William Crasby
William was born 10 November 1925.

11(12)224(11)3424   WEAVER, Layton Lee
Layton was born 14 September 1926.

11(12)224(11)343   EDWARDS, (Infant)
(Infant) was born 28 September 1898. (Infant) died 12 October 1898

11(12)224(11)35   HALSEY, John Cleveland
John was born 30 August 1872. He married **MCMILLAN**, Lelia 26 March 1899. John died 25 July 1946 at 73 years of age.

11(12)224(11)351   HALSEY, (Infant)
(Infant) was born 16 March 1900. (Infant) died 22 March 1900.**11(12)224(11)352 HALSEY, Zilphia Clyde**
Zilphia was born 29 June 1905. She married **COLLINS**, Wilburn Bryan 22 October 1930.

11(12)224(11)3521   COLLINS, John Bryan
John was born 31 January 1932. He married **LOVINGOOD**, Jane 29 December 1952.

11(12)224(11)35211   COLLINS, Kimberly Joe
Kimberly was born 29 March 1957.

11(12)224(11)35212   COLLINS, Mary Katheryn
Mary was born 5 October 1959.

11(12)224(11)35213   COLLINS, Thomas Bryan
Thomas was born 22 June 1962.

11(12)224(11)353   HALSEY, Edna Florence
Edna was born 27 June 1909. She married **THOMPSON**, Clive Allen in Grayson Co., VA, 29 June 1930.

11(12)224(11)3531   THOMPSON, Shirley Ann
Shirley was born circa 1936. She married **LAWS**, Jerry Holt 28 December 1957.

11(12)224(11)35311   LAWS, Allen Maurice
Allen was born 28 June 1958.

11(12)224(11)35312   LAWS, Eadye Jane
Eadye was born 2 April 1960. Eadye died 26 August 1972.

11(12)224(11)36   HALSEY, Mary Elizabeth
Mary was born 9 February 1875. She married **EDWARDS**, William Sabert 10 October 1894. Mary died 16 January 1965 at 89 years of age.

11(12)224(11)361   EDWARDS, (Infant)   (Infant) was born 8 April 1897. (Infant) died 8 April 1897.

11(12)224(11)362   EDWARDS, Verna Clyde
Verna was born 21 March 1900. Verna died 7 August 1974.

11(12)224(11)363   EDWARDS, Iley Emerson
Iley was born 20 November 1904. He married **RUSSELL**, Carolyn 17 April 1926.

11(12)224(11)3631   EDWARDS, John Emerson

John was born 17 November 1929.
11(12)224(11)3632   EDWARDS, Ann
Ann was born 30 December 1938.
11(12)224(11)37   HALSEY, Ira Reed 'lley'
Ira was born 6 July 1881. He married **ALEXANDER**, Imogene 4 July 1906. Ira died 17 January 1932 at 50 years of age.
11(12)224(11)371   HALSEY, Zeno Alexander
Zeno was born 16 September 1907. He married **GOAD**, Lula Mae 8 March 1941.
11(12)224(11)3711   HALSEY, Linda
Linda was born 8 January 1951.
11(12)224(11)372   HALSEY, Ralph M.
Ralph was born 5 June 1911. Ralph died 10 April 1930.
11(12)224(11)373   HALSEY, William Daily
William was born 19 June 1914. He married **PETTYJOHN**, Mattie 15 March 1942.
11(12)224(11)3731   HALSEY, Randall Daily
Randall was born 13 December 1944.
11(12)224(11)4 HALSEY, Tinsey
Tinsey was born 26 October 1822. She married **ROSS**, John 25 November 1839.
11(12)224(11)41   ROSS, William N.
His body was interred in Halsey Cemetery, Piney Creek, NC. William was born 28 March 1843. William died 15 May 1865.
11(12)224(11)42   ROSS, Nancy E.
Nancy was born circa 1847.
11(12)224(11)43   ROSS, John C.
John was born circa 1855.
11(12)224(11)44   ROSS, Mary J.
Mary was born circa 1859.
11(12)224(11)5 HALSEY, Sena
Sena was born 27 February 1825. She married **PARSONS**, Henry J. in Ashe Co. N.C., circa 1846.
11(12)224(11)6 HALSEY, Loucinda
Loucinda was born 21 October 1827. She married **PARSONS**, William C. circa 1846.
11(12)224(11)7 HALSEY, Mary Polly
Mary was born 19 July 1831. She married **HASH**, Lewis B. 12 September 1850. Mary died 15 May 1912 at 80 years of age.
11(12)224(11)71   HASH, William Weldon
William was born in Piney Creek, NC 15 February 1852. He married **HALSEY**, Juda Ennice 30 September 1883. William died 12 March 1912.
11(12)224(11)72   HASH, Allen Columbus
Allen was born in Piney Creek, NC 9 December 1853. He married **KIRK**, Rachel 9 August 1876. Allen died 1 July 1920 at 66 years of age.
11(12)224(11)721   HASH, Myrtle
Myrtle was born 10 August 1877. Myrtle died 24 February 1973.

11(12)224(11)722   HASH, Colonel Roy
>   Colonel was born 22 December 1878. Colonel died 7 November 1889 at 10 years of age.

11(12)224(11)723   HASH, Harlow W.
>   Harlow was born 23 March 1880. Harlow died 23 March 1880.

11(12)224(11)724   HASH, Robert Lewis
>   Robert was born 9 December 1889. Robert died 18 January 1967.

11(12)224(11)725   HASH, Garnet
>   Garnet was born 1 May 1893. Garnet died 16 February 1901.

11(12)224(11)73   HASH, Harlow W.
>   Harlow was born in Piney Creek, NC 17 February 1856. Harlow died 17 September 1881 at 25 years of age.

11(12)224(11)74   HASH, Alex Norman
>   Alex was born in Piney Creek, NC 1 January 1859. He married **KIRK**, Susie Carol 28 December 1879. Alex died 15 March 1930.

11(12)224(11)741   HASH, Colonel Lee
>   Colonel was born 1 April 1881. Colonel died 1 April 1959.

11(12)224(11)742   HASH, Mary Belle
>   Mary was born 24 February 1884.

11(12)224(11)743   HASH, Arthur Estel
>   Arthur was born 6 April 1886.

11(12)224(11)744   HASH, Charlie Gleason
>   Charlie was born 20 November 1888. Charlie died 4 May 1970.

11(12)224(11)745   HASH, Effie Stella
>   Effie was born 4 April 1891. Effie died 13 April 1946.

11(12)224(11)746   HASH, Cebert Carbet
>   Cebert was born 3 October 1893.

11(12)224(11)747   HASH, Ollie Mae
>   Ollie was born 1 February 1896. Ollie died 1 February 1957.

11(12)224(11)748   HASH, Zollie
>   Zollie was born 1 February 1896.

11(12)224(11)749   HASH, Albert Hobson
>   Albert was born 28 September 1898.

11(12)224(11)74(10)   HASH, Susie Viola
>   Susie was born 8 July 1901.

11(12)224(11)75   HASH, Glenna
>   Glenna was born in Piney Creek, NC 2 January 1861. Glenna died 11 March 1862 at 1 year of age.

11(12)224(11)76   HASH, Granville R.
>   Granville was born in Piney creek, NC 7 May 1863. He married **WYATT**, Cora Lee 5 October 1889. He married **ROSS**, Anna Lilian 30 April 1915. Granville died 1 September 1944 at 81 years of age.

11(12)224(11)761   HASH, George Lester
>   George was born 12 December 1890.

11(12)224(11)762   HASH, Dwight Reed
>   Dwight was born 10 March 1892. Dwight died 2 February 1947.

11(12)224(11)763   HASH, Paul Gary

Paul was born 31 December 1895. Paul died 28 February 1948.
11(12)224(11)77   HASH, Lindsay Roan
Lindsay was born in Piney Creek, NC 17 February 1866. He married **GAMBILL**, Jennie 3 January 1901. Lindsay died 27 September 1928.
11(12)224(11)771   HASH, Jessie E.
Jessie was born circa 1902. Jessie died circa 1945.
11(12)224(11)772   HASH, Pressie Louise
Pressie was born 25 February 1906.
11(12)224(11)773   HASH, Lenna Clyde
Lenna was born 3 July 1907. Lenna died 1 July 1979.
11(12)224(11)78   HASH, Mary Jane
Mary was born in Piney Creek, NC 3 April 1868. She married **MCMILLAN**, Walter Warner 28 September 1904. Mary died 6 January 1960.
11(12)224(11)781   MCMILLAN, Gayle
Gayle was born 2 May 1906.
11(12)224(11)782   MCMILLAN, Wiley Dean
Wiley was born 11 May 1908.
11(12)224(11)783   MCMILLAN, Warner
Warner was born 11 December 1910.
11(12)224(11)79   HASH, Lura Virginia
Lura was born in Fox, VA 20 July 1871. She married **LIVESAY**, Johnny Fielding May 1892. Lura died 3 March 1966 at 94 years of age.
11(12)224(11)791   LIVESAY, Geneva
Geneva was born 22 October 1895.
11(12)224(11)792   LIVESAY, Claire
Claire was born 7 September 1896.
11(12)224(11)793   LIVESAY, Georgio
Georgio was born 26 November 1900.
11(12)224(11)7(10)   HASH, Ira Cebert
Ira was born in Fox, VA 30 April 1873. He married **BRYANT**, Drucilla Moelick 8 August 1901. Ira died 3 November 1948.
11(12)224(11)7(10)1   HASH, DeEtte Moelick
DeEtte was born 29 May 1902. DeEtte died 23 March 1922.
11(12)224(11)7(10)2   HASH, Alta Helen
Alta was born 12 November 1904. Alta died 29 January 1905.
11(12)224(11)7(10)3   HASH, Sena Gladys
Sena was born 8 January 1906.
11(12)224(11)7(10)4   HASH, Cebert McB.
Cebert was born 9 October 1908. Cebert died 19 February 1951.
11(12)224(11)7(10)5   HASH, Mary Kate
Mary was born 11 April 1911.
11(12)224(11)7(10)6   HASH, Rex Bryant
Rex was born 20 December 1913.
11(12)224(11)7(11)   HASH, Rosa Eudora
Rosa was born 17 March 1877. She married **MCMILLAN**, Manley Eugene 19 November 1898. Rosa died 11 August 1935 at 58 years of age.
11(12)224(11)7(11)1   MCMILLAN, Marie

Marie was born 8 May 1900.

11(12)224(11)7(11)2   MCMILLAN, Kyle

Kyle was born 27 June 1903. Kyle died 27 June 1964.

11(12)224(11)7(11)3   MCMILLAN, Virginia Lee

Virginia was born 14 June 1906.

11(12)224(11)7(11)4   MCMILLAN, French Lewis

French was born 1 October 1908.

11(12)224(11)7(11)5   MCMILLAN, Eugenia

Eugenia was born 8 September 1914.

11(12)224(11)8 HALSEY, Sarah (Sally)

Sarah was born in Piney Creek, N.C. 12 December 1836. She married **MCMILLAN**, John Jr. 29 February 1852.

11(12)224(11)9 HALSEY, Nancy

Nancy was born 12 November 1837. Nancy died circa 1838.

11(12)23   HALSEY, Ananias

Ananias was born circa 1724. She married **LUDLOW**, Jemima 12 July 1753.

11(12)24   HALSEY, Joel

Joel was born circa 1726. He married Anne circa 1745.

11(12)25   HALSEY, Rebecca

Rebecca was born circa 1730. She married **STILES**, Deacon Ephriam circa 1750.

11(12)26   HALSEY, Eliha

Eliha was born circa 1732. He married **ELY**, Elizabeth 28 April 1763.

11(12)27   HALSEY, Hannah

Hannah was born circa 1734. She married **LOPER**, Lion 25 October 1768.

11(12)28   HALSEY, Elizabeth

Elizabeth was born 8 January 1743/4. She married **BURNETT**, Lindsley circa 1764.

11(12)3 HALSEY, Ezekial

Ezekial was born 12 November 1703. His great nephew, Isaac Halsey, wrote that he lived and died a bachelor. In 1753 he and William were the only Halseys listed on the NJ jury list. Dr. Jacob Green's notes, dated 1770, of the Hanover Church says he was not sure if Ezekial was a church member or not. According to the publication "Descendants of the Reverend Francis Higginson" by Thomas Higginson, published privately in 1910, Ezekial's property was in Lower Whippany and joined lands owned by the Johnsons.

11(12)4 HALSEY, Ananias

Ananias was born 10 January 1705/6.

11(12)5 HALSEY, Anna

Anna was born 29 July 1707.

11(12)6 HALSEY, Eunice

Eunice was born 3 March 1708/9.

11(12)7 HALSEY, Deborah

Deborah was born 7 February 1709/0. She married **HOWELL**,

Jeremiah before 1750.

11(12)71   HOWELL, Jonathan

Jonathan was born 12 October 1750. He married first, Hannah Williamson and second, Mary Howell.

11(12)72   HOWELL, Ezekiel

Ezekiel was born circa 1753.

11(12)8 HALSEY, Nathaniel, Jr

He married **HALSEY**, Experience. Nathaniel, was born 15 December 1713.

11(12)9 HALSEY, Phoebe

Phoebe was born 31 May 1714.

11(12)(10)   HALSEY, Moses

Moses was born 12 July 1716.

12   HALSEY, Isaac

His body was interred in Southampton, LI, g.y.. He married **BARNES**, Mary circa 1663. Isaac died 31 January 1724/5 in Southampton, L.I., NY. In a list of inhabitants of Southampton, LI, NY, in 1698, Isaac appeared along with several Halseys. He was named as a Trustee of Southampton, NY, December 6, 1686, in Gov. Dongan's patent. A broken stone in Southampton grave yard says, "Isaac Halsey d. Jan. 31, 1725." It's probably the grave of this Isaac.

121   HALSEY, Jemima

She married an unknown person 22 May 1683.

122   HALSEY, Isaac

His body was interred in Southampton g.y., LI. Isaac was born in Southampton, LI circa 1664. He married **HOWELL**, Abigail 28 November 1689. He married **HOWELL**, Phebe circa 1690. Isaac died 23 March 1751/2 at 87 years of age. The gravestone of Isaac Halsey at Northend burying grounds, Southampton, NY, was inscribed: "In Memory/ Mr. Isaac Halsey/ who died March/ 23, 1752 in ye/ 88th Year of/ his Age. He was called "Isaac of the North End" to distinguish him from his cousin Isaac, son of Thomas, Jr. and Mary Halsey. His will was dated 16 October 1750 and proven 26 May 1752.

1221   HALSEY, Jonah

1222   HALSEY, John

1223   HALSEY, Phebe

1224   HALSEY, Mary

1225   HALSEY, Isaac

Isaac was born circa 1697. Isaac died 3 January 1725/6.

1226   HALSEY, Joseph

Joseph was born after 1697/8.

1227   HALSEY, Job

Job was born circa 1714. Job died circa 1750.

123   HALSEY, Elizabeth

Elizabeth was born circa 1666.

124   HALSEY, Joseph

Joseph was born circa 1668. He married **ELDREDG**, Elizabeth 29

January 1696/7. Joseph died 17 April 1725 in Elizabeth, NJ.
1241   HALSEY, Mary
1242   HALSEY, Daniel
     Daniel died circa 1727 in Elizabeth, NJ.
1243   HALSEY, Elizabeth
1244   HALSEY, Anna
1245   HALSEY, Timothy
1246   HALSEY, Isaac
1247   HALSEY, Nathaniel
1248   HALSEY, General Joseph
     His body was interred in Pres. Ch. g.y., Elizabeth, NJ. General was
born circa 1695. General died 16 December 1771 at 76 years of age.
12481   HALSEY, Isaac
     Isaac was born circa 1741. Isaac died 24 November 1788.
124811 HALSEY, Jacob Benton
     Jacob died 24 June 1815 in Campton, NJ.
1248111   HALSEY, Charles Henry
     Charles was born 22 February 1810. Charles died 2 May 1855.
12481111   HALSEY, William Frederick, Sr. Captain
     His body was interred in Arlington, VA. He married **BREWSTER,**
Ann Masters. William was born circa 1853. William died circa 1920.
124811111   HALSEY, William Frederick, Jr. Admiral
     His body was interred in Arlington, VA. William was born in
Elizabeth, NJ 3 October 1882. He married **GRANDY**, Fannie in Norfolk, VA,
1 December 1909. William died 16 August 1959 at 76 years of age. Admiral
Halsey was one of the leading Naval commanders during World War II.
General McArthur called him "the greatest fighting admiral of W.W.II." He
became vice admiral in command of the Pacific carrier division in 1940. In
1942 he was given command of U.S. Naval forces in the south Pacific. He
assumed command of the Third fleet on June 15, 1944. President Truman
promoted him to the five-star rank of admiral of the fleet in December 1945.
He retired from active service in 1947. The Japanese later signed the
surrender documents on his flag ship, the battleship Missouri. He graduated
from the Navy Academy in 1904.
1248111111   HALSEY, Margaret
     Margaret was born circa 1910.
1248111112   HALSEY, William Frederick, III
     William was born circa 1915.
125   HALSEY, Daniel
     Daniel was born circa 1670. Daniel died August 1719 at 49 years of
age. His will was found in the Secretary of State's office at Raleigh, NC. It
was dated March 13, 1719. Daniel was a resident of Albemarle County, NC,
in the precinct of Chowan. As the Southampton records show no marriage
records for this Daniel, he probably married in NC in 1694. Some believe his
marriage was the cause of his removal from Southampton. The earliest
record of him in NC was by the General Court of North Carolina, at a session
held November 28, 1694, ordered payment to Daniel Halsey for attendance

as a witness. In October 1708, Deputy Marshall Daniel Halsey received writ for choosing Assemblymen, issued by Glover as President of the Council and acting Governor. This was the time of the famous fight for control of the Legislature of NC by the Glover and Carney factions.

1251   HALSEY, Nathaniel
He married Joan.
1252   HALSEY, Dorothy
1253   HALSEY, Martha
1254   HALSEY, William
William died circa 1756.
1255   HALSEY, Miles
Miles was born circa 1700.
1256   HALSEY, John
John was born circa 1705.
126   HALSEY, Joshua
His body was interred in Southampton g.y., LI. He married **WILLMAN**, Martha. Joshua was born in Southampton, LI circa 1674. Joshua died 1 June 1734 at 59 years of age.
1261   HALSEY, Abigail
She married **POST**, John.
1262   HALSEY, Irene
She married **FOSTER**, William
. **1263   HALSEY, Prudence**
She married **WOODRUFF**, David.
1264   HALSEY, Martha
She married **SAYRE**, Joshua.
1265   HALSEY, Joana
1266   HALSEY, Elizabeth
1267   HALSEY, Experience
She married **HALSEY**, Nathaniel, Jr. She was named in her mother's will in 1753. She was married to Nathaniel Halsey.
1268   HALSEY, Mary
She married **HALSEY**, Israel.
127   HALSEY, Mary
She married **HOWELL**, Abraham, Jr.. Mary was born circa 1678.
1271   HOWELL, Stephen
Stephen was born circa 1708.
1272   HOWELL, Matthew
Matthew was born circa 1710. Matthew died 20 January 1732/3.
1273   HOWELL, Philip
Philip was born circa 1712. Philip died 3 January 1715/6
1274   HOWELL, David
1275   He married **HOWELL**, Phebe. David was born circa 1714.
12741   HOWELL, Pamela
She married **HALSEY**, Zebulon, Jr.. Pamela was born 9 November 1725. Pamela died 2 June 1843 at 117 years of age.
127411 HALSEY, Andrew

He married **COOK**, Proculi.

1274111   HALSEY, Abagail

Her body was interred in Wickapoque g. y., Southampton, NY. Abagail was born 3 April 1837. She married **HALSEY**, William in Southampton, NY, 31 October 1865. Abagail died 27 March 1928.

12741111   HALSEY, Daniel

His body was interred in Southampton, NY. Daniel was born in Southampton, NY 1 June 1867. He married **HAND**, Fannie Gertrude in Southampton, NY, 21 November 1889. Daniel died 9 April 1963 in Southampton, NY, at 95 years of age.

127411111   HALSEY, Allen Hand

His body was interred in Southampton, NY. Allen was born in Southampton, NY 25 February 1899. He married **WHIPPLE**, Edna Alberta 12 July 1928. Allen died 1 June 1974 in Southampton, NY.

1274111111   HALSEY, Glenn Richmond

Glenn was born in Southampton, NY 8 March 1931. He married **CHAROS**, Margaret Ann in Southampton, NY, 27 June 1964.

12741111111   HALSEY, Glenn Richmond, Jr.

Glenn was born in Southampton, NY 27 June 1966. He married **RAYMOND**, Kimberly Ann in Old Saybrook, CT, 18 June 1994.

1275   HOWELL, Mary

She married **HOWELL**, Elisha. Mary was born circa 1715.

1276   HOWELL, Silas

He married **SANDFORD**, Susannah. Silas was born circa 1717.

1277   HOWELL, Charles

He married **JESSUP**, Deborah. Charles was born circa 1722.

128   HALSEY, Thomas

Thomas was born in Southampton, LI circa 1680. Thomas died January 1764 at 83 years of age.

1281   HALSEY, Ethan

1282   HALSEY, Phebe

She married **TOPPING**,

1283   HALSEY, Martha

She married **ROGERS**, Stephen in Bridgehampton, NY.

1284   HALSEY, Mary

129   HALSEY, Samuel

Samuel was born circa 1682.

1291   HALSEY, Samuel

1292   HALSEY, Benjamin

Benjamin was born 10 December 1721. Benjamin died 19 February 1788 in Morristown, NJ, at 66 years of age. He moved to Morristown, NJ., and bought property at Monroe, on south side dividing the townships of Hanover and Morris. He was one of the most prominent men in Morristown. Benjamin was called Captain, was a County Judge, County Collector during the Revolutionary War, and June 14, 1776, was appointed by the Provincial Congress as one of the five Commissioners to pay the bounty allowed to volunteers. In the winter of 1779-80, DuPortail, one of the French officers, with a guard of 25 men, made his headquarters at Benjamin's house. He was married three times.

1293   HALSEY, Ezra
Ezra was born circa 1727. Ezra died 31 October 1775 at 48 years of age. His will was dated 12 October 1775, as recorded at Trenton, NJ. He was a church elder.

1294   HALSEY, Jerushu
She married **WOOD**, Jonathan. Jerushu was born circa 1728. Jerushu died 21 April 1803 in Morristown, NJ, at 74 years of age.

13   HALSEY, John

14   HALSEY, Robert
His body was interred 28 October 1630.

15   HALSEY, Daniel
His body was interred in Wickapogue g.y., Southampton, NY. Daniel was born in England circa 1630. He married **WOODHULL**, Jemina circa 1668. Daniel died circa 1682 in Southampton, NY. Letters of administration given to his widow on 24 April 1682.

151   HALSEY, William

152   HALSEY, Abraham

153   HALSEY, Daniel, Jr.
His body was interred in Wickapogue g.y., Southampton, NY. Daniel, was born 31 August 1669. He married **LARISON**, Amy circa 1699. Daniel, died 28 February 1733/4 at 64 years of age.

1531   HALSEY, Abraham

1532   HALSEY, Daniel III
His body was interred in Wickapogue, L.I., Southampton, NY. He married Hannah. Daniel was born 21 March 1698/9. Daniel died 26 February 1733/4 at 34 years of age.

15321   HALSEY, Daniel IV
He married **STEVENS**, Elizabeth. Daniel was born 4 October 1732.

153211   HALSEY, Daniel V
He married **JAGGER**, Mary 22 October 1788. Daniel died 14 March 1823.

1532111   HALSEY, Daniel VI
Daniel was born in Wickapoque, Southampton, NY 1 April 1796. He married **ROGERS**, Louisa in Southampton, NY, 1 January 1824. Daniel died 23 August 1836 at 40 years of age. He was a teacher and poet.

15321111   HALSEY, William
William was born in Southampton, NY 28 December 1831. He married **HALSEY**, Abagail in Southampton, NY, 31 October 1865. William died 21 March 1890 in Wickapoque, Southampton, NY, at 58 years of age.

1533   HALSEY, Henry
Henry was born 28 February 1699/0. Henry died circa 1740.

1534   HALSEY, Amy
She married **HALSEY**, Abraham. Amy was born 17 August 1702.

1535   HALSEY, Elias
Elias was born 16 May 1707.

1536   HALSEY, Jesse
Jesse was born 5 August 1710.
1537   HALSEY, Silas
His body was interred in Wickapogue, L.I., NY. Silas was born in Long Island, NY 17 January 1717/8. He married **HOWELL**, Susannah 11 September 1742. Silas died 3 January 1786 in Ovid, NY, at 67 years of age. Silas was Chairman of the Committee of Safety for Southampton, Long Island, NY., during the Revolutionary War. He was a member of the Commission of Public Safety, proscribed by the British, sheriff of Suffolk Co., NY. He lead the first colony to south Seneca Co. and was it's first physician. Silas built the first mill, was the judge of Onondaga Co., supervisor, Assemblyman, a Delegate to Congressional Convention in 1801, and was county clerk for 15 years. He was a Congressman in 1804 and a State Senator in 1808.
15371   HALSEY, Catherine
15372   HALSEY, Silas, Jr.
Silas, was born in Southampton, L.I., NY 6 October 1743. He married **RADLEY**, Sarah 8 November 1764. He married **HOWELL**, Hannah 16 November 1780. He married **HOWELL**, Abigail 3 December 1815. Silas, died 19 November 1832 in Lodi, NY, at 89 years of age. Dr. Silas studied medicine in Elizabethtown, NJ, and practiced in Southampton from 1764 until 1776, wnen he fled Southampton, with other patriots, to Connecticut and lived for three years in Killingworth. His first wife died in1778, leaving him with four small children. In 1779 he returned to his home in Southampton by permission of General Erskine. The British had trashed his house. He later became sheriff of Suffolk County, NY, and held other offices untill 1792. In 1792 he relocated to Ovid (now called Lodi). He was a memberof the State assembly for eight years, representing Seneca County. He was a member of Congress during Jefferson's term as President and later became a State senator. He held offices of trust and responsibility for forty years.
153721 HALSEY,
153722 HALSEY,
153723 HALSEY,
153724 HALSEY,
153725 HALSEY, Nicoll
Nicoll was born 8 March 1782. He was a member of Congress.
153726 HALSEY, Lewis
Lewis was born in Southampton, L.I., NY 22 May 1783. He married **CLARK**, Fanny 23 November 1807. Lewis died 15 May 1842 in Trumansburg, NY(?), at 58 years of age.
1537261   HALSEY, William Clark
William was born in Trumansburg, NY 13 April 1815. He married **MARSH**, Hetta E. 18 October 1841. William died 25 October 1872 in Ogden, NY, at 57 years of age. He was an Ensign and Lieutenant in the New York Militia.
15372611   HALSEY, Lewis
Lewis was born in Trumansburg, NY 19 January 1843. He married

BARBER, Zada 12 September 1872. He graduated from Hobart College in 1868 with a BA & AM degrees. He was the Adjutant for the 50th regular National Guard of New York. In 1869 he was a professor of Latin and natural sciences in the Oxford Academy. He graduated from the Rochester Theological Seminary in 1872 and was ordained at Ogden, NY., that same year. He began as the pastor of the Farmer Village Baptist Church in 1874. Lewis wrote the "History of Seneca Baptist Association"; "Falls of Taughannock"; and of sermons, poems and addresses.

153727 HALSEY, Sarah Radley
    Sarah was born 28 February 1785.
153728 HALSEY, Frances
    Frances was born 20 December 1786.
153729 HALSEY, Jehiel
    Jehiel was born 7 October 1788. He was a member of Congress.
15372(10)   HALSEY, Mary
    Mary was born 16 May 1790. Mary died 27 September 1791.
15372(11)   HALSEY, Mary Ann
    Mary was born 30 March 1792.
15373 HALSEY, Susannah
    She married **HOWELL**, Sylvanus. Susannah was born circa 1747.
154 HALSEY, Richard
    Richard was born in Southampton, LI circa 1670. Richard died circa 1738.
155 HALSEY, Jemima
    Jemima was born circa 1671.
156 HALSEY, Elizabeth
    She married **HALSEY**, Joseph. Elizabeth was born circa 1675.
16 HALSEY, Elizabeth
    Elizabeth was born in England circa 1632. She married **HOWELL**, Richard in Southampton, NY, circa 1654. Elizabeth died circa 1710.
161 HOWELL, Elizabeth
    Elizabeth was born circa 1655. She married **MARSHALL**, Joseph 18 March 1672/3.
162 HOWELL, David
    He married **HERRICK**, Mary. David was born circa 1657.
163 HOWELL, Richard, Jr.
    He married Sarah. Richard, was born circa 1659. He resided in the village of Southampton, L.I., NY, at the South End, on the east side of Main Street.
1631 HOWELL, Dorcas
    She married Robert Norris.
1632 HOWELL, Abigail
    She married Silas Pierson.
1633 HOWELL, Hezekiah
    Hezekiah was born circa 1680.
1634 HOWELL, Sarah
    Sarah was born circa 1682. She married Martyn Rose.

1635   HOWELL, Edward
Edward was born circa 1684. He married Abigail Sanford.
1636   HOWELL, Christopher
Christopher was born circa 1689. He married Joanna.
1637   HOWELL, Obadiah
He married **JAGGER**, Patience. Obadiah was born circa 1696.
16371   HOWELL, Ryall
Ryall was born circa 1723.
16372   HOWELL, Obadiah
Obadiah was born circa 1725. He married Elizabeth.
16373   HOWELL, Richard
His body was interred in North End, Southampton, L.I., NY. Richard
was born circa 1727. Richard died 23 October 1793 at 66 years of age.
16374   HOWELL, Abigail
Abigail was born circa 1729. She married William Stephens.
16375   HOWELL, James
James was born 15 October 1734. He married Lucretia Havens.
16376   HOWELL, Sylvanus
He married **HALSEY**, Susannah. Sylvanus was born circa 1736.
1638   HOWELL, Arthur
Arthur was born after 1697/8. He married Hannah.
164   HOWELL, Isaac
Isaac was born circa 1663. Isaac died before 1696.
165   HOWELL, Ruth
Ruth was born 17 June 1669.
166   HOWELL, Josiah
He married **JOHNES**, Mary. Josiah was born circa 1674.
1661   HOWELL, Anne
1662   HOWELL, Ester
She married a Post.
1663   HOWELL, Phebe
She married Nathaniel Smith.
1664   HOWELL, Mary
1665   HOWELL, Abner
Abner was born 22 June 1699. He married Eunice Fithian.
1666   HOWELL, Josiah
Josiah was born 12 May 1709. He married first, a Mitchell and
second, Mary.
1667   HOWELL, Elias
He married **GELSTON**, Mary. Elias was born 8 January 1710/1. He
married **MULFORD**, Abigail in East Hampton, L.I., NY, 20 December 1744.
16671   HOWELL, Mary
16672   HOWELL, Ruth
16673   HOWELL, Elias
Elias was born 27 September 1745.
16674   HOWELL, Hannah
She married **JOHNES**, Paul. Hannah was born 4 February 1753.

She married **HALSEY**, Silas, Jr. 16 November 1780.

166741 JOHNES, Elias

Elias was born circa 1773. He married Jerusha Topping.

166742 JOHNES, William

William was born circa 1774.

166743 JOHNES, Elizabeth

Elizabeth was born 1 June 1776.

16675 HOWELL, Abigail

Abigail was born 15 February 1755. She married **HALSEY**, Silas, Jr. 3 December 1815. Abigail died 18 February 1831 at 76 years of age.

167   HOWELL, Hezekiah

Hezekiah was born circa 1677. He married **HALSEY**, Phebe 10 September 1702. Hezekiah died 4 December 1744 at 67 years of age.

1   HALSEY, Thomas, Sr.
                He married WHEELER, Elizabeth in
Cranfield, Bedfordshire, England, circa 1625. He married JOHNS, Ann
Mrs in Southampton, L.I., NY, 25 July 1660. Thomas, died 27 August
1678 in Southhampton, L.I. NY.
2   HALSEY ALIAS CHAMBERS, Robert
                Robert was born circa 1552. He married ALLEY ALIAS
COOKE, Ellen in Flamstead, Hertfordshire, England, 28 July 1577.
His body was interred 18 April 1610 in Flamstead, Hertfordshire,
England. Robert Halsey was of Holtsmere End, Flamstead, which was
located very close to the parishes of Redbourn and Hemel Hempstead,
when he made his will and where he died. He was taken to Flamstead for
burial. At Flamstead he was a church warden, as his signature attested to
the Bishop's Transcript of the parish registers in 1604. Robert Halsey of
Hemel Hempstead, Hertfordshire, made his will 3 April 1610.
3   ALLEY ALIAS COOKE, Ellen
                Ellen was born circa 1559. She married HALSEY ALIAS
CHAMBERS, Robert in Flamstead, Hertfordshire, England, 28 July
1577. After her husband, Robert Halsey, died there is no known record
for the burial or remarriage of Ellen. She probably relocated close to
Cranfield, Bedfordshire, where Robert, Ann and Thomas Halsey,
presumably her children, married Wheelers from at least two different
families there.
4   HALSEY ALIAS CHAMBERS, Thomas
Thomas was born circa 1522. He married Margaret circa 1543. His
body was interred 5 February 1592/3 in Hemel Hempstead,
Hertfordshire, England. Thomas Halsey is recorded making several land
transactions. "On 15 November 1550 he bought a cottage with curtilage
and two acres three rods of arrable land adjoining in Bircheley Field,
Great Gaddesden from Richard Pare of Enesham, Oxon., son and heir of
Richard Pare of Great Gaddesden, gent., deceased;" Some of the
witnesses were Robert Halsey, William Halsey, and William Halsey the
younger son of Robert Halsey. The younger William was the one called
"of the Wood". "On 1 April 1560, Thomas Halsey was admitted to an
acre of land in Barmar Field, Manor of Great Gaddesden, on the
surrender of Henry Hawseye, by the hand of Richard Knight in the
presence of William Hawseye, Senior. On 31 May 1574, Thomas Halsey
and wife, Margaret were admitted to a messuage and seventy seven acres
of land in the Manor of Great Gaddesden, upon surrender of Thomas
Halsey alias Chambers, by the hand of William Halsey of the Wood in
the presence of Gilbert Wells." "On 10 May 1591, Margaret Halsey alias
Chambers on surrender of her husband Thomas Halsey alias Chambers,
by the hands of John Munn, in the presence of Thomas Welles of
Coznor, was admitted to the cottage called Gorberdes and two closes of
arrable land belonging to the said cottage, containing three acres, and one
parcell of land called Wadlokes containing two and one half acres of land

parcell of land called Wadlokes containing two and one half acres of land
in the Manor of Great Gaddesden. Also on 10 may 1591, William Halsey
was admitted to this same land on the surrender of Margaret Halsey alias
Chambers, wife of Thomas Halsey alias Chambers." Thomas Halsey
alias Chambers, yeoman, of Hemel Hempstead, Hertfordshire, made his
will 16 November 1592, proved 28 May 1594. NOTE: According to the
Reference; "There were several contemporary Thomas Halseys born
about the same time as this Thomas Halsey. One, a son of the William
Halsey who was granted "the Parsonage", born circa 1520, was of
Berkhamstead; his mother named his children in her 28 August 1557
will; Fridswid, Ellen, William, Thomas, and Anne; they were
subsequently also namedin the son William's 1601 will." "Another
Thomas, born in 1521, died in May 1544, unmarried. Another, born
between 1528 and 1542, did have a brother Robert, and nothing more is
known of them, but that Thomas was too young to have children starting
in 1544."

5   **Margaret**
    Margaret was born circa 1523. She married **HALSEY ALIAS
CHAMBERS**, Thomas circa 1543. Her body was interred 13 January
1600/1 in Hemel Hempstead, Hertfordshire, England. Margaret Halsey,
widow, made her will 4 January 1601/2, proved 15 January 1601/2.
According to the reference neither Margaret nor Thomas named all their
children in their respective wills. A case in point is son Gilbert Halsey.
Gilbert's baptism was recorded at Flamstead, 22 January 1553/4 as the
son of "Thomas Hasye and Margerie". There being no other couple
named Thomas and Margaret Halsey at Flamstead, Gilbert had to be the
son of this couple. The reference contained further evidence in that the
26 January 1589/90 will of Thomas Halsey's brother Robert also
mentioned; "to Gilbert Halsey the money that he oweth me". Gilbert was
alive at the time of his father's will, baptisms of his children being
recorded as late as 1596. Continuing to quote the reference; "Considering
that both Thomas and Margaret named their son Thomas Halsey in their
wills, it is significant that Robert Halsey of Holtsmerend was named not
only in the will of his uncle Robert, but in the 3 April 1605 will of
Thomas Alley alias Cooke, whose sister Ellen was the wife of Robert
Halsey of Holtsmerend. The will referred to Robert and Thomas as
"brethern" in law, strongly suggesting that Thomas was a brother of
Robert, who was indeed the brother in law of Thomas Alley alias
Cooke."

6 **ALLEY ALIAS COOKE, John**
    John was born in Flamstead, Hertfordshire, England circa 1526.
He married Isabel circa 1554. His body was interred 5 April 1577 in
Flamstead.

7 **Isabel**
    She married **ALLEY ALIAS COOKE**, John circa 1554. Her
body was interred 8 January 1578/9 in Flamstead, Hertfordshire,

England.
8 HALSEY ALIAS CHAMBERS, John

John was born circa 1498. John died circa 1559 in Dunstable, Bedfordshire, England. John Halsey was probably married more than once, since he had two sets of surviving sons named Thomas and John. His widow was Agnes. According to the reference the key to John being an ancestor was that two of his sons were named Thomas and one was named Robert. The will of one of the Thomas' named his brother Robert; and the will of Robert later named his brother, Thomas Halsey, with no sign that the latter was dead. John Halsey alias Chambers made his will On 2 April 1559, proven on 23 October 1559.

12 ALLEY ALIAS COOKE, Thomas

Thomas was born circa 1495. He married Joan circa 1517. Thomas died circa 1548 in Flamstead, Hertfordshire, England. Thomas Aleye of Flamstead made his will 2 June 1548, proved 4 July 1548, naming his wife, Joan as executor.

13 Joan

She married **ALLEY ALIAS COOKE**, Thomas circa 1517.

24 ALLEY ALIAS COOKE, Hugh

Hugh was born circa 1469. He married an unknown person circa 1494. He was of Redbourn, Hertfordshire, England. Hugh Alee of Redbourn made his will 22 September 1531, proved 21 October 1531.

E

F

Farley
Cleo (-), 76
Sarah Elizabeth (1888-1982), 46
Farrnggia
Tony (-), 74
Fechko
Ilene (-), 66
Fellows
Richard (1928-), 26
William (-), 26
Fender
Ben (1903-), 183
Bruce (1895-), 183
Cornelia V. (1875-1953), 177
Paul (1898-), 183
Sue (1872-1960), 183
W. A. 'Bud' (1866-), 183
Ferguson
Shirley (Dawson) (1923-), 155
Fields
John Cam (-), 85
Nancy Rosamond (1941-1976), 85,
191
Finley
James (-dec.), 15
Finn
(1859-1859), 95
Charles Wilbur (1851-1851), 94
Henry E. (CA 1845-1857), 94
Leonora H. 'Nora' (-), 94
Lillian Estelle (-), 94
Lois E. (-), 94
Mabelle Maud (1860-1937), 95
Mary Evelyn (1849-1849), 94
Philander G. (1822-1901), 94
Robert W. (CA 1843-1863), 94
Finney
Ileta (1906-CA 1964), 166
Fischer
Lorraine Kay (1954-), 11
Fisk
Anthony (Fick) (CA 1828-), 6
Arthur (CA 1890-dec.), 6
Charles William (CA 1860-), 6
Ella Frances (CA 1855-), 6
Fitzgerald
Don (-), 32
Flach
Alice (-), 61
Fleshman

Linda Lou (1937-), 46
Foit
Wendy Lea (-), 52
Ford
Barbara Lynn (1961-), 52
Don (-), 32
Oley (-), 32
Peggy Ann (-), 32
Foster
Daniel (-), 4
William (-), 199
Fowler
Edna Belle (CA 1876-), 10
James (-), 68
Frampton
Lois Jane (-), 63
Francis
Elizabeth (-1913), 20
Karen (CA 1947-), 34
Frank
Jim (-), 71
Franklin
Ann Marie (1979-), 57
Charles Edgar, Jr. (1947-), 56
Charles Edgar, Sr. (1906-1989), 53
Connie Mae (1932-), 55
Danny Ray (1948-), 57
Donald Montgomery (-), 57
Frances Lillian (1937-), 56
Geneva Louise (1926-1998), 53
Gloria Dawn (1966-), 57
J. Warren (-), 154
Julie Lynn (1977-), 57
Michael Joe (1967-), 57
Reva June (1939-), 56
Velma Pearl (1929-), 54
Frauef
Debra Ann (1953-), 54
Freedline
Mary Frances (1950-), 54
Freeman
Byron (1931-), 191
Elizabeth Halsey (1974-), 191
Elvira (-), 27
Laura Landreth (1969-), 191
Friend
Renita Jean (-), 39
Fritz
Sabrina (-), 33

George (-), 40
Richard (-), 40
Gus
Robert (-), 66

H

Hackler
Doris (1914-), 80
Frankie (-), 146
Garfield (1824-1879), 79
Lewis W. (1904-1925), 80
Robert Halsey (1859-1933), 80
Vance Bain (1892-1892), 80
Hackney
Vergie (CA 1946-), 38
Haga
Jacob (-), 145
Hager
Gerald Edward (1947-), 47
Tammie Lynne (1973-), 47
Vanessa Ann (1978-), 47
Haines
Donn Vaughn (-), 158
Sarah (1730-CA 1813), 18
Hale
John (1844-), 108
Haley
Deborah (Debbie) (1964-), 9
Elizabeth (Beth) (1965-), 9
Theodore (Ted) (1970-), 9
Thomas (1938-), 9
Hall
Claudia (1930-), 152
Henry F. (-), 143
Kimberli (CA 1960-CA 1993), 37
Patricia Joan (1934-), 155
Robert (-), 43
Savannah (-), 149
William (-), 41
Halsey
(-dec.), 44
(1890-1890), 25
(1901-1901), 153
(1902-1902), 177
(1912-1912), 121
(CA 1922-), 162
(Infant) (1896-1896), 191
(Infant) (1900-1900), 192
A. Leota (1907-), 84
Aaren (-), 41
Abagail (1837-1928), 200, 201

Abigail (-), 199
Abigail (1673-1696), 93
Abigail (CA 1690-1696), 17
Abigail (CA 1760-), 88
Abigal (1732-), 16
Abraham (CA 1695-1759), 17, 201
Ada (Adie) (CA 1916-), 60
Ada Ann (1869-CA 1941), 80, 135
Ada Selina (1869-1948), 26, 176
Ada Virginia (1882-1889), 110
Adah Ann (1841-1922), 83
Agnes Kay (1935-), 46
Ahart (1814-1887), 109
Ahart (1887-1955), 125
Albert (1922-), 119
Albert Clay (1930-), 121
Albin Thomas (1928-), 76
Aldeen (1920-), 74
Alden (1931-), 82
Alex Addison (1874-1956), 183
Alice E. (1875-1902), 84
Alice Marie (1920-), 23
Allen Blake (Tom) (1929-), 138
Allen Hand (1899-1974), 200
Allen Jackson (1906-), 137
Allen Sampson (1923-1973), 114
Alma Ruth (1921-1924), 73
Almeda (-), 44
Almeda (1908-1955), 29
America Alice (1910-), 27
America J. (1861-1916), 176, 190
America Virginia (1873-1952), 105
Amos (-), 139
Amos (1913-), 124
Amy (1702-), 17, 201
Amy (1724-), 17
Ananias (1706-), 196
Ananias (CA 1724-), 196
Ananias (CA 1836-), 140
Andrea Michelle (1984-), 47
Andrew (-), 200
Andrew Albert (1882-1960), 46
Andrew Clyde (1891-), 179
Andrew Frank (1891-1964), 170
Andrew Jack (CA 1924-1994), 61
Andrew Jackson (1889-), 102, 112
Andrew Martin (1934-), 169
Andrew Martin 'Jack' (1907-1988), 168
Andrew McMillan (1843-1916), 168
Andrew Raymond (1907-), 169
Anice Lee (1951-), 48

227

Merry Alice (1950-1953), 8
William Edward (1919-), 7
William Robert (1953-), 8
Hartsog
James Keith (-), 60
Hartzog
James (-dec.), 144
Viola (1920-), 138
Harvey
Mary C. (-dec.), 18
Nadine (-), 32
Hash
(Infant) (1900-1900), 190
(Infant) (1902-1902), 190
(Unnamed Infant) (-1896), 102
Abel (1846-), 146
Abraham (CA 1830-CA 1902), 147
Ada Lucille (1917-), 81
Addie Carol (1908-), 25
Albert Garland (1913-), 163
Albert Hobson (1898-), 194
Alex Norman (1859-1930), 194
Alice (1863-), 146
Alice (1866-1926), 109
Alice (Cox) (CA 1860-CA 1909),
125, 132
Allen Columbus (1853-1920), 193
Alta Helen (1904-1905), 195
Andrew Jackson (1848-), 108
Annie Belle (1916-), 102
Ardith Adell (1926-), 81
Arthur Estel (1886-), 194
Bettie (1891-1973), 117
Bettie (CA 1891-), 132
Bonnie Sue (1945-), 125
Boyden (1866-1890), 145
Calvin (1840-), 146
Cansada (1851-1937), 112, 132
Carl Lewis (1887-1976), 190
Carrie or Caroline (Halsey) (1847-
), 108
Carrie Viola (CA 1899-CA 1916),
132
Cebert Carbet (1893-), 194
Cebert McB. (1908-1951), 195
Charlie Gleason (1888-1970), 160,
194
Charlotte (1918-), 160
Clarence Victor (1904-), 25
Clayton (1925-), 102
Cleveland, Dr. (-1898), 102
Colonel Lee (1881-1959), 194

Colonel Roy (1878-1889), 194
Curtis Dale (1936-1937), 25
Cynthia (1846-CA 1906), 145
DeEtte Moelick (1902-1922), 195
Dennis (1859-1941), 147
Donald H. (CA 1917-), 174
Donna Raye (1905-), 133
Drucilla Ann (1847-1916), 159
Dwight Reed (1892-1947), 194
Earl (1902-), 24
Earl McKey (1904-), 101
Effie Stella (1891-1946), 194
Electia Kate (CA 1919-CA 1921),
81
Eli G. (1835-), 145
Elizabeth (1842-), 146
Elizabeth Ann (1923-1971), 163
Ella Mae (1917-), 80
Ellen (-), 108
Ellen (CA 1889-CA 1911), 132
Elsie (1838-), 145
Emaline (1865-), 146
Emmett (-), 101, 112
Emmett, Jr. (1922-1946), 102
Emmie Caroline (1887-1937), 125
Emmie Caroline (CA 1887-1937),
132
Enoch D. (CA 1835-), 108
Etta (-), 131
Etta (1914-CA 1942), 80
Etta Mae (1896-), 133
Eugene (1886-1941), 80, 81
Eva Loucinda (1909-), 101
Flora Mahala (1899-), 24
Floyd (1847-1929), 145
Floyd Wilborn (1915-), 81
'Fronie' Sophronie (1863-1944),
109
Garnet (1893-1901), 194
Gary Rex (1960-), 154
Gelene (-), 161
George Lester (1890-), 194
Glenna (1861-1862), 194
Granville R. (1863-1944), 185, 194
Greek Garnet (1906-), 25, 81
Grover (1894-1964), 125
Grover Cleveland (1894-1964), 132
Guy Swanson (CA 1896-1905), 132
Harlow W. (1856-1881), 194
Harlow W. (1880-1880), 194
Hazel Beatrice (CA 1906-), 174
Hazel Gladys (1905-), 163

Robert Eugene (CA 1968-), 38
Robert Lee (CA 1940-), 34
Robert Lee, Jr. (CA 1961-), 34
Ronald (CA 1953-), 35
Samuel Harrison (CA 1948-), 35
Staci (CA 1990-), 34
Susan (CA 1967-), 34
Thomas Eugene (CA 1944-), 34
Timothy (CA 1971-), 34
Victoria Lynn (CA 1956-), 35
William Harrison (1895-CA 1988),
   33
William Harrison, III (CA 1946-), 35
William Harrison, Jr. (CA 1921-CA
   1990), 35
William Richard (CA 1939-), 33
Zelma Ruth (CA 1929-), 36
Jimenez
   M. (-), 67
Johnes
   Elias (CA 1773-), 205
   Elizabeth (1776-), 205
   Mary (CA 1681-1766), 204
   Paul (1748-1776), 204
   William (CA 1774-), 205
Johns
   Ann Mrs (CA 1600-CA 1680), 1,
      207
Johnson
   Anna Nancy (-1828), 15
   Clare (1955-), 53
   Elizabeth (-), 72
   Jean (-), 33
   Linda Mae (1948-), 54
   Mildred (-), 175
Jones
   Alice L. (1877-1964), 115
   Barbara Gail (1971-), 38
   Benjamin Allen (-), 168
   Caroline Alice (CA 1869-CA 1930),
      143
   Celia Ennice (1907-), 153
   Edith Mae (-), 136
   Evans (-), 136
   George (-), 74
   James William (-), 38
   John W. (-), 142
   Judy (CA 1951-), 36
   Malinda (1847-1925), 114
   Minnie (1891-1912), 121
   Mitchell (-), 107
   Namie (-), 115

Sarah Catherine (1872-), 143
Sollie (1892-1956), 126
Justice
   Cecil (-), 74

K

Keadle
   Virgie E. (1895-1992), 71
Keller
   William (-), 65
Kelly
   Barbara Jean (1933-), 10
   Betty (-), 71
Kennedy
   Micky (-), 69
Kenyon
   Mercedes (1909-1981), 23
Key
   Della (1926-), 152
Kingrea
   James (-), 38
Kirk
   Attie (1882-1901), 153
   Jones (-), 112
   Rachel (1855-1943), 193
   Susie Carol (1863-1956), 194
Kirkum
   Joann (-), 59
Kitchell
   William (-dec.), 13
Kline
   Michael (-), 66
   Mickey (-), 66
Knapp
   David (-), 41
Kobsieh
   Donald J. (-), 158
Kohl
   Alfred (-), 188
   Barbara M. (1957-), 188
   Diane V. (1964-), 188
   Edwin C. (1949-), 188
   Franklin A. (1959-), 188
   James W. (1954-), 188
   Shirley J. (1952-), 188
Kyker
   Ruby L. (-), 143

M

Robert Everett (1887-1974), 7
Robert Morgan (1920-), 8
Stephen Bolles (1922-), 8, 9
Stephen Campbell (1948-1968), 8
Stuart Morgan (1954-), 9
McNeely
Janice Lou (1940-), 47
McTigue
Jerry (-), 32
Mead
Josephine A. (-dec.), 18
Meadows
Alice (-), 64
Dayton (-), 69
James (-), 32
Joseph (-), 64
Means
Etta Louise (1925-), 187
Melody
Jean (-), 55
Mercer
Grant (-), 73
Martha Ann (1952-), 52
Meyer
Euginia Alice (1894-1982), 68
Kathleen Joyce (1935-), 188
Mickle
Clara (1866-1943), 179
Milan
Easter (-), 72
Miles
Bill (-), 53
Jamison Ian (1978-), 54
John (-), 163
John Richard (1955-), 164
Myrtle (1889-1965), 190
Patricia Ann (1945-), 164
Randall Kieth (1960-), 54
William Jesse (-dec.), 135
Miller
(Infant) (-CA 1886), 95
Albert (CA 1859-1919), 95
Barbara Innes (-), 95
Cynthia Dawn (1969-), 47
Dana Susanne (1978-), 96
Diana Lynn (1956-), 96
Don Eddie (1941-), 47
Douglas Alan, Sr. (1943-), 96
Douglas Allan, Jr. (1977-), 96
Granville Gould (1896-1971), 95
Gregory (1971-), 51
Halsey Wilkerson, Jr. (1930-), 96

Halsey Wilkinson, Sr. (1897-1964), 96
Joyce Truscott (1929-), 95
Kennith Paul (1967-), 47
Maud (CA 1887-CA 1888), 95
Shelia Dawn (1960-), 47
Susan Linda (1965-), 96
William Al (1899-1995), 47
William Darrell (1940-), 47
Mills
Carole (1948-), 33
Ruby Jean (1945-), 54
Vertle (1914-), 46
Mink
Grace (-), 142
Joseph E. (-), 142
Minton
Michelle Lynn (1971-), 41
Walter Lee (1944-), 41
Mitchell
Anna (1893-), 25
Moody
Maxine (-), 43
Mooney
Retha (-dec.), 128
Moore
Dwight (1948-), 49
Garry (-), 66
Joseph (BEF 1661-1726), 4
Robert D. (1977-), 49
Sarah (1683-dec.), 4
Valerie E. (1980-), 49
Moores
R. B. (CA 1805-), 12
Morgan
Aaron (1924-1998), 62
Almira Smith (1890-), 7
Billy (-), 62
Clarence (CA 1903-dec.), 62
David Gray (1979-), 48
Deborah Ann (1953-), 48
Gregory Dean (1963-), 42
Henry (-), 78
Herbert (CA 1908-dec.), 62
James (-), 62
James (1889-1937), 62
Jo Ann (1933-), 90
Laurence "Ted" (CA 1905-dec.), 62
Leona (-dec.), 62
Mary Lynn (1928-), 89
Miranda Kay (1986-), 42
Mona (-), 62

R

Georgia (1903-), 21
Tullium
 Steve (-), 106

U

Uhl
 Zachery (-), 70
Underwood
 Joan (-), 71

V

Van Boven
 Raymond O. (-), 56
Van Ness
 Debra (1966-), 52
Vanhoy
 Liza Jane (-), 68
Vannoy
 Nathaniel (-), 139
Vaught
 Blaine (-), 159
 Erdice Sue (1953-), 164
 Gincy (-), 147
 Harold Eugene (1946-1946), 164
 Hobson T. (1912-), 164
 Hobson T., Jr. (1955-), 164
 Shirley Ann (1949-), 164
Vazquez
 Peter (1940-), 53
 Piper Angela (1964-), 53
Vickers
 James C. (CA 1923-), 148
 James Glenn (CA 1949-), 148
 Robert Laird (CA 1952-), 148

W

Waddell
 Jones Huston (1870-CA 1971), 115
 Linda Sue (1953-), 66
 Norman (-), 66
 Zenna (1909-), 82
Wagg
 Annie Mae (1912-), 162
 Hale (-1934), 174
 James W. (-), 174
Wagner
 Debra Ann (1956-), 40

Ernest (1934-), 40
 Ernestine (1961-), 40
 Sue (CA 1946-), 34
Wagoner
 Fred (1888-), 104
 Neal (1914-), 104
Waldron
 Arthur (CA 1860-), 6
 James (CA 1836-), 6
Walker
 Eugene (1944-), 191
 Houston (-), 147
 James (1942-), 191
 Nona (-), 49
 Ralph (1905-), 191
Walters
 Mavis Adell (1920-), 9
Wampler
 Gus (-), 38
Ward
 Clarence S. (1898-), 176
 Evaline (-), 146
 June Elizabeth (1926-), 176
 Nathan (-), 146
 Sallie (CA 1830-CA 1862), 147
 Stewart Elmore (1921-), 176
Warden
 Angelia Faye (1941-), 189
 Charles Franklin (1926-), 189
 J. Garfield (1900-1954), 189
 Mabel (1921-), 189
 Madge Janet (1923-), 189
 Mildred Irene (1924-), 189
 Rex Savannah (1902-1965), 189
 Rex Savannah, Jr. (1932-), 189
 Ruth (1904-1953), 28
 Vonnie Wave (1936-), 189
Watkins
 George (-dec.), 29
Watson
 David James (1979-), 11
 Robecca Lolita (1977-), 10
 William Robert (CA 1953-), 10
Watts
 Deena (-), 56
Weaver
 Annie (-), 148
 Donald Watson (1894-1961), 191
 Donald Watson, Jr. (1921-), 192
 Edward Maurice (1923-1945), 192
 Felix Johnson (-), 170
 Layton Lee (1926-), 192

Emma (-dec.), 64
Etta Pearl (1909-), 65
Harry (CA 1945-), 65
Howard (-), 64
Josephine Ennis (-), 65
June (-), 64
Mary (1943-), 65
Richard Sterling (1920-1986), 68
Ronald (1941-), 65
Thelma Mae (1927-), 68
William Coy (1902-1981), 64
Wingate
  Alexander Mitchell (1908-), 107
  Barbara Jean (1938-), 104
  Cecelia (CA 1922-), 108
  Charles Curtis (1928-), 106
  Charlie (1910-), 104
  Claude (1904-), 104
  Cora Lee (1896-), 105
  Curtis (1902-1971), 104
  Danny (1951-), 106
  Emily (1941-), 107
  Eugene (CA 1910-), 107
  Eugene Mitchell (1907-1907), 105
  Frances Irene (1922-), 106
  Garnett Smith (1924-), 106
  Geneva (1898-1932), 105
  Geneva Louise (-), 106
  Gordon (1932-), 106
  Gwyn (1906-), 107
  Harmon (1892-), 104
  Hobert Banks (1909-), 107
  Horner (1901-), 104
  Hurley (1896-1962), 104
  Ina Jane (1912-), 105
  James (CA 1917-), 108
  James Richard (1924-), 86
  Jerry (1933-), 105
  Josephine (1930-), 106
  Kyle (1907-), 107
  Lelia (1900-), 104
  Lenna (CA 1913-), 107
  Lessa (1898-1900), 104
  Lester (1897-1969), 104
  Letcher Carlisle (1898-), 106
  Lettie Rosmond (1903-), 107
  Lillian Virginia (1904-1904), 107
  Lillie Rose (1900-), 105
  Lura Marie (1905-), 107
  Mae (1877-1954), 176
  Margaret Ann (1931-), 106
  Mary Lucille (1925-), 106

Mava (1949-), 107
Myrtle (1894-), 104
Myrtle Carolyn (1914-), 107
Paul Jones (1911-), 107
R. Verdigan 'Dock' (1869-1949), 104
Raymond Claude (1922-), 86
Richard Elmore (1872-1950), 105
Robert W. (1914-), 104
Rush (1880-), 107
Ruth (1909-), 104
Stella (1906-), 104
Suzanne (-), 106
Troy William (1894-1969), 86, 105
Vilace (1905-), 105
Walter Lee (1896-1965), 105
Wayne Robert (1946-), 104
Wright (1869-1943), 104
Wright McCamant (1900-), 106
Zollie Virginia (1899-), 105
Wingler
  Joe (-), 29
  Sharon (1950-), 29
  Tatsey (1955-), 29
Wolf
  Helen (1925-), 58
Wood
  Eva Ann (1886-), 118
  Jonathan (-), 201
Woodard
  Christine Edith (1958-), 11
Woodhull
  Jemina (CA 1646-), 201
Woodruff
  David (-), 199
  Elizabeth (-1831), 19
  Flora (1874-1896), 191
  Harriett (CA 1854-), 98
  P.B. (-), 71
  Sadie W. (1892-), 190
  Sarah (-), 18
Woods
  Harold Gray (1934-), 163
  John Wythe (1909-1979), 163
  John Wythe, Jr. (1929-), 163
  Sallie Elizabeth (1945-), 163
  Walter Ralph (1931-), 163
Workman
  Earl Ann (-), 74
  Earl Carson (1913-1992), 74
  Okey (-), 74
  Roy B. Jr., (-), 74

ADDENDUM

11822223311132   MILLER, Robert Gregory
Robert was born in the Bethesda Oak Hospital, Cincinnati, Ohio on 21 January 2000. He arrived at 8:44 am EDT at eight pounds and 11.5 ounces.
(See parents page 51)

1182222331142   PHILLIPS, Darrell Ellery
He married **COMMERFORD, Adrienne** on 2 October 1999.
(See page 53)

1882222331151   VAZQUEZ, Piper Angela
She married **McCOY, Franklin** on 24 April 1999.
(See page 53)

BIBLIOGRAPHY

Halsey, David Halsey, "Halsey Genealogy Since 1395 A.D.", Heritage Books, Inc., Bowie, MD, 1995

Halsey, Rufus Clinton, "Halsey Genealogy", Sparta, NC. 1980; (lithographic offset, Publisher unk.)

Halsey, Jacob Lafayette & Halsey, Edmund Drake, "Thomas Halsey of Hertfordshire, England, and Southampton, Long Island, 1591 to 1679, with his American Descendants to the Eighth and Ninth Generations", Morristown, NJ., Printed at "The Jerseyman" Office, 1895

Howell, M. A., George Rogers, "The Early History of Southampton, L.I., New York, With Genealogies", second edition, Albany, NY., Weed, Parsons and Company, 1867; Facsimile reprint by Heritage Books, Inc., Bowie, MD, 1989

Bowman, Mary Keller, "Reference Book of Wyoming County History", Parsons, WV., McClain Printing Company, 1965 & reprinted 1981

Halsey, Abigail Fithian, "Halseys in Old Southampton", New York, NY., Columbia University Press, 1940

Cussans, John Edwin, "History of Hertfordshire", volume 3, London, England, Chatto and Windus, 214, Piccadilly, Hertford, Stephen Austin & Sona, 1879-1881

Seversmith, Herbert Fuman, "Colonial Families of Long Island, N.Y. & Conn.", Volume 2 (1939) Library of Congress, Typescript, 1939

Coddington, John Insley, "The Wheelers of Bedfordshire and New England", Arlington, VA., The American Genealogist, Volumes 27 & 28, 1951

Wheeler, Raymond David, "The English Ancestry of Thomas Halsey of Southampton, Long Island", (unpublished, available through "The Thomas Halsey Family Association, Southampton, L.I., NY) October 1994

www.ingramcontent.com/pod-product-compliance
Lightning Source LLC
Chambersburg PA
CBHW061719270326

41928CB00011B/2042